Multiplexity of Postcolonial Literature

Multiplexity of Postcolonial Literature

Sunil Kumar Navin
T Sai Chandra Mouli

AUTHORSPRESS
Publishers of Scholarly Books

Worldwide Circulation through Authorspress Global Network
First Published 2010
by
Authorspress
E-35/103, Jawahar Park
Laxmi Nagar, Delhi-110 092
e-mail: authorspress@yahoo.com

Multiplexity of Postcolonial Literature
ISBN 978-81-7273-554-8

Printed in India at Tarun Offset, Delhi.

Preface

Indian English writers have carved a niche for themselves and they have won accolades—prestigious awards and prizes—making significant contributions to literature of the world. They have successfully articulated in the chosen language human passions and aspirations, human virtues and vices. Not a facet of life is there which has not been genuinely addressed. The anguish and bitterness Indians felt during the colonial rule; the sting of subjugation that pierced Indian psyche, the poverty caused by economic exploitation by the colonisers and the exhilaration on account of hard-won freedom from foreign rule, have successfully been depicted by Indian English writers. Besides, they have given expressions to discrimination of Dalits by the upper caste Indians; wretched condition of Indian women under the system of patriarchy; the ever widening gulf between the rich and the poor; their joys and sorrows. Indian English literature abounds in writings from ethical elevation to spiritual deprivation.

A vast number of cultural critiques of the Empire and its aftermath have been designated with the label 'postcolonialism' published in the last two decades. Disparities of perspective and subject-matter apart, they all have a common reference point. They are all broadly concerned with experiences of cultural, political, social and economic exploitation of the colonised and resistance under systems of colonial control. The term 'postcolonialism' thus addresses itself to the historical, political, cultural and textual ramifications of the colonial encounter between the West and the non-West, dating from the sixteenth century to the present day. It considers how the encounter shaped both parties—the colonisers as well as the colonised. Studies of postcolonial cultures, texts, and politics are interested in responses to colonial oppression which were (and are) sensitive or contentious.

Postcolonialism is, thus, a name for a critical theoretical approach in literary and critical studies. It also designates a politics of transformational resistance to unjust and unequal forms of political and cultural authority which extends back across the twentieth century and beyond. In academic discourse postcolonial approach is commonly associated with names such as Edward Said and Gayatri Spivak. It is also important to underline the importance of anti-colonial nationalist thinkers and theorists like Gandhi and Fanon in shaping postcolonial concepts of opposition and self-determination.

We believe that this volume will prove to be useful to readers to understand postcolonial perspectives in Indian English writing, for it incorporates responses to the works of a wide range of Indian English authors in different genres. An interview with a creative writer on postcolonial perspectives will certainly be illuminating. Healthy criticism and suggestions are most cordially invited which will only help in making it worthier in future editions.

We gratefully acknowledge the encouragement given by Prof. Avadhesh Kumar Singh, Vice-Chancellor, Dr. Babasaheb Ambedkar Open University, Ahmedabad, Prof. C.R.Kar, and Prof. Shubha Tiwari. We place on record the support of Dr. Rajiv Kumar Mallik, Dr. Sudhir K. Arora, Dr Jaydeep Sarangi and Dr. Krushna Chandra Mishra. We are beholden to all the scholars who have enriched this volume with their erudite research papers. It is due to the blessings of elders and well wishers this volume could acquire a shape.

We express our heartfelt gratitude to Prof. A.S.Meena, Principal, Nabira Mahavidyalaya, Katol for encouraging us to take up this invaluable project.

We sincerely thank Sudarshan Kcherry of Authorspress, New Delhi, for bringing out this volume with love and affectionate concern.

Sunil Kumar Navin

T. Sai Chandra Mouli

List of Contributors

Ajay B. Kukade, Mahatma Fule College, Warud (Maharashtra).

Avadesh Kumar Singh, Vice-Chancellor, Dr. Babasaheb Ambedkar Open University (Gujarat).

B. Kavya, Research Scholar, Dept. of Englsih, Mysore University, Mysore. (Karnataka).

Beena, Lad, Asst. Prof. of English, Govt. K.R.G. College, Gwalior (M.P).

Charu P. Gidwani, R.K.T. College, Ulhasnagar, Thane (Maharashtra).

Dinesh Kumar, V.J. Vaze College, Mulund, Mumbai (Maharashtra).

G.A. Ghanshyam Associate Prof. Govt. M.L.Shukla College, Seepat, Bilaspur (C.G.).

Jaydeep Sarangi, Head, Dept of English, Sevabahrati Mahavidyalaya (Vidyasagar University), Kapgari, Paschim Medinipur (W.B.).

Jaukkalkar Sd. Imtiaz, S.P.M. College, Nandura (Rly), Buldhana (Maharashtra).

Krushna Chandra Mishra, S.G. Lecturer in English, Govt. College, Bomdila (Arunachal Pradesh).

Madhu Kamra, Head, Dept. of English, Durga Mahavidyalaya, Raipur (C.G.).

Mamta Kori & Dr. Shubha Tiwari, Research Scholars, A.P.S. University, Rewa (M.P.).

Mukti B. Shah, Naran Lala College of Commerce & Management, Navsari (Gujarat)

P. Gopichand, J.K.C. College, Guntur (Andhra Pradesh).

P.Nagasuseela, J.K.C. College, Guntur (Andhra Pradesh).

Pragyasa H. Upadhyaya, Research Scholar, Nabira Mahavidyalaya, Katol, Nagpur (Maharashtra).

Prantik Banerjee, Hislop College, Nagpur (Maharashtra).

Pratima Das, Smt. C.H.M. College, Ulhasnagar, Thane (Maharashtra).

Priti D. Thakre, V.N. College, Mangrulpir, Washim (Maharashtra).

Rajiv K. Mallik, Head, Dept. of English, K.P. College Murliganj, Madhepura (Bihar).

Ram Sharma, Sr Lecturer in English, J.V (P.G.) College, Baraut, Baghpat (U.P.).

Shubha Tiwari, Head, Dept. of English, A.P.S. University, Rewa (M.P).

Soma Banerjee, S.F.S.College, Nagpur (Maharashtra).

Sunil Kumar Navin, Associate Professor Dept. of English, Nabira Mahavidyalaya, Katol, Nagpur (Maharashtra).

Sunila Pillai, R.K.Talreja College, Ulhasnagar, Thane (Maharashtra).

Sunita S. Gharge, Chh. Shivaji College, Satara, (Maharashtra).

Sushama Tiwari, Head, Dept. of English, Arts & Comm. Girls' college, Raipur (C.G.).

T.S. Chandra Mouli, Former Associate Professor of English, Railway college, Lalaguda, Secunderabad (Andhra Pradesh).

V. Pala Prasada Rao, J.K.C. College, Guntur (A.P.).

Contents

1

Writing Postmodernism and Postcolonialism in India

—Avadesh Kumar Singh

Ours is an age of "isms" in which we are fated to define and measure our pre-suffixed and hyphenated existence in terms of these "isms". However, in the obtaining of "three minutes's culture", nothing lasts, leave alone a particular "ism". With every new morning some or other "ism" becomes old and falls, as it heralds the advent of "neo"/new, "pre" or "post" either by post-speed or ordinary post—or by *poste* that in French stands for a TV station and can serve a befitting metaphor for media—print or electronic.

Of all these "isms" in the later half of our century, "one of the meanest, cruelest, bloodiest in human history," as Peter Drucker called it, "post-modernism and postcolonialism have had more enduring life than their other counterparts. So much so that by the end of the century the subscribers of the postmodernism and postcolonialism have come to be known as the "po-mo" and "po-co" generation.

Postmodernism has been, and still remains, the most fashionable word in the world outside the First World for the reasons whose explanations may lie in post/colonialism, making our yoking of postmodernism with postcolonialism in our context considerably legitimate. The fervid interest in postmodernism and its uncritical reception in the so-called postcolonial Third World (I use the term for the sake of convenience and brevity. Given a choice I would prefer the "Pre-First World" to it) and in the countries like ours in particular, as the West with all its media gives us these "isms", a la Shakespeare, "in the throat, as deep as to the lungs," should surprise all sensible people and attract their critical attention also. Coming as I do from a "Third World" country I find it difficult to pronounce altogether so favourable a sentence upon postmodernism, as do the greater mortals from the First or even the so-called Third World, not entirely without susceptible formulations.

Postmodernism is a consequence of change in the West's understanding of man and the world. The West understands man and the world with its three discourses: metaphysical discourse of the ancient world, the theological discourse of the medieval world and the scientific positivistic view of man. These three ways of perception or discourses went through the states of disintegration leading to an unprecedented state in which the West seems to have no clear way of understanding the nature of man, his position in the universe or the purpose of his life. Consequently the West is 'really' lost for the first time a fluid and extravagantly chaotic state that McIntyre referred to in his book *After Virtue*. He further remarked that in the West we have not only lost our morality but even the notion of morality is completely lost. Confusion is all, nay, greater confusion is all, as postmodernism celebrates, and also wants us to do so, the carnival of confusion and uncertainty.

Ours is no flattering state-rather worse, for we are consumers of this postmodernism without going through the stages and states that the West went through. In India we have had modernism without modernisation. Modernsim is an essence or pickle of modernisation. It is fragrance of the dough called modernisation that is a consequence of industrialisation that leads to modernism and the way it affected the West. Industrialisation in India, however, has been slow and very uneven, and so it remains even in its post-colonial era, say nothing of it in the colonial era that witnessed systematic unsetting of indigenous industries and institutions. And whatever leftovers of the so-called industrialisation were thrown at us was more aimed at exploitation of native natural resources, consolidation and preservation of colonialism thereby serving colonial interests.

If postmodernism has anything to do with modernism, with post-scientific positivism or post-industrial society, then it is almost inconceivable to think of postmodernism in our country. Only our naivity would have persuaded us to believe and accept that we have had modernism, and are in the post-modern era now. But the ground reality has a different story to tell, if we are willing to listen to it. Postmodernism neither grows in our climes, nor does it even sit well on us, if we put it on us to appear fashionable. 'Isms' like postmodernism and postcolonialism are not products of hot houses but of certain eco-socio-political order and culture that forge condition, mood or perception called postmodernism.

Ironical it is that postmodernism is being used as category, label or brand, at least in our literary and critical discourses. This happens to be a fashionable trend, as it comes from the West, and a convenient category for our critical reputations to measure our literary and critical endeavours. A considerable number of our literary writers and literatures seem to be vying with each other to earn this label or category. In Hindi, for instance, Sudheesh Pachouri is the wholesale dealer of postmodernism. It is discernible in a few articles such as "Post-modern Gujarati Story" by Ajit Thakore (with no ostensible reference or discussion to post-modern phenomenon in it or discussion of Gujarati Short Stories in the Post-modern Mode) or "Games of Fiction: Search for Post-modernist Mode in the Malayalam Fiction of 1990s" by E.V. Ramakrishanan (the redeeming features of this enabling endeavour of the critic is that it focuses on a "search" for the post-modernist mode without being obsessed with it). Ironically these two are not mere critics but writer-critics. And if our writer-critics do not resist the invasion of alien "isms "and "post", then there is something wrong with our "post-colonial" condition. One of the notable exceptions among Indian critics is Namvar Singh who has questioned and resisted postmodernism in his article, "Shatabdi ka Avasan aur Uttaradhunikata" (1984). However, a successful Hindi novelist like Manohar Shyam Joshi listlessly longed to place his novel *Hariya Hercules Ki Hairani* in postmodern category as the dust-jacket of the novel states. The temptation of postmodernism as a category is so irresistible for the author that he suggested that his novel is postmodern in its carft and narration. By doing so he prescribed consideration of his novel as a postmodern novel to be received with post-modernist tools.

In the process, he inversely suggests lack of faith in prospective critical intentions and abilities to locate the text properly. The novelist, thus, strives to condition and control the role of reader critic. With his author/ity he othered the critic; whereas postmodernism is supposed to accept the "other". Is it the spirit of post-modernism? Is the author dead? Long live the author! Is it not the anxiety of being postmodernism? Isn't it the anxiety of earning a label like "post-modern" or "post-colonial" that comes from the First World? Is it postcolonialism? And if this is postcolonialism, then what is colonialism?

Imperialism, Edward Said informs us, is "the practice, the theory and the attitudes of a dominating metropolitan centre ruling a distant territory, colonialism is almost always a consequence of imperialism of the implanting of settlements on distant territories." To Said imperialism and colonialism are not merely acts of accumulation and acquisitions. They are sustained by and gain impetus from impressive ideological formulations that include ideas that people of certain territories require and beseech domination and also forms of knowledge related to it. The civilising project of the West led to colonisation of "a grand total of roughly 85% of the earth" by 1914 from "55% but actually...35% of the earth's surface" (Said : 6). The cultures of these colonies were impacted by the imperial and colonial processes in different measures in different parts of the world. Colonising forces are still active, though their ways and methods of operation have become subtler, sharper and more dangerous. These forces have coopted postmodernism as a tool to serve their purposes. Postmodernism is the philosophy of neocolonialism, and consumerism is its culture. Ironical it is that the first post-colonial nation, if political independence is the criterion, is the foremost neocoloniser today.

Admittedly, postmodernism is the only philosophy or discourse from the West that at least in principle proclaims that there are others. It valorises heterogeneity of con/texts and interest groups. So far, so good. Acceptance of existence of others should, however, rest, on modesty and piety, not in their Christian sense but in their Indian sense of *vinamrata* or *bhakti* towards others. Postmodernism was supposed to wage a war against totalisation in principle but the way it is (being) peddled by the West with arrogance in the non-Western world, has made it a totalising concept. In practice, postmodernism is nothing but an empty slogan used as camouflage by the neocapitalist culture which, equipped with its means, methods and modes of consumption and media, imposes a homogenising super voice, language and culture over others proposing neo-universalism of its kind.

Postmodernism is one of the outward teeth of the elephant called neocapitalism. This elephant tramples others, though it remains invisible. That makes neocaptilism more dangerous than capitalism was. It reaches nooks and corners of hearts and houses with air and waves. It seduces others with its tempting "little revolutions" that happen so often with "extra", "new" or "super" added to everything that it is almost impossible to sustain oneself. Postmodernism acts as a handmaid of neocapitalism, for it provides theoretical and philosophical framework to neocapitalism and to its consumerist culture.

The neocapitalist consumerist culture sees everything in terms of resources, productivity and commodity and profit to the detriment of the consumers. It has led to commodification of art and literature and their consideration by non-literary, non-artistic criteria. Frederick Jamson had tried to locate the postmodern as a condition arising out of the development in the sixties of the consumerist capitalism. Within a decade and half after Fredric Jameson's critique of postmodern and late capitalism, the neocapitalism, keeping its pernicious consequences in the rear, rages ahead, accentuated by the highly sophisticated interaction through technological means. The subtle hyper-mercantile ways of neocapitalism have proved hollowness of postmodernism and also of postcolonialism. Neo-capitalism is the reigning reality of the so-called postcolonial societies. These societies remain consumers of postmodern and postcolonial discourses of neocolonial countries and their East India Companies. Neocolonialism of neocapitalist countries fuelled and fawned by flamboyant consumerist culture survives and thrives on its ability to transform itself and hide its colonial colours and tantalising telos. 'Others' can exist, and do so too, but on the terms of arrogant neocolonisers as the neocolonies and consumers. Resistance to neocolonial ways, if any, is anticipated, appropriated and hijacked by neocolonisers and their agencies.

In this context, I am reminded of Udai Prakash's story about a dog. On a Diwali night a few children tied a string of crackers to its tail and set fire to its end. The dog barked, cried, ran and fell. Vinayak Dattatrey threw a few pieces of bones towards the dog that chewed the bones and yelped out of fright of bursting crackers. Vinayak laughed at this bizarre tragicomic sight. When asked by people he said about the cause of his laughter, "See this dog. It is a true consumerist of the Third World. A horrible instance of postmodern consumerism" (Hans, February. 1997). In the context of our endeavours to understand ourselves, this story becomes a pertinent comment on our so-called post-independent postcolonial situation in the Third World in general and ours in particular. Post-colonialism, unattended by intellectual independence, does not mean much. Even at the risk of being called a pessimist I must state that the postcolonial state is a mirage, colonialism is ever always present. Only its colour, external appearance or demeanour changes. Its nature remains the same. Colonialism yields place to neo, new or newer colonialism.

Neocapitalist forces accompanied by the philosophy of postmodernism, culture of neo-consumerism operate in ways subtler than ever before facilitating replacement of visible capitalist colonialism with neocolonialism. Colonialism was like a mountain but neocolonialism is an iceberg whose tip only is visible; that too, to a few. It deceives the best of our perceiving reputations making the task of our writers and critics more difficult and complex. It cannot be ignored or rejected. It can be understood, gnawed at and resisted.

Postmodernism has no fixed referent. "We begin our definition with Postmodernism is... and are already in trouble" (Marshal, 3). It is written differently by different people with a hyphen and without it (as I do to disentangle it from modernism and stress the changed perception), in past or present tense, in singular and plural. "What is/are/was/were/ postmodernism (s)?" (Woods, l). What this term refers to is not specifically clear, as it is "stretched in all directions across different debates, different disciplinary and discursive boundaries, as different factions seek to make it their own, using it to designate a plethora of incommensurable objects, tendencies, emergencies" (Hebding, 181). In this free play of postmodernism "you get the postmodernism you deserve" (David Antin, "Modernism and Postmodernism", Bounday, 2, l, 1972).The only place where it is fixed is the dictionary where it is sandwiched between postmaster and postmortem. Coming as it does, it is posted to us by the West. In fact the West is the writer, processor, pack (ag)er, postmaster and distributor of postmodernism. Its uncritical acceptance or celebration will tantamount to postmortem of our own living bodies.

Whatever postmodernism is, in whatever manner our society, our critical and literary faculties are responding to it, it has to be admitted that we can love it or loathe it but cannot be indifferent to it, for it is inconceivable to escape it. It has attained so much currency that it cannot be wished away. It is still happening to us. Rather than regretting it what is needed is to understand it and its condition (s), its strategies and the ways of operation. Societies like India have to prepare their strategies, receive and respond to it. Our literatures and criticism can play their own roles in bearing its ugly hidden face by penetrating under the skin of its connivance and thereby resisting whatever is inimical to our national and social interests with our counter-strategies. We can respond to it in some of the following ways: (i) we can reject it and without taking note of it, we can allow it to thrive around us, and get throttled in the process; (ii) we can accept its currency and supremacy, and surrender ourselves to it; (iii) we can celebrate it and commit intellectual and cultural suicide; (iv) we can receive it proactively, understand it and resist and reject whatever is negative in it, and accept pragmatically whatever is of use to us in it; and (v) we can think of alternatives to it, and redefine it or reconstruct our theory or model from our texts, though that may be a sort of complicit participation in it.

Of all the alternatives to postmodernism *deshivad* or *nativism* is the most potent. Before discussing *deshivad* in the Indian context it shall not be incongruous to consider some of the aspects.

Let us unhesitatingly accept that nativism is not a politically innocent construct. It shares its etymological root "nasci" or "natus" with nation—a loaded term relating nativism—to birth in its narrow sense. Incidentally indigenism and *deshajvad* are also related to "gen" or "gene" (birth). At times *deshivad*, the Indian counterpart of nativism, lays emphasis on language so excessively that the notion appears to be a linguistic construct. This reliance on language is justifiable because language is related to *rachana-*

chetana (consciousness of creation), *rachana* (creativity) and *rachana-aswad/sweekaran* (reception). Whatever may be the limitations of language yet it is the only medium by which we can express our experience—fictive or factual—reposed in our conscious, subconscious and unconscious mind. Moving a little further, it is a language through which we take cognisance of the world. The language gets mixed with our consciousness and like paint becomes the integral part of a canvas. The moment we try to pull and tug the paint from the canvas, a few shreds of the canvas also come out. Hence, *deshivad* insists on language for the sake of fidelity and sincerity of expression of experience.

Deshivad and *nativism* share quite a bit of premises, yet the synonymity of the two would amount to mortgaging our specificity, though Professor Bhalchand Nemade, one of the precursors of this movement, and the subsequent subscribers like Ganesh Devy and Makarand Paranjape do not mind using the terms as it is in English. *Deshivad* is not celebration of ghetto culture. Nemade is against those pseudo-claims of catholicity and universalism as against narrowness. He is unopposed to cosmopolitanism or universalism with full cognisance of its limitations. But he is aware of inherent contradictions of internationalism. He observed in his seminal essay, "Even theoretically, internationalism without nativism as its basis is impossible, because, nativism is a multi-centred, descriptive and real concept, whereas internationalism is an artificial and parasitic concept."

Though *deshivad* relies heavily on language, there is no reason at least for us in India to seek divorce between *deshivad* (nativism) and nation. In the so-called post-nation society, a term accepted by some of us to measure our Post-Independent State, we must note that in the West the nation was an organisation of interest groups. With these organised interest groups the West saw the other races and societies as its adversary and either annihilated them or colonised them. They reaped the harvest by exploiting non-Western societies and communities economically, culturally and intellectually. The *nemesis* did await them in the form of the World Wars. The West then pronounced it as an evil—a position subscribed to by quite a few non-Western scholars like Rabindranath Tagore. He could not transcend the then historical pressures that led to the formation of the organised modern nation, as his lectures on nationalism reveal.

To me *deshivad* or nativism is not disengaged with nation—not the rigid exclusive of the West of Tagore but of Gandhi—inclusive one leading to happy internationalism. The Western society may have reached the post-national state, that need not mean that we too have also touched that state and reject the notion of nation altogether. Reject we must the modern Western notion of nation but not Gandhi's. For us the nation is the unit with which we can resist the onslaught of the postmodernist, neocoloniser, neocapitalists and mindless Westernisation. This relationship between *deshivad* and nation proposes *deshivad* as a strategy which with its insistence on identity, specificity and authenticity resists direct or indirect culture or intellectual invasion or encroachment by "other" or alien homogenising forces, and disallows being used as data. Moreover, our *deshivad* is more inclusive than nativism in the way Gandhi's concept of nationalism is from the Western nationalism. *Deshivad* for us cannot afford to exclude the *dalit*, feminist/ womanist, labourers' and farmers' discourses, much in the same way it cannot exclude Gandhi's nation.

Deshivad encompasses all aspects of economic, political, intellectual, cultural and social life but if I focus on literature only, then it is more for critics than for writers, for no true writer of substance would like to write under any "ism" or "*vad*". If s/he does, s/he will be faithful not to the experience but to the *vad*. What is of interest to me as a member of the Indian pluralistic society is that the *deshivad* does not allow me to accept those standards, criteria and categories that are not approved of by my own experience. Therefore it is the duty of the critics, and of the critical faculty of the creative writer, to keep reminding the creative faculty about the role of the consciousness, experience, culture and medium of creative writing.

Deshivad does not need my advocacy when history supports it. Let me take a few instances from the Western history. In the sixteenth century with the rise of English nation the British society was faced with the question: What should be the course of the developing British drama and poetry? On the one hand were native forms of drama like the Mystery, Miracle, Morality and Interlude; and on the other hand was the rich tradition of Greek and Roman plays prescribed then in schools and colleges. Sir Philip Sidney, Gabriel Harvey, Spenser, Ben Jonson and their Areopagus favoured the rich classical yet foreign tradition of antiquity. On the other hand, the Cambridge School of Thomas Wilson, John Cheke and Roger Ascham supported the native literary forms. They admired Rome but loved London. The conflict was between the native and the foreign literary forms. All students of English literature know it well that it progressed by exquisitely balancing its native traditions with their alien counterparts in the sixteenth century, as William Shakespeare resisted and even assimilated the systematic foreign modes with his native wild wood notes.

The Americans also found themselves on the crossroads of history where they had to encounter their moment of choice. R.W. Emerson delivered his famous lectures "American Scholar" on October 31, 1837, almost 61 years after the political independence. The lecture was hailed as a declaration of independence from literary colonialism. His quest for the American scholar was a part of the debate between the subscribers of the nascent American and the established Greek-Roman European traditions. Regarding myth his friend Margaret Fueller opined that they (the Americans) were the direct descendents of the Europeans, so the Greek and Roman myths were their own. Hence, they can be used for their literary creativity. But mythology needs a past that America did not have then. And the past cannot be manufactured, else the Americans would have. Emerson constructed a new definition of myth, as he wrote in his journal that myth is what is believed in by most of the people on most of the occasions in most of the places. It was in perusal of this project that the myth of the Frontier, the Road, the American Dream, the American Adam, and the Success were constructed and made use of by the novelists and later dramatists in such a way that American literature not only carved a particular niche for itself in the world literature by the advent of the twentieth century but also its identity distinct from English literature.

There are two principal fears of provincialism and revivalism often raised against nativism. The fears of suppression of "little voices" by the dominant hegemonic power groups trying to impose homogeneity and of the rise of "little nationalities" due to insistence on specificities are not absolutely baseless. They can bring the pluralist India on the brink of disintegration, particularly when these little nationalities begin to clash against each other. As far as the charge of narrow parochialism against nativism is concerned, it has to be admitted that even Shakespeare would have been a parochial writer if, by the standards of sceptics of nativism, English unattended by their traders, pirates and army and consequent colonisation of a large part of the world, were not to become an international language.

The critics of nativism see the seeds of revivalism in it. Quite natural. Narrow rigid nativism may lead towards revivalism. But it has to be borne in mind that "revival" *per se* is not as bad as revivalism is. Revival attempted after considering the questions—what should be revived and what should not be?— is not always either unwarranted or unwanted. Unwise it would be to consider the past traditions as a useless lump and discard them altogether. It may prove fatal for new creativity, for the fears of revivalism inveigle upon them to sever links with the tradition. For instance, the most of our twentieth century problems are descendents of their nineteenth century counterparts. Hence it is imperative for us to go to the reformers, thinkers and writers and the model that they had constructed to examine them in their complexities in order to eradicate them. To take whatever suits our purpose of preparing our strategy to respond to our obtaining problems is neither retrogression nor revivalism. Is return to the Indian literary and critical traditions to seek and revive, whatever has possibility of regeneration, or revival? If it is so, then this revivalism is better than the slavish imitation of Western theories, a rampant practice. Did the Western criticism not revive rhetoric for its own development? The rhetoric belonged to the ancient Greece and Rome not to the twentieth century.

Almost a century ago Vivekananda after his return from the West was concerned with the question pertaining to revival in religion in particular. In his "Reply to the Address of Welcome at Madurai" he spoke on different aspects of revivalism: "There is danger ahead as well as glory; for revival; sometimes breeds fanaticism, sometimes goes to the extreme, so that often it is not in even in the power of those who start the revival to control it when it has gone beyond a certain length. It is better, therefore, to be forewarned. We have to find our way between the Scylla of old superstitious orthodoxy and the Charybdis of materialism of Europeanism, of soullessness, of the so-called reform which has penetrated to the foundation of Western progress. These two have to be taken care of. In the first place, we cannot become Westerns; therefore imitating the Western is useless.... In the second place, it is impossible."

In his "Reply to the Address of Welcome at Ramanad" on 25 January, 1897 Vivekananda spoke to the then generation caught in the warp of the Westernisation and native Indian tradition. It was a question that haunted him and he responded to it again almost in the same idiom by probing further into the issue every time with his arguments. The question, like one of Yasksn's, still haunts the Indian society:

> There are two great obstacles on our path in India, the Scylla of old orthodoxy and the Charybdis of modern European civilisation. Of these two, I vote for the old orthodoxy, and not for the Europeanised system; for the old orthodox man may be ignorant, he may be crude, but he has a faith, he has strength, he stands on his feet, while the Europeanised man has no backbone, he is a mass of heterogeneous ideas picked up at random from every source and these ideas are unassimilated, undigested, unharmonised. He does not stand on his feet and his head is turning round and round. *(151)*

Vivekananda may be accused of advocating "old orthodoxy" and of willingness to be co-opted by the revivalist Hindu fanatics. But he needs none. At least me, to support him against the sceptics. He was fully aware of the dangers implicit in revivalism, as he forewarned us against consequent fanaticism. But he preferred orthodoxy to Europeanism. We need not subscribe to his views or be an alarmist or a rejectionist. But we have to bear in mind that the obtaining Westernism conditions and controls the other by determining its choice. What we need is to prepare a strategy of revival for survival. Everything is not to be revived. The important question is: What should be revived? And what should not be revived? Some of our sage writers have left a few pieces of advice for us in this regard. "In Conversation" with me Namvar Singh, the noted Hindi critic, referred to Tulsidas who said in the sixteenth century, *Sangraha tyagu na binu pahachane.* (Acquisition or rejection without recognition—both are dangerous.) Tulsidas forewarned us against "unrecognised" accumulation or rejection of our past and condition. In the twentieth century Suryakanta Tripathi also said:

> *Bhram mein jo liya gayan mein lo tum gin gin.*
> *Bhram mein jo diya gayan mein do tum gin gin.*

(Whatever you accepted in ignorance, you should accept in the state of knowledge; whatever you reject in ignorance, you must do so in full knowledge.)

Acquisition of something new or alien or abandonment of one's own without recognition or consideration, both are equally dangerous. Whatever is rotten should be forsaken as surgeons remove the malignant from the good. But what harm is there in accepting what has the possibility of life and regeneration? Instead of wailing over the fear of revivalism what is needed is pragmatic, progressive and positive revival of our tradition. "So we will have to understand the difference between ignorance and knowledge like the proverbial blind man who threw way valuable gold and diamonds and kept stones. We have almost thrown away our ancient poetics and *alamkarshastra*. The Westerns on the other hand have been taking out gold from their patchwork and developing theories for long. We must also do the same. In this sense revival is not bad, if it is done with discretion, discrimination and wisdom," observed Namvar Singh.

To conclude let me go back to *deshivad*. Postmodernism and postcolonialism can be suitably written as *deshivad* or should be written with full consciousness of *deshivad*. Concerned it is with roots but it should not be forgotten that even the birds do not make their nests in roots. Human beings also do not make their home "in" the foundation but "on" it to look beyond in the sky above. Our love for our roots should not inveigle upon us to keep holding our roots or tie them around our necks. That would prove suicidal. Despite this there are some legitimate reservation against *deshivad*. K. Satchidanandan has referred to some of the legitimate fears like parochialism, revivalism and dangers of disintegration in his article "Nativism and its Ambivalances". And if our fears and anxieties pertaining to *deshivad* persist, it becomes imperative for us to reconsider and redefine the term keeping our obtaining context and situation in mind. We can look back and go beyond Nemade if not as far as Bhartendu, Chiplunkar, Narmada, or Bankim in the nineteenth century—for a new dimension that Gandhiji gave to *deshivad* which to some critics has always ever been present in the twentieth century with his *Swadeshi*. His *Swadeshi* was a strategy or an alternative against *videshi* or *pardeshi*. As of now politically the problem of *pardeshi* or *videshi* is over, though indirectly it challenges other voices, cultures, literatures and societies. There is no denying the fact that we have to take even form *videshi* whatever is useful for us in it. And if our *deshivad* has failed to remove our fears and anxieties of our own people, it should be redefined. Gandhiji had to make a choice between *swadeshi* and *pardeshi/videshi*, we have to make a choice between *kudeshivad* and *sudeshivad*. And our choice should fall on *sudeshivad*—positive, pragmatic, inclusive, swastha (swa + stha = located in one's self). The alternative to postmodernism is *sudeshivad* whose alternative there seems to be none.

2

Towards a Comprehensive Theory of Literary Criticism in English in India

—*C.R. Kar*

Which comes first—creativity or criticism? Obviously, creativity and criticism go hand in hand. The author is the first critic. His perception of the world is no doubt a critique of what and how things, events, characters around him are at his disposal. "Theoretical perceptions relate to shared experiences and in aesthetics they evolve out of experiences" (Jain, 2000, 40). Dryden, Wordswoth, Coleridge, T.S. Eliot, Tagore, W.B. Yeats, James Joyce, Aurobindo, etc. are no less critics than writers in their times because writers re-create as do careful or responsive readers.

In this sense, criticism may be taken as re-creation. And no writer writes as he imagines rather he leaves it incomplete, as Paul Valery puts it, "a poem is never completed, it is only abandoned." This also means that the reader too creates and re-creates and it never ends, "The literary man is philosophically eclectic because what makes him literary also makes him long for possibilities which are not available in the philosophy of his choice. The literary man, like the artist, wants to live a hundred lives. Whitman's statement about himself applies to the literary class as a human type which includes all those literary imaginations that do not produce literary works" (Ezekiel, 2000, 102).

> Do I contradict myself?
> Very well, then, I contradict myself.
> I am large. I contain multitudes. (Song of Myself)

The last line clearly reverberates the vedic hymn: *aham brahmasmi, ekoham bahusyama.*

While confronting with a variety of literary theories in the last four decades, there are hardly any careful readers left without confusion. It is because the theories put forth are least helpful in clarifying the meaning and theme of the text. "Several schools of criticism in the west in competing with each other have made the study of literature a cerebral exercise" (Das, 2001, 11-12).

Literary criticism in English in our country shows a very negative side of the picture as Kapoor (1998, 2) has rightly put:

1) The relationship between Indian and Western scholars has been restricted to a one-way receiver-donor relationship generating a subordination of mind which is evident in the almost mechanical adoption and application of changing theoretical critical models (with the necessary time-lag).

2) The Indian scholar has become an uncritical receiver, for he has not been provided access to the alternative (native) ground from where he could have actively evaluated Western systems.

3) University research / thinking has been limited to applying, in respective fields, the newest Western proposals, uncritically received in the first instance, to Indian regional data. This theory-data relationship is attested by thousands of theses/ dissertations lying in the cupboards of university departments.

4) As Rege (1988, xxii) has pointed out, it has delayed the proper fulfilment of scholarship in Indian thought because:

    a) Indian systems of ideas are selected for research for their pertinence or relationship to some Western system;

b) the interest in Indian systems is by and large merely historical and the systems remain unexpounded); and

c) as undertaken by Western trained Indian scholars, the Indian concepts are not articulated as parts of a total conceptual scheme. There is, hence, a need to expound the Indian systems.

5) The possibility of the Indian intellectual tradition opening out of its self-imposed isolation has not been fully realised. This could have been realised if some sort of mobility and continuity had been established between the traditional and the new centres of learning and through translations of primary classical texts into all contemporary Indian languages.

6) Finally, the advantage of true and proper encounter between the relativity stable Indian systems and the dynamic Western systems in diverse disciplines has not been recognised.

To overcome this pathetic situation, mere comparison will not be of any great avail. Instead we need to devise a cohesive scheme of literary analysis in such a way that "The line which has existed so far between Western criticism and Indian poetics will have to be effaced. Instead of comparing the two traditions to establish that we are better, we shall have to use our critical tradition in Sanskirt and regional language in international critical debates. In a discussion of metaphor, for example, we can bring together western and Indian views on this central literary device, point out where Indian and western critics are right or wrong, and evolve our concept of the nature and function of metaphor" (Rajnath, 2001).

In trying to evolve a comprehensive theory of criticism, we must not forget that any single theory or any single school of criticism does not and cannot cover the whole of literary analysis. Furthermore, a theory must not underscore the work of art, for, "Creative writing generates the parameters for its own evaluation, very often the form and experimentation in itself is either an exposition of an existing framework or a questioning. It makes a shift in the nature of aesthetics, the development of the genre, the nature of imagination or the relationship of the writer with society. To separate writing from theory as raw material and finished product is to miss the point" (Jain, 2000, 17).

In an appropriate approach to literary studies we have also to remember that "In the mind of the reader a book by a talented writer usually stands as an integral whole and indeed it is profound, organic unity for which the writer always strives" (Khrapchendo, 1977, 89). Kshmendra (11th century A.D.) treats *auchitya* (propriety or appropriateness) the central element of literariness. He defines *auchitya* as the property of an expression (signifier) being an exact and appropriate analogue of the expressed (signified)" (Kapoor, 1998, 27).

The reader, while reading a piece of literary work, encounters\ language first. Roland Barthes thinks, "While the work is held in the hand, the text is held in language: it exists only as discourse. The text is not the decomposition of the work rather it is the work that is the text's imaginary tail. In other words, the text is experienced only in an activity, a production" (1985, 414-415).

However, "in a literary creation the function of language goes much beyond that of denotation and connotation. Language here does not only 'mean', but also 'exists': it does not only refer to objects of the outside world, but becomes an object itself" (Srivastava and Gupta, 1987, 17:36). This object is, what Paul Valery suggests, "a language within language" (1958, 64).

Thus, literary language, as a discourse, encompasses the whole context of its use, viz., the author, the style, the content or subject-matter, the theme, the time, the space, and the social customs and systems relevant to the work of art and, as Bhattanayaka says, it neither undermines the author, the protagonist, nor the reader/ receiver to create a balance between the two and bring harmony in the trio and being of that text as co-text by way of deconstruction *vis-a-vis* re-creation by the reader/receiver. So to speak, a comprehensive theory of literary criticism would be one that fulfils this criterion of balancing and harmonising. "Indian Poetics banks heavily on the reader's/ spectator's identification with the creative writer for aesthetic delectation" (Pathak, 1998, 68).

An Elizabethan spectator, M.C. Bradbrook, attests this fact as follows:

> The way in which an audience was delighted or ravished or charmed in Elizabethan times implies their collective assent beyond the level of everything feeling.... Abhinavagupta, five hundred years before Zeami, maintained that the spectator participates imaginatively but actively in the play. He tastes the emotion as immediate experience through an imaginary identification, but it is gereralised in his lived or pre-reflected consciousness. To achieve this he has to be trained in feeling, as the actor trained in movement and speech has to be a qualified spectator, an *adhikarin* (1972, 42).

The above paraphrase of Bhattanayaka's term "sadharanikarana" has been translated by Pathak as "transpersonalisation" (1998, 68).

What actually makes an author identifiable amongst others is his style—the way he uses his language—words, phrases, idioms, proverbs, symbols, myths, metaphors, imagery, fantasy, etc., the characters, the themes, all couched in language. "Indian literary theories are constitutive theories, i.e. they are concerned with analysing how *meaning* is constructed, through what devices of cognition and communication, and how the work succeeds in giving enjoyment, *ananda*, to the *sahrdayas*. There is a pervasive consciousness of the linguistic materiality of texts and a concern for craftsmanship and form, as it is believed that it is HOW something is constructed that constitutes the element of beauty in a composition and is the source of delight. The major concern, therefore, is chiefly HOW and secondarily WHAT (meaning) to the extent that *what* is involved in explaining *how*. This explains the exhaustive enumeration and examination of *alamkaras*, the figures of speech—a subject that remains central throughout the tradition of literary thinking. These devices are not seen as merely 'ornaments' but as integral to the constitution of meanings—as the poet's epistemology, his mode of perception" (Kapoor, 1998, 45-46). This is why the poets were also called 'alamkarins' in ancient times.

This HOW must not be, in any case, thought of as the western 'style' which does only analyse the choice of language, deviation, and parallelism in a stereotyped way rather it is the harmonious cohesion of *reeti, vrtti,* and *pravrtti,* in which *reeti* is the author's craft, *vrtti* the power or vigour of language, and *pravrtti* the social/geographical trends in vogue.

Language is culture, i.e., language is cultivated as is culture cultivated. Literary language is the recultivation by an author. This is the starting point of all Indian aestheticians or poeticists when they variously emphasise on the harmonious relation between the word (signifier) and its meaning (signified) which, nonetheless, has a free play in the making of the text as a 'meta-sign' (*mahavakya*) — a discourse. And it is needless to say that the signifier-signified relationship can be evaluated only by those who are both critics and grammarians (linguists) as *Anandavardhana* (9th century A.D.) puts it:

> shabdarthashasanajnandmatrenaiva na vedyate
> vedyate sa tu kavyarthatattwajnairaiva kevalam
>
> *(Dhwanyaloka, 1.7)*

Which is paraphrased by Halliday as:

> Linguistics is not and will never be the whole of literary analysis and only the literary analyst—not the linguist— can determine the place of linguistics in literary studies. (1966, 42-55)

To conclude, let the critic be an intermediary between the author and the reader not by complicating but by explicating the text. While doing this, the critic must not undermine language as merely an instrument or medium of communication. Roman Jakobson has rightly proposed:

> A linguist deaf to the poetic function of language and a literary scholar indifferent to linguistic problems and unconversant with the gains and insights of linguistics are hardly better than flagrant anachronisms (1960 : 377).

Works Cited

Anandavardhana, *Dhwanyalokalochana, cf,* Pathak, 1998, 67.

Barthes, Roland,"From Work to Text", *Literary Criticism: A Reading,* B. Das and J.M. Mohanty (eds.), Calcutta, Oxford University Press, 1985.

Das, Bijay Kumar, "Whither Literary Criticism", *The Ravenshaw Journal of English Studies,* Vol. XI, Nos. 1-2, Jan.-Dec., 2001, 7-16.

Ezekiel, Nissim,"Philosophy of the Literary Man", Jain (ed.), 2000, 96-103.

Halliday, M.A.K., "Descriptive Linguistics in Literary Studeis". Angys McIntosh, M.A.K. Halliday (eds.), *Patterns of Language: Papers in General, Descriptive and Applied Linguistics,* London, Longmans, 1996, 42-55.

Jain, Jasbir, ed., *Creating Theory : Writers on Writing*. Delhi, Pencraft International, 2000.

Jakobson, Roman, "Linguistics and Poetics", in *Style in Language,* Thomas A. Sebeok (ed.), Cambridge, Mass, 1960.

Kapoor, Kapil, *Literary Theory: Indian Conceptual Framework.* New Delhi, Affiliated East-West Press Pvt., 1988.

Khrapchenko, M., *The Writer's Creative Individuality and the Development the Literature* (Trans. from Russian by Natalie Ward), Moscow, Progress Publishers, 1977.

Pathak, R.S., *Comparative Poetics,* New Delhi, Creative Books, 1998.

Paul Valery, *The Art of Poetry* (Trans. D. Folliot), London, 1958.

Rajnath, "Literary Criticism in the New Millenium", In *Littcrit,* 27: 1-2 (June-Dec.) 2001, 14-26.

Srivastava, R.N. & Gupta, R.S, "Language(s) in Literature: A Semio-Linguistic Approach", *Language Forum,* Vol. 13, Nos. 1-14,1987, 17-37.

3

Universality of Colonial Experience

—Shubha Tiwari

"Erstwhile colonies of the world unite!" sounds a loud call. Nevertheless, the loudness of the call does not undermine its relevance and legitimacy. The politics of colonisation has been such that countries that had been close historically and culturally in the past, have now been distanced. Countries that would have been natural friends have become enemies. For example, Thailand, Myanmar and Singapore are very near to Indian culture and ethos. But the significant part of their trade and bilateral dealings are with Europe. The fact that our colonisers were the same people and they exploited and ransacked our different lands should actually kindle sympathy. Ironically, it is not so.

In the literary field, there are universal echoes in the expression of colonial experience and postcolonial response to it. When Gabriel Garcia Marquez defies the Western cannon of decent, rational writing and fills his tales with unfathomed mysteries, fountains of eternal youth, hems with tiny lumps of gold, witches and spirits, the Western mind boggles but we as Indians find exact affiliation with that kind of writing. In a country like India where ghosts, spirits, gods and goddesses have been integral part of the tapestry of life, there is no problem in understanding Marquez. When we study the Nobel Lectures by Marquez or Octavio Paz of Pablo Neruda, their concerns seem to be exactly ours. The social agenda in which literature is an important crystallising catalyst of all erstwhile colonies is quite similar. We may take note of the following words of the Nobel Lecture by Marquez, "... the Europeans of good will and sometimes those of bad as well, have been struck with ever greater force by the unearthly tidings of Latin America, that boundless realm of haunted men and historical women, whose unending obstinacy blurs into legend."[1]

We cannot miss the irony of these words. The so-called civilised world is entertained by 'unearthly' land and its people. The Third World is out for sale. We are out to entertain the rich men and women of rich nations. The rich nation need situations and people whom they can pity; no matter they themselves have been the cause of the ruin of the pitiable masses. The coloniser comes for poverty tourism. We may be millionaires but we may remember that we are slum dogs.

I find postcolonialism to be a cry against the unjust world order. The rich, mysterious, proud and boundless past of the erstwhile colonies on the one hand and utter penury, lack of self-respect and today's state of disfigured mentality on the other, put the erstwhile colonies in tongue-less solitude and loneliness. They are in a bewildered state. After being repeatedly looted, they do not know where they stand or what they should say. This is a pathetic state indeed. We are not honoured by our own honours. We do not judge ourselves by our own yardsticks. We are not even elated by our own beauty. "Pappu ki aakhein light blue, Pappu dikhta angrez hai." For being handsome, Pappu must look like an 'angrez'.

Postcolonialism challenges those parameters with which the dominant European culture judges other cultures. Alien yardsticks applied to the history, culture and literature of erstwhile colonies have no validity. Life, breath, history, geography, fervour, art, food, ways of worship, thinking and parenting—just everything is different in any given two distinct territories of the world. Why should rules and values of one area be applied to the others? This is absolutely unjust. Marquez says in his Nobel Lecture, "The interpretation of our reality through patterns not our own, serves only to make us even more unknown, ever less free, ever more solitary."[2] Every nation has to undergo the painful process of birth in order to be recognised and respected. There is no cake walk alternative. Marquez urges the European world to "reconsider their ways of seeing us." Every nation should have its own agenda, its own priorities and techniques of achieving its desired aims. Marquez uses a beautiful phrase 'solidarity with our dreams!' One's dreams should be one's own; every nation should stand by its own dreams. The point is to drive home the cruelty of colonisation and resultant unjust world order. The unjust world order has denied the erstwhile colonies of establishing their own goals and means of achieving those goals. In today's world, no nation can survive without being at the mercy of the rich nations.

When we look at the Middle Eastern countries, we will again find similar patterns of chaos and disorder. The tale of these countries could have been the tale of India or Pakistan or Myanmar. In 2004, Labri Sadiki wrote *The Search for Arab Democracy: Discourses and Counter-Discourses*. The book is an eye opener. Most of the Middle Eastern countries are facing the severe problem of loss of identity. More than three-quarters of a century after the disintegration of the Ottoman Empire, from which most of these countries emerged, these states have been unable to define, project and maintain a national identity that is both inclusive and representative. Independence and political end of colonisation have ended in social fragmentation and war in the Middle East. Whenever a reference to Middle East is made, the picture of perpetual conflict, war and poverty comes to our mind. The problems of today's Middle East can be traced back to imperialism and colonialism because European colonial powers drew borders ignoring the roots of the region, ancient tribal boundaries and local histories.

It is opined this is exactly the manner in which disputes between India and Pakistan ought to be viewed. The lean man with a *lathi* might have been killed for this but the fact remains that division of India was done on unjust grounds.

When we see the African situation, we are surprised to note that the strongest postcolonial notes come from this part of the world, yet the interiors of Africa were not colonised until almost the end of the nineteenth century. Africa was looted faster and more intensely than any other colonial region in the world. Perhaps that is the reason for the sharpness in the postcolonial voice from Africa. The British Empire tried to overlook and ignore the African empires of the precolonial era. The British tried to build one single railroad throughout the whole continent and thus 'educate' the lot in one go. I am again reminded of a short story by Marquez titled *The Sea of Lost Time* where Mr. Herbert arrives on an untouched, virgin island and slowly eats the very spirit of the island and its people. He offers huge money to natives for receiving 'his' education and finally succeeds in corrupting all that was once pure and original.

Chinua Achebe from Nigeria and Ngugi wa Thiongo from Kenya have been powerful postcolonial voices. The African voice is full of pain for the inhuman treatment of the natives. Achebe's call is basically for considering the viewpoints of the non-Westernised nations. He suggests ways of considering effects of colonialism. His classic criticism (1975) of Conrad's *Heart of Darkness* echoes our criticism of novels or films that project our country in bad light. What we often say about Arvind Adiga's *The White Tiger* or Arundhati Roy's *The God of Small Things* or movies like *Slumdog Millionnaire* directly echoes what Achebe says of Conrad's book. Damaging stereotypes of the erstwhile colonies must not be perpetuated.

French voice against colonialism in the form of Frantz Fanon's *The Wretched of the Earth* (1961) and Albert Memmi's *The Coloniser and the Colonised* highlight use of violence in establishing the new world order. Fanon's words echo the voice of extreme rightists in India who openly say that bloodshed and the path suggested by the likes of Bhagat Singh and Subhash Chandra Bose would have produced greater national solidarity among Indians.

Edward Said (1978), through his *Orientalism*, does not say anything with which we do not feel instant affinity. The book is basically a protest against the (mis) presentation of the Orient by the Occident. He has convincingly and powerfully shown the repetition of damaging and incorrect projection of the orient by the Occident. Said openly discards writers like Edward William Lane who spend two to three years in Egypt and come with an entire book on Egyptians, *Manners and Customs of the Modern Egyptians*. The book became the Bible of knowing Egyptian culture in Europe. This is how wrong constructs go abounding in literature and society alike. We can find countless parallels of our Indian society's faulty description by the colonisers. The recent public movement in our country to call the events of 1857, the first War of Independence, instead of the Mutiny can be cited as one example. Even sympathetic books like A.L. Basham's *The Wonder that was India* cited as a classic by many, eventually end up making India even more unknown and inscrutable for the rest of the world. The countless works on our spiritual traditions, on India's poverty and its alleviation and various other issues come under this kind of knowledge.

What is needed is a living model of postcolonialism. We have enough of disinterested, dispassionate, 'unfeeling' literary criticism. We must find universal patterns in the postcolonial voices and envisage common strategies to resist neo-colonialism in the form of catchy phrases like globalisation and postmodernism.

Z. Sardar in his book *Postmodernism and the Other: The New Imperialism of Western Culture* says:

> Colonialism was about the physical occupation of non western cultures. Modernity was about displacing the present and occupying the minds of nonwestern cultures. Post modernism is about appropriating the history and identity of non western cultures as an integral face of itself, colonising their future and occupying their being.[3]

Similarly, R.I. Young in his book *Post Colonialism: An Historical Introduction* says:

> To sweep colonialism under the carpet of modernity, however, is too convenient a deflection. To begin with, its history was extraordinary in its global dimension, not only in relation to the comprehensiveness of colonisation by the time of the high imperial period in the late 19th century, but

> also because the effect of the globalisation of western imperial power was to fuse many societies with different historical traditions into a history which, apart from the period of centrally controlled command economics, obliged them to follow the same general economic path. The entire world now operates with the economic system primarily developed and controlled by the west and it is the continued dominance of the West, in terms of political, economic, military and cultural power, that gives this history a continuing significance. Political liberation did not bring economic liberation and without economic liberation there can be no political liberation.[4]

We as educators must be alert to multi-culture contexts. If we are chauvinistic and elitist in our approach, we cannot be said to be practising postcolonialism. We must have our own education system. We must be sensitive to those segments of society that have been marginalised over the ages by forces such as religion, tradition, mythology, trade or system of government.

It was Lord Buddha who for the first time in the history of human kind spoke of 'Gantantra' He visualised representatives of the different sections of the society coming together and solving all issues pertaining to polity. We have to be careful in guarding ourselves against reverse racism. Every person in the society has a right to speak for every other section of the society. Our education system is hopelessly repetitive and orientated towards cramming. Noam Chomsky says, "Far from the democratic education we claim to have, what we really have in place is a sophisticated colonial model of education designed primarily to train teachers in ways in which the intellectual dimension is often devalued. The major objective of a colonial education is to further de-skill teachers, and students to walk un-reflectively through a labyrinth of procedures and techniques."[5]

We must evolve our own pedagogy which is more inclusive and more elastic. De-centralisation of education is an immediate need. Good quality education must be provided in ali towns, big or small. Hierarchy in education is the most dangerous trend that a society can actually face. McLaren and Torrese have opined in *Critical Multiculturalism: Rethinking Multicultural and Anti Racist Education*:

> Critical educators must always ask themselves tough questions what is the hidden history of otherness contained within our narratives of liberation? Whom do they exclude, marginalise, repress? How can we re-gather what has been lost and fill the empty space of despair with revolutionary hope? Hope stipulates an 'other' who stands before us?[6]

When we reject the signifying system of imperialism, that rejection should percolate in our own society as well. We need to replace the system of colonial thought with our own patterns and styles. For example, cold theorising has had a dampening effect on many non-Western societies. Non-Western societies are warmer in their human relationship. The people of these societies speak more; they are more informal in their behaviour; they weep more openly; and they are basically storytellers. Many great writers like Marquez, Achebe, and Rushdie have gone directly to precolonial style of storytelling. This is an effective tool.

Payne declares:

> Since scientific descriptions have traditionally enjoyed a higher truth status in Western culture, postmodern expositions tend to give more attention to the previously undervalued narrative mode....But in a post–modern perspective it is assumed that it is our immediate, day to day, concrete, personal apprehension of our lives- expressed through the 'stories' we tell ourselves and others about our lives- that is primarily predictable. The stories are also influential. In a postmodern perspective these stories or narratives form matrix of concepts and beliefs by which we understand our lives and the world in which our lives take place; and there is a continuing interaction between the stories, we tell ourselves about our lives, and the further stories we then tell.[7]

It is a common accepted fact that traditional societies, particularly their women, communicate better through experiences, life stories and anecdotes. In this regard folk literature projects and programmes on oral literature can be effective tools of ending colonial mindset. Stone–Mediatore says, "Many third world women in particular, have found theoretical discourses inadequate and have turned to experience oriented writing to communicate their struggle against an array of patriarchal and neo-colonialist institutions. When scholars focused on criticising experience we alienated our work from these practical struggles. We may address other's stories as sites for deconstructive analysis, but we forfeit learning from them and building theories responsive to them."[8]

So our own encounters with any kind of colonial attitude or racism become relevant to the practice of postcolonial theory. Once my uncle, while on a visit to London, asked a Londoner as to where he might get clothes. Critically looking at my uncle's skin, the Londoner said, "Rags are sold over there, especially for Asian." My sister, currently living in Barack Obama's America, tells that whites do not prefer to mix with coloured people. All those who are in touch with international media (through internet, of course) know about British media's constant description of Janjaweed militants of Sudan as 'Arab' ! People of Sudan speak Arabic, wear Dish-dasha (the flowing dress of men) and are Muslims. Apart from these affiliations to Arabic nations, we all can locate that Sudan is not an Arabic nation. But the feeling of alienation, of self-encased identity is such among all of us that Sudani people become African people. We are all suffering from 'I, Me, Myself' syndrome.

Postcolonialism is about breaking this rigidity. We have to be involved and concerned in matters of national and individual dignity. In this manner we can actually contribute to a world which is run by justice, transparency and honesty. It is very difficult to decolonise minds. We have taken layers and layers of borrowed training. Postcolonialism is not averse to new ideas. It only urges us to negotiate well with the bombardment of trends and formally establish ourselves. We might be silly, passionate, touchy and what not, but the best agenda is to be ourselves. We have swallowed so much from the West that to undo all that is definitely a huge task. But we can always try. To quote a few lines from a poem *Don't Say* by Ludy Massamba (1988):

> Don't say you love me
> Because you must know the meaning of love
> Before saying it

Don't let I love you sound like the English
'Good Morning, How are you?'
Don't say
Don't say you care for me
Because one must care for herself
Before caring for someone else,
So don't say you care for me
When you don't care for yourself
Don't say
Don't say you will do anything for me
When you cannot do a thing for yourself
Don't say
Don't say you will never lie to me
Because you are doing it
Don't say

I find this poem not only beautiful but also a strong statement against Westernisation. We are Indians. We need to speak our own language; the mood and tone must be ours.

The best way of practising postcolonialism is to be ourselves. Postcolonial is often criticised for its fixation to the past. But without proper understanding of the past, there can be no future. Postcolonialism is simply sensitising a person about any kind of unjustified misappropriation, dominance or oppression. We totally agree with R.J. Young when he says, "Postcolonial critique is a form of activist writing that looks back to the political commitment of the anti colonial liberation movements and draws its inspiration from them, while recognising that they often operated under conditions very different from those that that exist in the present."[10]

References

1. www.noblelectures.org
2. Ibid.
3. Sardar Z., 1998, *Postmodernism and the Other*, London: Pluto, 13.
4. Young, R.J., *Postcolonialism: An Historical Introduction*, 2001, Oxford: Blackwell, 5.
5. Chomsky, Nom, *Chomsky on Miseducation*, 2000, Lanham: Rawman and Little Field Publishers, 3.

6. May, S. ed., *Critical Multiculturalism: Rethinking Multicultural and Antiracist Education,* 1999, London: Falmer Press, 208.
7. Payne, M, *Narrative Therapy*. 2000. London: Sage, 20.
8. Stone, Mediatore, 2003, *Reading Across Borders: Story – telling and Knowledge of Resistance,* New York: Palgrave, Macmillan, 1.
9. www.africana.com.
10. Young, R.J., op.cit, 10.

4

Understanding Postcolonialism

—*Sunil Kumar Navin*

The ascendency of Barak Hussein Obama, an African-American, to the US presidency has ultimately broken the myth of the long-drawn racial conflict which has always been the key issue of postcolonial study. Equality of races, irrespective of caste, creed and colour, region and religion, has been the objective humanity has been aspiring to achieve and thus make this lovely blue planet a place worth living.

A large number of cultural critiques of the empire and its aftermath published in the past two decades and designated with 'Postcolonialism' are chiefly concerned with experienecs of exclusion, denigration and resistance under systems of colonial control. To be precise, the term postcolonialism addresses itself to the historical, political, cultural and textual ramifications of the colonial encounter between the West and the non-West dating from the sixteenth century to the present day. It studies how this encounter shaped the destiny of the colonisers as well as the colonised. Particularly the study of postcolonial cultures, texts and politics brings to light the responses to colonial oppression which were oppositional and contestatory. It predominantly manifests resistance of the colonised to unjust and unequal forms of political and cultural authority.

The publication of *Orientalism* in 1978 was epoch making and marked the beginning of postcolonial studies. Gayatri Spivak and Homi Bhabha have been closely associated with postcolonial approach. However, it is equally important to recognise the legacy of anti-colonial nationalist thinkers and theorists like Mohandas Gandhi and Franz Fanon who have contributed significantly to shaping postcolonial concepts of opposition and self-determination. The immediate purpose of both of them was to ensure first human rights and *Purna Swaraj*.

Without going into a debate on whether postcolonialism should have a hyphen or not, it should be considered in a broad sense as a critical approach which questions, overturns and/or critically refracts colonial authority—its epistemologies and forms of violence, its claim to superiority. Postcolonialism, therefore, refers to those theories, texts, political strategies and modes of activism that engage in such questioning that aim to challenge structural inequalities and bring about social justice.

Freedom struggle movements in countries like India, Egypt, Algeria, Ghana, Kenya and in the Caribbeans forced the colonisers to bring about political and cultural reforms. Limited representation of the native in the colonial set-up was allowed, but they were not prepared to dismantle the social, economic and political hierarchies on which their control rested. This aggravated the native people and anti-colonial nationalist movement became aggresively confrontational. Nor was it complete independence (*Purna Swaraj* in India, *Ujamaa* in Tanzania, *Amandla* in South Africa) from the colonial hold that was at the top in the nationalists' agenda. It meant liberation of political structures as well as obliteration of what the revolutionary seer Aurobindo Ghosh in Bengal in India or Fanon in Algeria first named the colonisation of the psyche.

Owing to growing militancy in the 1960's, countries like Ghana, Nigeria, Algeria, Jamaica and Kenya became free. The indigenous culture in these countries became the most important vehicle of self-expression. The once colonised people derided the culture of the coloniser as uncouth, uncivilised, inarticulate and irrational. Nationalist leaders and intellectuals like Gandhi and Nehru in India, Fanon in Algeria and Kwame Nkrumah in Ghana helped define the major ideologies of postcolonial liberation. They shaped and gave substance to some of the definitive concepts or paradigms of what have become postcolonial studies, especially as later interpreted in the work of the critic Edward Said. These great intellectuals understood the anti-colonial struggle as a Manichaean or binary conflict of us against them, of self versus 'other'. The natives or others were always seen as secondary figures, imperfect replicas of the coloniser, wearers of borrowed cultural rags. The native society was invariably represented as disorderly or ethically degenerate. The immediate challenge for them was to remake themselves. It was important that they reconstitute their identity on their own terms, that they Indianise, Africanise or Caribbeanise themselves. What was most important for them was to have their own new identity to speak in a language that was chosen, not imposed.

The liberation struggle involved a tripartite process. The anti-colonial nationalist like the Bengali radical Aurobindo Ghosh in *The Doctrine of Passive Resistance* (1910), Frantz Fanon in *the Wretched of the Earth* (1961) or the Lusiophone African revolutionary activist Amilcar Cabral in his speech 'National Liberation and Culture' (1970) considered that the process led from attempted cultural assimilation with the colonisers through attempts at political reform (sometimes of an intensively radical kind). But if the colonial state proved uncompromising, as it so often did, forceful self-assertion developed a possible militant resistance.

It would be in the fitness of things to elucidate the views on postcolonialism of great thinkers like Frantz Fanon, Edward Said, Gaytri Spivak and Homi Bhaba. Frantz Fanon holds that the first phase of colonial assimilation will inevitably lead the colonised on to a second phase of disturbance, and this second phase involves the reconstitution of identity through reclamation of local culture and traditions. From this phase might eventually emerge a third or fighting phase. According to him the native intellectual instead of losing himself in the people will shake the people. Thus, he would seize freedom by violent means and assert political power. He would retrieve a selfhood that was damaged under colonial oppression.

Fanon's ideas had a telling impact on revolutionaries across the colonised world. He did believe that revolutionary violence had cleansing properties. Here he departs widely from the strategy of non-violence that Gandhi advocated. Gandhi's method was to expose the inhumanity of the coloniser. However, Fanon changed emphasis within his own tripartite system and hoped to find possibilities of healing under colonialism. He seems to have reconciled with the claim that the cathartic ejection of the coloniser forms the most important part of that healing process, and the basis of a reconstituted humanism.

Edward Said's Orientalism enlarged the scope of the postcolonial approaches by exposing the Eurocentric universalism which establishes Western superiority over the East, identified as the 'other'. He showed that Foucault's idea that power operates through systems of knowledge applied to the ways in which authority was exercised in the colonial world. The natives were seen as masses and not as individuals. They were held to be weak-willed, inferior, secondary, effeminate and unable to rule themselves.

Said's proposition that all empires functioned in similar ways did not go uncontested. This generalisation and universalisation was targeted and vehemently challenged. He also asserted an alternative humanism or human-centredness directed against the tainted humanism of oppressive empires. He also held that the colonised peoples were utterly silenced by being made into the object of Western systems of knowledge. The theory of Said seemed to say that the colonised lacked strategies and languages to resist oppression and decry objectification to answer back. Building on the practice of post-independence writers, such as Salman Rushdie, and theorists of anti-colonialism, like Fanon, Said traces sources of resistance in processes of reading and writing against the grain and names such resistant reading contrapuntal. He further argues that postcolonial writers are competent enough to take on or appropriate the forms, styles and symbols of the dominant texts and myths of colonial Europe. While so doing they successfully express their own perceptions of the world. He holds that postcolonial independence involves not only the recovery of geographical region, but also the reclamation of culture. Thus he shares his opinions with Bill Ashcroft, Gareth Griffiths and Helen Tiffin, the authors of *The Empire Writes Back*.

No discussion can be said to be compete unless Gayatri Spivak's critical insight is given due consideration. *Can the Subaltern speak*? she wrote and by 'subaltern' she meant the oppressed subject, non-elite social classes, groupings like proletariat, tribals, downtrodden and outcasts, untouchables and even women. Utterly unanswerable, half-serious and half-parody, the question spins round the self-conscious scene of postcolonial texts, theory, conferences and conversations. Spivak goes on to conclude that the subaltern cannot speak. She has been primarily concerned to point to the differences which separate and divide those called natives or the colonised. She emphasizes how different forms of *othering* under colonialism, even within the category of the oppressed, were not necessarily commensurable the one with the other. She laments that women have not been offered their due space; instead they have been subordinated in the traditional patriarchal structures.

The critic Homi Bhabha's contribution has been to theorise ambivalence as operating within the apparently binary colonial system itself. From this he goes on to measure what the possibilities for resistance within the system might be. In his comments on Fanon's *Black Skin, White Masks* he announces that memory is the necessary and sometimes hazardous bridge between colonialism and the question of cultural identity.

Remembering, he writes, "is never a quiet act of introspection or retrospection. It is a painful *re-membering*, a putting together of the dismembered past to make sense of the trauma of the present." The theoretical re-remebering of the colonial condition is called upon to fulfil two corresponding functions. The first is the simpler disinterment of unpalatable memories which seek to uncover the overwhelming and lasting violence of colonisation. The second is reconciliatory in its attempt to make the hostile and antagonistic past more familar and therefore more approachable. The fulfilment of the latter project requires that images expelled by the violence of the postcolonial be reclaimed and owned again. Thus it can be concluded that the forgotten content of postcoloniality effectively reveals the story of an ambivalent and symbiotic relationship between the colonisers and the colonised.

Over the last few decades, postcolonial study has emerged both as a meeting point and battleground for a variety of disciplines and theories. While it has enabled a complex interdisciplinary dialogue within the humanities, its uneasy incorporation of mutually antagonistic theories, such as Marxism and post-structuralism, confounds any uniformity of approach. As a consequence, there is little consensus regarding the proper content, scope and relevance of postcolonial studies.

Works Cited

Boehmer, Elleke, Postcolonialism, *Literary Theory and Criticism*, ed. by Patricia Waugh, Oxford University Press, 2006.

Memmi, Albert, *The Coloniser and the Colonised*, Boston: Beacon Press, 1965.

Gandhi, Leela, *Post-Colonial Theory*, Oxford University Press, 1998.

Kar, P.C. (Ed.), *Critical Theory (Western and Indian)*, Pencraft International Delhi).

Krishnaswamy, N., *Contempory Literary Theory*.

Mishra, Sunita, *A Student's Companion*, Verghese John, Macmillan India Ltd.

5

Strategies to Devalue a Nation's Past and Postcolonial Resistance

— V.Pala Prasada Rao

The main argument of the essay is to deconstruct the Euro-centric norms, universalistic and other colonial practices which had long been in vogue until such overriding claims were dismantled by postcolonial critics. It is remarkable to note that this has been the fulcrum of endeavours of Frantz Fannon, Edward Said, Gayatri Spivak, Homi Bhaba, Bill Ashcroft and scores of other postcolonial critics. Though colonialism was defunct, it is likely to resurrect in various hidden forms and so the creative writers would seek to debunk it with all informed fervour in their novels. This paper attempts to study wiles of the colonial powers who seek to employ all means to keep the natives under their sway. In their polemical work on colonialism, *The Empire Writes Back* (1989) Bill Ashcroft, Gareth Griffiths and Helen Tiffin show how Eurocentric norms and practices are being promoted by a sleight of hand to an elevated status, and all others correspondingly relegated to subsidiary, marginalised roles. The British rule in the colonies demonstrated the fact how the natives were let to indulge in internecine quarrels. It is clear that the British took advantage of it, encouraged it, and helped it reach the monstrous proportions that it ultimately did in 1946-47.

Colonial authorities followed a policy of divide and rule, promoted communalism, accentuated communal conflicts and used communalism to perpetuate their rule. In other words, colonial state made consistent attempts to accentuate all actual or potential antagonism within Indian society. In the end they banked heavily on communal antagonism. In the novel, *Tamas* (1987), Richard, the highest official of a district in North West Frontier Province, becomes the mouthpiece of British imperialism when he takes upon himself the task of putting into practice the policies and imperialist designs of the British ruling class. This is clear when he confides to his wife: "When the people fight among themselves the ruler is safe" (Bhisham Sahni, 45).

With an intention to protect the interests of the empire at any cost Richard in *Tamas* is prone to play off one community against the other. The delegates belonging to all religions come to seek his help, as there is an impending riot. He knows the explosive situation in the city owing to a carcass of a pig thrown on the steps of a mosque. But he is not inclined to stave off the imminent riot. Hence, he pays scant attention: "The usual routine stuff ... some tension in the city. Between the Hindus and the Muslims. But that is nothing new. You find this all over the country" (*Tamas*,44). Their promptitude to initiate action against the warring groups was suspect. The conversation between Lizza and Richard reveals that the British rulers did play vital role in the promotion, spread, growth and ultimate success of communalism. Their role became crucial precisely because they held the state power, which was an important determinant in toning down the differences. They could prevent Indians from fighting in the name of religion. This is clearly told with great candour by Bakshiji when he curtly puts it to Richard: "Everything is under you, Saheb. If only you have a mind to" (Bhisham Sahni,74). But Richard is quick to add arrogantly that the problem should be brought before Pandit Nehru or Baldev Singh. The fact is that Richard is reluctant to keep the city under control at least for the time being. It is obvious from his explanation to his wife, Lizza that if Indians join hands and fight against them, the British and the Empire would be at stake. He knows Indians' psychological make-up, their impetuosity and their morbid fascination with religion. In fact, knowledge and power go hand in hand.

As Edward Said observes in *Orientalism* (1983): "The only way to subjugate natives and dominate them is in the process of knowing them" (Said, 54). It becomes very easy for Richard to rule Indians because he "knows" (my emphasis) much about them.

It should be noted that the British Indian administration did support a particular community not solely for the love of fomenting communalism. The aim of the British policy of divide and rule was to curb their consolidation and unification and to disrupt the process of the Indian nation-in-the-making. Once the anti-imperialist nationalist movement arose, the policy was also directed towards checking its growth, dividing its actual or potential supporters and preventing Muslims in particular from joining it.

To confront effectively the nationalist onslaught in order to perpetuate their hegemony, the British needed some anchor among some sections of the Indian people to create political support. The long-term policy adopted was that of stimulating communal antagonism, communal politics and organisation through appropriate short-term administrative policies. These policies could have a certain diversity to suit the given moment as well as the personalities and the outlook of the administrators. This would divide Indians and make them fight each other as enemies and secure the active or passive support of communal forces for colonial rule because they would treat the other community as the main and immediate enemy. The protagonist in Balachandra Rajan's *Dark Dancer* (1976) Krishnan disdainfully debunks the British rulers for the rise of communalism: "It's your fault ... you made this awful thing to grow. For a whole generation you British have stirred up the trouble. It's you that made the religious divisions take priority over our common political interests. Communal electorates, communal representation in the civil service. Communal this and communal that. Even the cricket matches were communally organised" (*Dark Dancer*, 159-160). It is clear that the colonialist ideology aims at, as Frantz Fanon affirms in his *The Wretched of the Earth* (Fanon, 1961): "To devalue the nation's past" (Fanon, 47).

Communalism is the mischief of Englishman in the observation of Government House Gardener who figures in Bapsi Sidhwa's *Cracking India* (1988): "The English's mischief ... They are past masters of intrigue. It suits them to have us all fight" (Bapsi Sidhwa,152). Instead of toning down the differences they played "divide-and-rule monkey tricks" (Bapsi Sidhwa, 63) culminated in communal riots. Bapsi Sidhwa does not spare the accountability of the British in "inciting one against the other". She depicts a realistic rendering of the British motives in *Cracking India*. Mr. Singh is of the opinion that the British has long been supporting the Muslim League for some ulterior, self- seeking reasons. He bandies words with the British officer, Inspector-General Rogers who throws his weight behind the Muslims. Rogers presents Britishers' staying in India a must because all Indians would "bloody' fall at each other's throat" if "the British quit India" (Bapsi Sidhwa, 62). Here, the colonial administrators present communalism as the problem of the defence of minorities. It became a major part of the theory of imperialist legitimation, as its other components—welfare of the colonised, civilising mission, white man's burden, etc.—got increasingly discredited. The imperial statesmen, officials and ideologues at that stage say that Britain had to continue to rule India because it alone could protect the minorities from domination and suppression by the majority.

The struggle for domination can be both systematic and hidden. There was an increasing interaction between classes, nations, power centres and regions seeking to dominate and displace one another. But what made the struggle more than a random tooth-and-claw battle was that a struggle of values was involved. At this juncture, it is pertinent to observe Edward Said's view in *Culture and Imperialism* (1993): "What distinguishes the modern European empire from the Roman or the Spanish or the Arab is that they are systematic enterprises, constantly reinvested" (Said,75). They did not move into a country solely to loot it and leave. What kept them there was not simple greed, but massively reinforced notions of the civilising mission. For the protagonist in Rudyard Kipling's *Kim* it was India's best destiny to be ruled by England. All the ambivalences and contradictions of the novel emerge from its unquestioning acceptance of the efficacy of British rule. This was the notion that imperial nations have not only as the right but the obligation to rule those nations "lost in barbarism". As Italian Marxist, Antonio Gramsci has observed, hegemony arises from the power of the ruling class to convince other classes that its interests are the interests of all. Looking from this perspective, Inspector General Rogers in *Cracking India* (1988) appears to serve only as the mouthpiece of the British that came to be conceived, as synonymous with "the best that has been thought and said".

It should be remembered in this context that the communal division was not the only constituent of the policy of divide and rule just as divide and rule was the only weapon in the armoury of colonialism for its preservation and continuance. Every effort was made to set as many groups against one another. They endeavoured to find and widen as many social gaps as possible. Different permutations and combinations were tried at different times to split up the Indian people and arrest their emerging unity. Bhisham Sahni provides an accurate representation of this phenomenon. He shows this when Richard says: "Indians came from the same stock" (*Tamas*, 53). He does know that Indians know nothing about it. Nor does he want to make Indians know these facts because "the rulers don't look for similarities among the ruled. They are only interested in finding out what can keep them apart" (*Tamas*, 42). Sahni shows how the British have exploited the element of communalism for they knew that communal division could survive to the end and was the most serviceable.

The effects of the British policy branched off into the policies of post-independent India. When the British were in power they exploited the Babri mosque issue to their advantage. The British acknowledged that a mosque had been built on the site of the temple. But they felt they could do nothing about it because they did not want to risk a law and order problem. Taking the cue from the British, the Hindu communalist, Ram Charan Gupta in *Riot* (2001), seeks to exploit the issue. He quotes the British magistrate's judgment: "It is most unfortunate that a masjid should have been built on land specially held sacred by the Hindus .... But as the event occurred 356 years ago it is too late to remedy the grievance. All that can be done is to maintain status quo" (*Riot*, 120-121). The words in the judgment were deliberately chosen to keep the spark of communalism alive which continues to keep some parts of independent India aflame.

As one begins to read, not univocally but contrapuntally— a form of 'reading back' from the perspective of the colonised— as posited by Edward Said in *Culture and Imperialism* (1983) — one finds the ubiquitous presence of the colonial power in all areas.

Contrapuntal analysis uncovers the large role of colonial policy, the basic causative role or primary responsibility of colonialism and the colonial structure in the growth of communalism. It is the logic of the colonial structure that provided the parameters within which communalism grew and functioned. It is the colonial structure, the resulting economic under development and the scarcity of economic opportunities, which created conditions conducive to communal antagonism on the one hand and the successful result of the colonial policy of divide and rule on the other. In fine, as Sudhamoy in Nasreen's *Lajja* (1993) reflects, the British wanted to perpetuate their presence in the subcontinent "by inflaming the existing feelings of ill-will between Hindus and Muslims" (*Lajja*,180).

The seeds of suspicion, thus taken root with the complicity of the colonial power, spread rapidly as both the communalists, Hindu and Muslim adopted diametrically opposite and hostile position with their faulty understanding of history. In fact, a communal and distorted unscientific view of Indian history especially of its long chequered history belonging to ancient and medieval periods was used by the colonial power as a major instrument for the spread of communal consciousness. What Rudyard Hart said to Mohammed Sarwar in *Riot* stands as a pertinent revelation: "I'll tell you what your problem is in India. You have too much history. Far more than you can use peacefully. So you end up wielding history like a battle axe, against each other" (*Riot*, 205).

While using history Muslim communalism depended more on religious and minority feelings for creating a psychosis of fear. The Hindu communalist could hardly do so successfully in view of the Hindu majority in the present. They, therefore, relied upon the past for the purpose. The two communal interpretations were based by those earlier put forward by British historians like James Mill, H.M. Elliot and others. Of these, the former was responsible for the periodisation of Indian history into Hindu and Muslim periods. Many of the historians were often guided by narrow-minded considerations other than those of historical enquiry. They showed that the Indian people had always been ruled by cruel tyrants and uncontrolled despots. Consequently, there was nothing wrong if the British rule too was autocratic or despotic;

only it was benevolent and just operated under the rule of law. Moreover, Muslims were also foreigners just like the British; therefore, the British had not introduced foreign and inhuman foreign rule with a humane and civilised foreign rule. The historians also evinced that Muslims had oppressed and maltreated Hindus whereas the British had virtually 'liberated' them. They also asserted that Hindus and Muslims were always divided and at each other's throat and therefore, they could never live amicably with other in the absence of the British.

In *Cracking India* British Inspector General brings in the justification for the communal periodisation of history: "If we quit India today... You'll bloody fall at each other's throat" (Bapsi Sidhwa, 62). Like English philosopher, John Stuart Mill (1806-73), who states that the British are in India because India requires them and without them these are territories and peoples who beseech domination from us and that without the English India would fall into ruin. It is worthy to note that postcolonial criticism exposes such false pretensions of the civilising mission and other such high-brow attitudes.

Works Cited

Ashcroft, Bill, Gareth, Griffiths and Tiffin, Helen, *The Empire Writes Back,* London: Routledge, 1994.

Chaman, Nahal, *Azadi.* New Delhi: Orient Paperbacks, 1979.

Edward Said. *Orientalism.* New York: Vintage, 1978.

______________ *The Text and the Critic,* London: Faber, 1984.

______________, *Culture and Imperialism,* London: Chatto & Windows, 1993.

Fanon, Frantz, *The Wretched of the Earth,* London: Penguin, 1961.

______________ *Black Skin White Masks,* New York: Grove Press, 1967.

Nasreen, Taslima, *Lajja.* Trans. Tatul Gupta, New Delhi: Penguin, 1993.

Sahni, Bhisham, *Tamas.* Trans. Jai Rajan, New Delhi: Penguin, 1987.

Sidhwa, Bapsi, *Cracking India.* New Delhi: Penguin, 1988.

Singh, Khushwant, *Train to Pakistan,* Bombay: India House Pvt. Ltd., 1975.

Spivak, Gayatri Chakravorthy: *In Other Worlds: Essays in Cultural Politics,* Rouledge: New York & London, 1998.

Tharoor, Shashi, *Riot,* New Delhi: Penguin, 2001.

Chomsky, Noam, *Necessary Illusions*, London: Pluto Press, 1989.

McLeod, John, *Beginning Postcolonialism*, Manchester: Manchester University Press, 2000.

Naik, M.K. *A History of Indian English Literature*, New Delhi: Sahitya Academy, 1982.

Rangeya Raghava, Sulochana, *Sociology of Indian Literature*, Jaipur: Rawat, 1987.

Thapar, Romilla, *The Past and Prejudice*, New Delhi, National Book Trust of India, 1975.

6

Issues in Colonial and Postcolonial Literature: A Probe

— *Sushama Tiwari*

Colonialism usually works through the use of brutal force employed by one country to exploit another community and obtain economic wealth. Colonialism most commonly was the abuse of native people. The postcolonial perspective emerged as a challenge to this tradition and legacy, and it attempts to criminalise the idea of establishing power through conquest.

Without colonialism there would be no postcolonialism. Colonialism is about the dominance of a strong nation over another weaker one. Colonialism happens when a strong nation sees that its material interest and affluence require that it expands outside its borders. Colonialism is the acquisition of the colonialist, by brute force of extra markets, extra resources of raw material and manpower from the colonies. The colonialist, while committing atrocities against the natives and territories of the colonies, convinces himself that he stands on high moral grounds. His basic assumptions in defence of his actions are:

1. The colonised are savages in need of education and rehabilitation.
2. The culture of the colonised is not up to standard of the coloniser and it's the moral duty of the coloniser to do something about polishing it.
3. The colonised nation is unable to manage and run itself properly, and thus it needs the wisdom and expertise of the coloniser.

4. The colonised nation embraces a set of religious beliefs incongruent and incompatible with those of the coloniser and consequently, it is God's given duty of the coloniser to bring those stray people to the right path.

The colonised people pose dangerous threat to themselves and to the civilised world if left alone, and thus it is in the interest of the civilised world to bring those people under control. As a result of this the white Europeans ventured adventurously into the so-called underdeveloped countries in Africa and Asia and dominated greater geographical spaces there. They subjugated the natives, imposed their will at large on them. They eroded the native cultures and languages, plundered the natives' wealth and established their orders based on settlers' supremacy.

There is no denying in that oppression dehumanises both the oppressor and the oppressed. Thus, in the thickness of colonialism national movements and most of them were radical and violent in their approaches, emerged to encounter the aggression of colonialism.

There are so many views on the effects of colonialism. Some claim that in spite of the ugly face of colonialism, it did a lot of good to the colonised. It brought to the colonised a new vision of life, mainly Western and advanced. It fostered a strong sense of national unity. It brought industrialisation and modern economy to the colonies and above all it advanced cultural life where it occurred. Implicit in these claims is the colonisers' high moral grounds mentioned above. On the other hand, there is the view that colonialism is pure oppression, immoral, evil, and nothing more than a form of a neo-slavery. As a result, no possible good can come out of such evil and it should be combated with sheer force. This radical view not only denies any positive effect of colonialism, but also incriminates those so-called apologists for colonialism.

Some of the results and effects colonialism has are put in the following ways:

1. There is total or partial erosion of the colonised culture.
2. There is mediation of the identity and subjectivity of the colonised.
3. There is total rejection by some elements among the colonised of everything Western as a form of reaction and protest against the coloniser.

4. There is categorisation of the world into ranks, such as first world, second world, the West and the rest with all the subsequent stereotyping and prototyping that follows. The emergence of different forms of fundamentalism that aim at purifying their local culture from that residues of the colonial past.
5. There is emergence of bourgeois classes in the colonies, modeling themselves after their masters, who endeavour to maintai· their *status quo* by getting closer to Western culture.
6. There is emergence of societies with a lot of contradictions and split loyalties.

When looking at precolonialism we see the area's original culture. Their beliefs and customs run smoothly and they are a functioning society. Colonialism changes everything. In almost all cases of colonialism, the norms, beliefs and cultural values of the larger power are forced upon all of the natives of the colonies. This is because the coloniser believes that the natives are "savages" and they need to be civilised. The natives have no choice but to accept these new ways of life. The settlers' technology is móre advanced and they could easily wipe out all natives who refuse to conform to the new culture. This is where the depletion of the culture of the colonised begins. Natives stop practising their religion. In most cases they convert to Christianity, mainly because it is forced onto them. In order to communicate with the colonisers/ settlers, they start speaking the settlers' language. Soon enough their own is lost.

After so many years of colonialism, the natives become similar to their colonisers. The colonisers control education, therefore they control the thoughts and ideas absorbed by the youth. Native children absorb the new culture and ideas at a young age. Because of this, the original culture is lost in new generations. The coloniser uses brute force to oppress the natives. In the plight of this oppression, independence is fought for and a culture that has almost been forgotten is once again sought after. Finally, an independence day comes. The larger power no longer has control of the colony or rather, former colony. New postcolonialism takes place. The subject of culture is deeply explored in postcolonial literature.

In essence, what post colonialism as a movement does is to expose to both the coloniser and ex-colonised, the falsity or validity of their assumptions. The pioneers of postcolonialism like Edward Said, Franz Fanon, Homi Bhabha among others concerned themselves with the social and cultural effect of colonisation. They regarded the way in which the West paved its passage to the Orient and the rest of the world as based on unconfounded truths. They asserted in their discourses that no culture is better or worse than other culture and consequently they nullified the logic of the colonialists.

In their readings of colonial and postcolonial literature and other forms of art, postcolonial critics relied heavily on other available literary theories. They manipulated Marxism, new historicism, psychoanalysis and deconstruction to serve their purposes.

Postcolonial theory is built in large part around the concept of otherness. There are however problems with or complexities to the concept of otherness, for instance:

1. Otherness includes doubleness, both identity and difference, so that every other, every difference is dialectically created and includes the values and meaning of the colonising culture even as it rejects its power to define.
2. The Western concept of the oriental is based, as Abdul JanMohamed argues, on the manichean allegory (seeing the world as divided into mutually excluding opposites): if the West is ordered, rational, masculine, good, then the orient is chaotic, irrational, feminine, evil. Simply to reverse this polarising is to be compplicit in its totalising and identity-destroying power (all is reduced to a set of dichotomies, black or white etc),
3. Colonised peoples are highly diverse in their nature and in their traditions and as beings in cultures they are both constructed and changing, so that while they may be "other" from the colonisers, they are also different ones from another and from their own pasts, and should not be totalised or essentialised through such concepts as a black consciousness, Indian soul, aboriginal culture and so forth.

Postcolonial theory is also built around the concept of resistance as subversion or opposition or mimicry but with the haunting problem that resistance always inscribes the resisted into the texture of the resisting. It is a two-edged sword. As well the concept of resistance carries with it or can carry with it ideas about human freedom, liberty, identity, individuality etc., which ideas may not have held or held in the same way in the colonised culture's view of humankind.

Postcolonialism deals with the aftermath of colonialism. It's about the struggle of being independent. One main concern in a post colonial nation is its government. After being controlled by the large power for such a long time, they need to establish their own way of running things. It's difficult because their cultural identity is in question. Governments are supposed to act in the best interest of the people but what do the people want? The society is no longer being oppressed, they're independent, free to be themselves again. However they've changed, their culture has changed now and they need to figure out who they really are.

Postcolonial literature is a body of literary writings that react to the discourse of colonisation. Postcolonial literature often involves writings that deal with issues of de-colonisation or the political and cultural independence of people formerly subjugated to colonial rule. It is also a literary critique to texts that carry racist or colonial undertones. Postcolonial literature, finally in its most recent form, also attempts to critique the contemporary postcolonial discourse that has been shaped over recent times. It attempts to re-read this very emergence of postcolonialism and its literary expression itself.

Postcolonial literature tends to answer the following question: Should there be an attempt to restore the original culture, conformity to the culture presented by the settlers or the creation of a new culture which combines both? If a novel answers and explores the above question it may be considered postcolonial literature. When trying to identify postcolonial literature, it is important to recognise whether the ex-colony in question is actually independent or considered independent, but reliant on its former colonist.

Despite the reservations and debates, research in postcolonial studies is growing because postcolonial critique allows for a wide-ranging investigation into power relations in various contexts. The formation of empire, the impact of colonisation on postcolonial history, economy, science and culture, the cultural productions of colonised societies, feminism and postcolonialism, agency for marginalised people, and the state of the postcolony in contemporary economic and cultural contexts are some broad topics in the field.

How did the experience of colonisation affect those who were colonised while also influencing the colonisers? How were colonial powers able to gain control over so large a portion of the non-Western world? What traces have been left by colonial education—science and technology in postcolonial societies? How do these affect decisions about development and modernisation in postcolonies? What were the forms of resistance against colonial control? How did colonial education and language influence the culture and identity of the colonised? How did Western science, technology and medicine change existing knowledge systems? What are the emergent forms of postcolonial identity after the departure of the colonisers? To what extent has decolonisation (a reconstruction free from colonial influence) been possible? Are Western formulations of postcolonialism overemphasising hybridity at the expense of material realities? Should decolonisation proceed through an aggressive return to the precolonial past? How do gender, race and class function in colonial and postcolonial discourse? Are new forms of imperialism replacing colonisation and how?

Along with these questions there are some more that are particularly pertinent to postcolonial literature: Should the writer use a colonial language to reach a wider audience or return to a native language more relevant to groups in the post- colony? Which writers should be included in the postcolonial canon? How can texts in translation from non-colonial language enrich our understanding of postcolonial issues? Has the preponderance of the postcolonial novel led to a neglect of other genres?

There is more to postcolonial literature than reading of colonialist narratives only. Generations of writers and intellectuals who are born under and after colonialism write inspiringly about the struggle for independence. They write about the conflicting interests of the natives under and after colonialism. Other writers direct their attention to the conflict between the natives and the newly appointed regimes that supplanted the colonialists. Many others write about fossilised social habits and customs in need of rehabilitation or replacement. Some writers exhibit a high level of animosity to the colonialist and their agents, others are less aggressive in their representation of the colonial past and the postcolonial present.

7

Tagore: Indianness in the Face of Colonialism

— *Charu P. Gidwani*

British domination was on its rise in India ever since their victory in the Battle of Plassey. The influence of English culture with its insistence on the English language was gaining fervour rapidly, knowing the English language was a symbol of social superiority. According to Nirad Chaudhari, to be educated was to know English; a person who had mastered Sanskrit was a Pundit; it was the English-speaking person who was educated.

In these times young Rabindranath was studying English literature at London in the university there. He was 17 years old then. A written exercise required him to write an essay. In this, his first known essay in English, he drew attention to the improper behaviour of British officials in India. Henry Morley, his teacher, spoke highly of the piece of writing and also read it out to the other students. Clearly, Rabindranath Tagore was not awed or overwhelmed with the English presence in India; instead he asserted his identity as an Indian in the face of the coloniser. This essay clearly reflects that Rabindranath did not believe in the superiority of the British; also through the essay, he attempted to command respect for India and for Indians. However, it is significant to see that in doing so, he did not reject anything simply because it was Western.

His first musical drama *Valmiki Pratibha* (The Genius Of Valmiki) was a result of his study of combined melody, Indian and European. This play is a fine example of a skilful blending of these melodies.

Clearly, Rabindranath was not cowed down by Western ideas and neither was he unequivocally full of praise for everything Indian; what he was simply doing was asking the coloniser—the British—to meet him—the colonised Indian with due respect on an equal platform. He asserted his Indianness and commanded respect for it; he refused to look down at himself as the slave or up to the English as the master.

Where many other leaders in India emphasized on education in English, Tagore believed in education through one's mother tongue. He believed that the mind can exercise freely if one studies through the mother tongue. The appetite for knowledge dies before the pupil can bite through the hard rules of grammar if he has to learn a foreign language. Rabindranath had clearly taken upon himself the self-assigned task of reminding the Indians carried away by everything English, to respect their mother tongue, their Indianness. All his writings depict characters and situations from rural Bengal — the Bengal that was closest to his heart. His keen interest in folk literature and folk music is clearly reflected in his short stories, plays, poems and novels.

When leaders of the Indian National Congress attended sessions in the English dress, Rabindranath, the young man, shocked them by appearing for these sessions dressed in typical Bengali dhoti, kurta and scarf. At one of the sessions of the Congress, he again shocked the gathering by summing up the chairman, Rev Kali Charan Banerjee's English speech in Bengali. He was first attempting to awaken the Indians to their Indianness before he could move on to the British. He was carrying forward the work that the legendary Bankim Chandra Chattopadyay had left behind. On the one hand, he was collecting folk songs and folk poetry of Bengal, on the other, he was trying to awaken his countrymen to the greatness of their heritage through poems, narrating the glorious incidents in the history of India and through the message of the *Upanishads*. All of these were published in a book called *Katha* (Narrative Poems).

This was also the time when Tagore delivered lectures on *The Creative Ideal, The Poet's Religion,* etc in English to the Western world. These essays are fine pieces of what makes fine art, what the major points of difference are between playwrights of the East like Kalidasa and those of the West like Shakespeare. His selected poems from *Gitanjali, Kheya,* and other collections, which he translated into English and for which he was awarded the Nobel Prize, are poems offering the philosophy of India to the West.

Tagore's poem in honour of Charles Freer Andrews, a missionary, who was totally awed by Tagore (he in fact referred to Tagore as the Christ of the Orient) is an indication of Tagore's utmost desire that the East meets West.

From the shrine of the West
You have brought us living water,
We welcome you, friend.
The East has offered you
Her garland of love,
Accept it and welcome, friend
Your love has opened
The door of our heart;
Enter, and welcome, friend.
You have come to us
As a gift of the Lord,
We bow to Him, friend.

These lines, keeping in synchrony with Tagore's ideas based on the *Upanishads,* echo the principle of unity in Indian life. The Westerner is God sent and welcome to stay in harmony with the East; the relationship is one of love.

Yet another one of the lesser-known poems of Tagore, in English, is the one he read out at the Calcutta Congress Session in 1917. The poem titled *India's Prayer* is further proof of his unwavering faith in the principle of oneness of the universe that is, the principle of unity:

Let this be our prayer to Thee-
Give us power to resist pleasure
Where it enslaves us,
To lift our sorrow up to Thee
As the summer holds its noonday sun
Make us strong that our worship may flower in love,
And bear fruit in work.
Make us strong that we may not insult
The weak and the fallen,
That we may hold our love high

Where all things around us are wooing the dust.
They fight and kill for self-love,
Giving it Thy name,
They fight against Thine anger and die.
But let us stand firm and suffer with strength
For the true, for the good, for the eternal in man,
For Thy Kingdom is the Union of heart
And for the freedom which is of the soul.

The lines "make us strong…that we may hold our love high" are reinforcement of Tagore's love for India.

By the year 1920, twenty books of Tagore were translated and published in English and other European languages. Foreign readers had become acquainted with his poems, plays, stories, novels, essays.

Tagore humbly attributed the respect he got all over the world to humanity so deeply embedded in the heart of India. Through his writings, he had only been instrumental in winning the respect due to India from the West. Here was an Indian who had met the English on an equal footing; he had made them look at India with respect and awe by throwing light on her spirit, her philosophy, on her Indianness through his writings in English!

Works Cited

Tagore, Rabindranath, *The English Writings of Rabindranath Tagore,* Sisir Kumar Das, ed,. New Delhi Sahitya Akademi, 1994.

Roy, Kshitis, *Rabindranath Tagore: a Life Story*; Publications Division, Ministry of Information and Broadcasting, Government of India, 1980.

8

Postcolonial Element in the Life and Works of Baba Saheb Ambedkar

—*Mamta Kori & Shubha Tiwari*

Baba Saheb's time was that of the rise of postcolonialism in India. The whole nation awoke against the atrocities and exploitation of the Indian masses. Ambedkar was not untouched by the strong waves. In his path-breaking work, *The Problem of the Rupee: Its Origin and its Solution*, we can see his keen insight at work. He clearly saw, understood and explained the cruel politics played by the British in the economic field. He explains how the British conspired to devalue rupee in comparison to the pound. This work is very relevant today when the rupee is still facing a deflation problem. We can see that the colonial mindset has not ended. They want to be at the top at any cost.

When Baba Saheb was studying the method and techniques employed by the British to weaken the Indian economy, he also realised the *modus operandi* of the elite class in India. What the British were doing to India, the high class Indians were doing to the downtrodden section of the society. The elite Indian were brown British. Suffering from all the complexes of the colonial rules, the high class Indians were targeting the downtrodden section.

Through this research paper, we want to extend and enlarge the meaning of postcolonialism to protest against any kind of oppression. If we protest against the British, it becomes postcolonialism. If we protest against sections of our own society, which have been unjust to us for centuries, that should also be read as postcolonialism.

Our next contention is that the wave of postcolonialism in India inspired Dr Ambedkar. The Renaissance produced Shakespeare. The French Revolution produced poets like Wordsworth, Coleridge, P.B. Shelley etc. In the same manner waves of nationalism, postcolonialism and rebellion against the Western forces produced Dr. Bhimrao Ramji Ambedkar.

When we study Dalit literature, the text of Ambedkar must be studied first. We cannot understand the dynamics of Dalit literature, its inherent patterns of meaning, the pain expressed therein and loss of identity of the Dalit self, if we do not fully grasp works like *Who Were the Shudras*.

Bhimrao Ramji Ambedkar, popularly known as Baba Saheb, is the chief architect of the Indian Constitution, and is regarded as one of the most learned personalities ever born in India. He was born in a Mahar family in Mhow on 14 April 1891. At the time of his birth, untouchables were illtreated, humiliated and deliberately isolated. The time of his birth can be considered the most significant years in the life of any Indian because those were the years, when the nation was in a state of unrest due to the rising sentiment of nationalism among Indians struggling for independence. Anarchy and chaos were widespread and there were cries of love for the nation and bitterness against the British colonial rulers. But ironically there was a serious problem within the nation. While India was fighting tooth and nail against the exploitative British, she herself was guilty of exploiting a large chunk of its population: the Dalits. They were discriminated and subjected to untold sufferings and miseries.

Ambedkar belonged to a family of so-called low caste. He had to tackle several financial and social obstacles to finish his education. Nevertheless, he became one of the first untouchables to obtain college education in India. He went to the USA and England for attaining higher education. There he acquired a degree in law and also numerous doctorates for his research in law, economics and political science. He returned to India as a renowned scholar and practised law for a few years. Then he began publishing journals. Through these works, he encouraged political and social awareness for the freedom of the untouchables in India.

The socio-political reforms brought about by Ambedkar have a deep impact on modern India. His genre of thinking commands deep respect across the political spectrum of post-independence

India. His programmes have changed the face of India's socio-economic policies and education system. His reputation as a scholar led to his appointment as the first Law Minister of free India and also as the chairman of the committee responsible for drafting the Indian Constitution. It is because of his efforts that India is the largest democratic republic in the world.

Ambedkar condemned the orthodox Hindu society, which was gripped with casteism. He also criticised the narrow doctrinaire positions in Islam. His condemnation of Hinduism and attacks on Islam made him unpopular. But his conversion to Buddhism sparked people's interest in Buddhist philosophy in India.

As a leading Dalit scholar, Amedkar was invited to testify before the Southborough committee. This committee was preparing the Government of India Act, 1919. At this hearing, he put forth the proposal of creating separate electorates, reservations for Dalits and other religious communities. In 1920, a remarkable event took place in his life. The event was the start of a Marathi weekly paper *Mook Nayak* under the editorship of Nandram Bhatkar in Bombay. He used the expression *Mook Nayak* meaning the leader of the dumb, to amplify the insensitivity and wickedness of the treatment faced by depressed classes in a country where freedom struggle was on its peak point. The first issue of the paper published Ambedkar's rebellious words:

> The Hindu society is like a tower of many storeys. It has neither a ladder nor a door to go out.. A society which believes that God exists even in inanimate things, also says that people who are a part of that very society should not be touched.[1]

Through the means of his journals, he tried to fight caste discrimination. He openly criticised orthodox Hindu politicians and their reluctance to fight for the plight of the Dalits in India.

In 1923, Ambedkar was awarded a D.Sc. degree for his thesis "The Problem of the Rupee—Its Origin and its Solution." In this thesis he had revealed how the relationship of the rupee to the pound was manipulated to the great profit of the Britishers and the resultant hardship to the Indian people. In 1924, he founded the Bahishkrit Hiktarini Sabha with the primary objective of creating awareness among the depressed classes about their importance as human beings. It aimed at encouraging Dalits to educate themselves and attain a respectable position in the society He went around with the slogan "Educate-Agitate-Organise" for eradicating the caste system and reconstructing the Indian society on the basis of equality of human beings.

Ambedkar was not just against Hindus and Hinduism. He spoke of reforming all social evils. This is evident in his critical approach to the practice of untouchability in the Indian Muslim society. In his acclaimed publication "Pakistan and the Partition of India" he wrote that while Islam spoke of brotherhood, the practice of slavery and caste discrimination were widespread in the Muslim society in South Asia, such as the Ashraf/Ajlaf caste divide and the major discrimination against the Arzal castes or Dalit Muslim as untouchables.

In 1926, he was nominated member of the Bombay Legislative Council. Then he decided to launch active movements against untouchabiliy. To prove that his speeches were not merely empty words to liberate people from the brutality of casteism, he led a march at Mahad in Maharashtra. His sole purpose was to show people how they could pull themselves out of the clutches of casteism with their own efforts. Chowdar Tank Satyagraha marked the beginning of anti-caste and anti-priest movement. The Bombay Legislature passed a bill declaring that all public tanks and wells were accessible by all the members of the society. But the law remained only on paper. He decided to give it a practical shape. The animals were allowed to use the water of the Chowdar Tank in the Mahad town of Maharashtra. But untouchables were barred. This glaring manifestation of inhuman attitude of the society was challenged by Dr. Ambedkar. On 20 March 1927, he marched towards the Chowdar Tank and drank water from it. Then his followers followed suit. Thus he broke the tradition of centuries, which had debarred untouchables from going even near the tanks. Thus he found at least some relief from the torture that had been meted out to him as a child when he had attempted to drink water from a well.

To encourage people he said:

> You must abolish your slavery yourselves. Do not depend for its abolition upon god or a superman. Remember that it is not enough that a people are numerically in the majority. They must be always watchful, strong and self respecting to attain and maintain success. We must shape our course ourselves and by ourselves.[2]

However, even this did not move the religious fanatics. Soon, the tank's news spread like fire along with the rumour that Ambedkar and his followers were planning to enter the Veereshwara temple. Hindus attacked Ambedkar and his men. Many satyagrahis were injured by them. Some of them took the Chowdar matter to court, but the court gave the verdict that tanks were public property.

The name of Mahad town is also permanently linked with human rights because of one more reason. Dr. Ambedkar organised a conference of satyagrahis on 25 December 1927 in which the *Manusmriti* was burned. It was a red letter day, in the history of India. This day, he not only burnt the *Manusmriti* but also asked for a new one so as to reshape the Hindutva that will treat all the untouchables as touchable Hindus.

These struggles opend a new era of struggle in the country. The orthodox section of the vast majority of Hindus got a rude shock due to the changing attitude of untouchables towards their own social status. The government too realised the change and began to pay more attention towards the welfare of the depressed classes.

On 29 July 1927, Ambedkar started his fortnightly Marathi paper *Bahishkrit Bharat,* in which he wrote, "If Tilak had been born among the untouchables, he would not have raised the slogan Swaraj is my birth right, but he would have raised the slogan Annihilation of untouchability is my birthright." In March 1930, he also launched another Dalit movement that led the untouchables to the Kalaram temple in Nasik.

Meanwhile, during this period, the British invited several Indian leaders to participate in the Round Table Conference to discuss all the problems faced by Indians under the British rule. During the first Round Table Conference attended by Ambedkar, he made a sweeping impression on the members. He maintained his ground that the deprived classes didn't enjoy equality even under the British rule; the British were simply following the ways of the other Hindus. He unflinchingly opposed the Indian patriotic hero of those times, Mahatma Gandhi. He made a memorable speech on this occasion:

> While I want to emphasise the fact that one fifth of the total population of British India – a population as large as the population of Britain, has been reduced to a position worse

> than that of serfs or slaves. However, I maintain that the untouchables in India were also for replacing the existing Government by a Government of the people, for the people and by the people.[3]

Ambedkar posed some direct and inconvenient questions to the British Government. He said:

> When we compare our present position with the one in pre-British days, we find that, instead of marching on, we are marking time. Before the British, we were in the loathsome condition due to our unsociability.... Has the British Government done anything to remove it?... Our wrongs have remained as open sore and they have not been righted, although 150 years of British rule have rolled away. Of what good is such a government to anybody?[4]

During the second Round Table Conference in 1931, he succeeded in securing separate electorates for the untouchables. With this the untouchables got the right to elect their representatives separately. But Gandhiji realised that such an act would separate the Hindus from the Harijans and the gap between them would never be bridged. He opposed it. He started a fast against separate electorates and proclaimed ceaseless fast to end either with his death or with the reversion of the decision. Many Congress leaders went to Ambedkar for saving the life of Mahatma Gandhi. Then he signed an agreement with the leaders in Poona. According to this agreement, ten per cent seats were reserved for the untouchables in the legislature. This agreement came to be known as the Poona Pact. Ambedkar did it only on humanitarian grounds to save Gandhiji's life.

Ambedkar's analysis of the origins of the untouchability and his action plans for its eradication were different from the approach and practice of the Dalits themselves. This perspective led him to think differently from the dominant stream of social and political thought of his time. His major works on *Caste in India: Their Mechanism, Genesis and Development, Who were the Shudras? The Untouchables: Who were They,* and *Why they became Untouchables* are testimonies to his independent and original thinking. He smashed the mythological basis of untouchability and laid bare its economic roots.

Between 1941 and 1945, he published a large number of highly controversial books and pamphlets. These included *Thoughts on Pakistan* in which he criticised the Muslim League's demand for a separate Muslim state called Pakistan. His passionate attacks on Gandhi and the Congress can be seen in this book. Asking 'What have Congress and Gandhi done to the Untouchables?' he charged them with hypocrisy. One of the extracts from this book is given below:

- On Gandhiji's support for the Hindu Caste System, albeit devoid of untouchability.

> The social ideal of Gandhism is either caste or varna. Though it may be difficult to say which, there can be no doubt that the social ideal of Gandhism is not democracy. For whether one takes for comparison caste or *varna* both are fundamentally opposed to democracy.[5]

In his book *Who were the Shudras*? he explained the formation of the shudras, i.e., the lowest caste in hierarchy of the Hindu caste system. He also elucidated on how the shudras were separate from the untouchables. He built a strong case against the birth thesis of untouchability which foreclosed all the ways for Dalit emancipation. He exhorted its victims to oppose it tooth and nail, declaring:

> It is disgraceful to live at the cost of one's self respect. Self–respect is the most vital factor in life. Without it, man is a mere cipher. To live worthily with self-respect one has to overcome difficulties. It is out of hard and ceaseless struggle alone that one derives strength, confidence and recognition.[6]

He drew a distinction between merely living and living worthily. For living a worthy life, he said that society must be based on liberty, equality and fraternity. For him social tyranny was more oppressive than political tyranny and a reformer who defied society, was much more courageous man than a politician who defied the government.

Ambedkar disapproved of Islamic practice in South Asia. He was also against the practice of child marriage in the Muslim society. The ill-treatment of women troubled him a great deal. He also denounced the caste practices carried out by the Muslims in South Asia. He was critical of slavery in Muslim communities. He was disturbed by the plight of women in the Muslim society. The women had to adhere to the oppressive purdah system. He asserted that while the purdah was also practised by Hindus, only among the Muslims was it sanctioned by religion.

Ambedkar raised his voice against women's discriminatory situation in the society. He gave new direction and dimension to the feminist movement in India. He always involved women in his struggles. He struggled for their equal rights as in the case of the Hindu Code Bill. Ambedkar who was born in an untouchable family, carried on a relentless battle against untouchability throughout his adult life. In the last part of his life, he renounced Hinduism and became a Buddhist. According to him, Buddhism stood for social, intellectual, economic and political freedom. It is noteworthy that he embraced Buddhism because it was a religion born on the Indian soil and is an integral part of the Indian culture.

He did not fight against any section of society; he fought against social evils. Gandhiji and Ambedkar, both reformers, had a vision of equality, but for Ambedkar equality meant not only equal status of *varnas,* but also equal social, political and economic opportunity.

References

1. www.Aambedkar.org
2. www.rohanbooks.com. *Illustrated Biography of Dr. B.R. Ambedkar,* Delhi: RBC International Publication, 2004, p. 35.
3. Alam, Firoz, *Dr. Bhimrao Ambedkar,* Delhi: Sahni Publication, 1992, 69.
4. Shahare, M.L., *Dr. Ambedkar Bhimrao: His life and Work,* New Delhi: NCERT, 1987, 41.
5. Ambedkar, B.R., *What have Congress and Gandhi done to the Untouchables*?, Delhi: Gautam Book Centre, 2002, 38.
6. Ambedkar, B.R:., *Who were the Shudras*?, Delhi: Gautam Book Centre, 2002, 49.

9

Mulk Raj Anand: A Major Postcolonial Short Story Writer

—Ajay B. Kukade

The Indian Short Story in English is a comparatively late product, but Short Story in India is an age-old phenomenon. Though Indian English short story is, in a sense, "postcolonial", the roots are to be seen in Indian traditional tales. Both the ancient Indian fable and the ancient Indian popular tale have helped the Indian short story writers in English in giving the stories a definite shape. Apart from these fables and tales, the West too has influenced these writers a lot.

In 1898, Kamala Sathianadan's *Stories from Indian Christian Life* was the first published English short story collection by any Indian. The Indian classic tales have inspired the writers like Manjeri Iswaran, Raja Rao, Mulk Raj Anand, R. K. Narayan a lot. Mulk Raj Anand appeared on the literary scene in 1929 with the publication of his first short story, often called as a prose poem, *The Lost Child*. The post-independence works of Anand show a much matured and bitter view. He was deeply influenced with the ancient classic tales. He openly admits that and says:

> I have always thought of this as a symbol of the highly finished art of story-telling in India.

For him *Katha Sarit Sagar* (Ocean of Stories) always remained a source of inspiration. He remarks:

> One of the oldest books of stories in India was entitled 'Ocean of Stories'. I have always thought of this book as a symbol of the highly finished art of story telling in India. I read it at an early age and was inspired by it to read and hear many of the folk stories told in my country.

R. K. Narayan and Mulk Raj Anand are contemporaries and are called the pioneers of the great tradition of Indo-Anglian literature. In fact, Anand and Narayan are the two writers to get international readership. Anand is a real "postcolonial" writer who presented a realistic picture of 'Postcolonial India'. He is convinced that no literature can ignore the people in the society. So it is evident that his principle was 'art for the sake of society'. He is concerned with social problems and eradication of the evils in modern society. He gives voice to the peasants, workers and suppressed members of society. English was not the first language of the writer and the characters. So the writer's aim was to write in English only to convey his message satisfactorily. For him the short stories were a medium to bring to life some of the beautiful and tragic characters from small parts of India.

Anand's short stories show no significant change in his attitude towards colonised and postcolonial India. For him the social scene everywhere was just the same, even after independence. The social injustice and discrimination in the so-called 'Postcolonial India" is a matter of have for some but a fact for many. The hate and anger for British Raj is clearly visible in *On the Borders*. Karima, the heroine of the story, is the victim of an Angrezi Sarkar near Peshawar. The postcolonial Indian malpractices are primarily shown in the stories. In *At What Price My Brothers?* Tara Singh practises various corruptions. Also in *The Man who was too honest for his job* every official is engaged in corrupt practices to earn a commission. Through his story *The Price of Bananas* the materialistic mentality of the businessmen is exposed.

Anand is always accused of being a propagandist. He himself feels annoyed with such judgment being passed on him. In one of his letters addressed to S. Cowasjee he sadly mentions that people will accept Tolstoy, Dickens and Hardy, but an Indian trying to portray the peasants of India will merely be a communist for them. He says:

> The western readers never accuse me of propaganda at all. It is in India that a few members of the Cultural Freedom Group come into the cold war and try to destroy the new myth of love among human beings, however, lowly which I had been building up to my works.

Anand seems to suggest that freedom from untouchability alone cannot guarantee man a full flowering of his personality. For a harmonious growth he has to wage a war against his own foibles.

Most of Anand's characters come from socially and economically backward classes. Srijut Sharma (*The Gold Watch*), Chandu (*The Barber's Trade Union*), Dhandu (*A Rumour*), Saudagar (*The Cobbler and the Machine*), Nur (*Lament on the Death of a Master of Arts*) are all economically suppressed ones. Anand always had a sympathetic attitude for women. This is clearly visible through his depiction of the characters of Sawitri (*Between Tears and Laughter*), Gujri (*The Watch*), Roopa (*The Tamarind Tree*), Lajwanti (*Lajwanti*), Karima (*On the Border*). Here Anand scores above R. K. Narayan, as the former's women characters are more powerful than those of the latter.

The free use of Hindustani words is another prolific feature of Anand's writing. He never cared a damn for the reactions of the critics. He wanted to create an everlasting impact on the readers' mind. Though the stories are in English, the bold use of Hindustani words like *'Hanji'*, *'Ao ji Ao'*, *'But Hujur'*, *'Are ja Seth'*, *'Chana jor garam'*, *'Ram he Ram'* suddenly makes the reader feel close to the characters. Thus, Anand is really the pioneer of effective Indian English short stories. His fiction is really an escape into life, always bitter but true. Though his fiction is rooted in the soil of his time, the artist in him carries it far above. His stories truly have a "universal appeal" in it.

We Indians always look to the West for inspiration and references. It is a tragedy that though Kalidasa was born much earlier than Shakespeare, we say, "Kalidasa is the Shakespeare of India". Considering this M.R. Anand holds a very high place not only in Indian English literature, but also in the whole literary world. To honour his work a very apt remark is made by Marjori Boulton, when she says:

English people will not trouble to write their own language well enough ought to be shamed by reading the English of such Indian writers like Mulk Raj Anand.

Works Cited

Anand Mulk Raj, *Preface, Selected Stories.*

Cowasjee, S., *Author to Critic.*

Venugopal, C.V., *The Indian Short Story in English.*

Boulton, Marjori, *The Anatomy of Prose.*

10

Bhabani Bhattacharya's *So Many Hungers* as a Postcolonial Text

—*Krushna Chandra Mishra*

Bhabani Bhattacharya (b. 1906) was honoured with the coveted Sahitya Akademi Award in 1967 for his novel *Shadow from Ladakh*. He has to his credit five other novels – *So Many Hungers, Music for Mohini, He Who Rides a Tiger, A Goddess Named Gold, A Visit to Hawaii* and a collection of short stories – *Steel Hawk and Other Stories*. He is a writer with a distinct faith in the possibility of the rise of man. He is a believer in Gandhism. He is interested in global peace which could ensure lasting human bond of love and lead mankind on the path of development via freedom and creativity. He recognises the role of de-instrumentalised reason in the making of an enlightened world order. Cooperation, mutual trust and an interest in the over-arching progress of all are the ways he finds useful to the construction of a new world, where race/caste discrimination would not be present and colonisation in any form would be absent. As colonisation projects man standing utterly de-humanised, he believes de-colonisation would serve to the glorification of the humanity. His vision has been considered to be an affirmative vision of life.

This paper studies his first novel, *So Many Hungers,* as a postcolonial text. In three convenient parts it develops the argument: the first part looks at how literature is responsible for colonisation and how it could appropriately be made to lead to freedom; the second part deals with only two characters – Kunal and Kajoli – to bring out the exploitative and degrading potential of colonialism while also to show how with the example of these two characters the postcolonial sensibility of the writer manifests itself; the third part deals with the postcoloniality of the text wherein the scope for Gandhism, ethics and a global order based on love and equality and freedom is explored.

Literature and Society in Postcolonial Perspective

Literature as 'critism of life' method (Arnold) must have to look at how life obtains in the world. In its use of language, it enters into a limited society with a distinct culture that has managed to emerge in conformity to a given social structure (Durkhim). In a colonial society the colonised are educated, when they are all educated in an alien language as the medium of instruction; in an alien literature developed in societies and context entirely different; in cultural and historical traditions, quite alien and without the least similarity.

In India the study of English literature and Western literatures was introduced to help protest against British interests with people who could 'help them rule a vast and unruly land'. (Macaulay 1972: 249 as in Loomba 2001: 85). Since teaching takes place in a mode to confirm to 'utilise' the colonised, a poorer self-image at a collective level is developed. Creativity involving one's own culture and traditions of the colonised suffers as a result. Literature as a civilising cultural tool then harms the natives, unless interpretations are not creatively made away from Eurocentric critical analysis lines (Said 1995). For Edward Said, it is crucial to read outside Western culture, to become comparative in a new sense: "to read Austen without also reading Fanon and Cabrel... is to disaffiliate modern culture from its engagements and attachments" (1995, 38, Loomba 2001,93). So long as the indigenous cultural tools are not applied in a true way in a bid to sustain the literary texts for general universal benefit of the humanity by the colonised who in most untaught of ways are subjected to exploitation and oppression, literature studies mostly go to create havoc and therefore potentially unchallenging natives among the educated ones who in their turn never grow to lead the oppressed masses to freedom. Loomba (2001) holds: "The study of colonial discourse (as in teaching of literature of the coloniser's location tongue) ought to lead us towards a fuller understanding of colonised institutions rather than direct us away from them" (97). "In Africa and India, by attributing particular characteristics to specific tribes or groups, colonial authorities entrenched divisions between the restive population" (97). "In India they carried strong underpinnings of caste divisions." (98)

In the context of postcolonial theory it is useful, maintains Loomba, "that literature or literay texts be read in fuller, more contextualised ways, so that ideological and rhetorical strategies' in the 'social and historical processes' as 'textual'. focuses could be grasped well"(2001,94). The study of colonialism in relation to literature and of literature in relation to colonialism has thus opened up important new ways to look in at both. Even more important perhaps is the way in which recent literay and critical theory have influenced social analysis (2001, 94). Emphasising the role of literacy texts in giving rise to anti-colonial urges Loomba holds: "Literacy texts are crucial to the formation of colonial discourses... they also militate against them (the dominant ideologies), or contain elements which cannot be reconciled to them." (2001,74).

Explaining why literature is worth bothering about J. Hillies Lilur (who however also ignores the postcolonial) says: "Works of literature do not simply reflect or are not simply caused by their contexts. They have a productive effect in history. This can and should be studied. To put this in their way, the only thing that sometimes worries me about the turn to history now as an explanatory method is the implication that I can fully exclude every text by its pre-existing historical context. But the publication of works was itself a political or historical event that in some way changed history. I think if you don't allow for this, literature is not much worth bothering about."(1991, 152-3 as in Dennies Walder (1998) 2002,190-191).

So Many Hungers—A Study in Colonialist Exploitation *vis-á-vis* the Postcolonial Expectation

As against Paul Scott's *A Jewel in the Crown* in which British colonial cultural mission is justified (Loomba 2001, 80), Bhabani Bhattacharya's *So Many Hungers* in its rape of Kajoli by the British soldier leading to abortion and birth of her dead child depicts the coloniser as essentially evil and uncultured though the soldier's taking Kajoli to the hospital for treatment shows the repentance that comes to him after the act (rape) was done. This is indicative of the fact that essential humanity lies brutally and deliberately suppressed by the coloniser. As humanity is a cultural treasure of far greater worth the coloniser, even when he inflicts wounds on the poor, hapless, hungry colonised Indian girl in the name of giving her food ('bread' here), he is capable of shedding his racial arrogance and submitting to the humanity's more celebrated norms of decency, sympathy and help.

Again when Scott is trying to deflect attention from the issue in spite of the racialist struggles at their height, Bhattacharya insistently portrays the coloniser's nature as immoral and bestial. When Scott justifies the civilising mission, Bhattacharya criticises such a stand of the colonialist and exposes his standards of morality. The 1920's novel of E.M. Forster *A Passage to India* portrays rape to present the Indian man as lacking in moral strength, while the actual effort is to hush up an apparent charge on grounds of morality against the Jallianwallah Bagh massacre of hundreds of defenceless Indians in March, 1919 (Loomba 2001, 80). Bhattacharya's efforts are geared to achieve what Loomba (2001) considers necessary. "Nevertheless, turning away from colonial culture is often a necessary precondition for paying serious attention to the literatures and cultures devalued under colonialism." (92-93).

Coming back to Kajoli's rape issue one may refer the incident to the mother image she had come to acquire for her in her sacrifice (by exhibiting her bare breast to earn favour from the foreign soldiers) for helping her hungry destitute brethren. Her rape is a metaphor for Mother India's rape and her abortion and still-birth of her baby may explain why after that unholy and lustful ravishment of our land virtually every effort on our part to grow rich, strong and dynamic has become in effect infructuous. Bhattacharya's presentation of the rape phenomenon is the colonised literary intellectual's most poignant and telling of creative responses glossing over Indian independence as virtually a blood-besmeared abortive experience on Mother India's part where a still-born child is born just to be thrown away and thereby painfully separated—could it not be a nightmarish, blunt reference to the pain of partition!

The scar lives on and the offender appears not to be in any easy mood by the self-image-conscious novelist to be granted a 'forgive and forget' kind of farewell. The wound on the subcontinent's psyche continues to be raw and fresh in the least. Poverty so acutely grinds, the countrymen go with a begging bowl to the foreigners for sympathetic favours. It is Bhattacharya's satiric way of projecting the situation where the double shame of being raped and further helped by the rapist colonialist exploiter needs to be avoided, for otherwise disgrace would cross all bounds. Said refers to such a practical wisdom to be mustered in due course when he suggests that the "intellectual stirrings of anti-colonialism can only be properly realised when nationalism becomes more 'critical of itself'—when it proves itself capable of directing attention 'to the abused rights' of all oppressed classes." (Said 1993, 264 as in Leela Gandhi 1999, 82).

In *So Many Hungers* the novelist is keenly awake to such needs. The novel coming in October 1947, just in two months of India's Independence, is a powerful instructive piece in political wisdom that Indian nationalist leaders did probably need to follow to enlist the deepest and most genuine, most urgent of the problems that the nation faced, namely, the rampant poverty that was an eye-opener, equivalent to death. Bhattacharya's commitment to the 'social purpose of his art' is vindicated in his interest in history that could guide him with a vision of security, dignity and development of country along with his firm grasp of the contemporary as well as immediate future's imminent and inevitable problems at the national scale that India was sure to face on attaining freedom. This very ability of the writer to see the truth, comprehend it and explain its meaning to the colonised people is in itself enough of a postcolonial stance.

The colonialism's success lies in denying all possible ways to the colonised, the true understanding of the reality. A concocted, highly twisted nature of truth was presented. Homi Bhabha's kind of 'hybridity' and 'liminality' in this identity development of the colonised individual makes it an untenable proposition. In *So Many Hungers,* thus, the theme he reflectively chooses is that of *death* on an unimaginable and unprecedented scale in the most devastating of conditions—the man-made war and the famine that was a natural calamity but rendered more devastating due to the man-made scarcity of the food items, especially rice.

All the hungers are of a secondary importance once the hunger of hungers, as in the passion and desire to live, asserts itself. Bhattacharya's insightful choice of the theme of certain death from which escape is impossible in the way the circumstances loomed under the colonisers with the capitalist greedy local forces firming up a nexus deserves critical acclaim of the highest order for much before postcolonial consciousness could formulate itself somewhat coherently as a typical Third World concept about the abysmal wretchedness of the once colonised peoples all over the globe. Bhattacharya could foresee the kind of hard identity-crisis freedom would lead to when management of freedom in the sanest of ways eludes the newly freed nations like India. Begging and borrowing are going to lead the people nowhere except to humiliation. To be 'self-reliant' is today India's Prime Minister's vision. If this vision is pursued steadfastly, perhaps, India can recover from the pathetic condition in which she is left after gaining Independence. Bhattacharya's novel *So Many Hungers* in its recognition of the mind-boggling circumstances to follow and in its prescription of the mantra of self-reliance proves itself as the earliest of post-colonial texts to have come close.

Kunal's disappearance in Italy (like Subhash Chandra Bose's) in that Second World War time when British sought support against fascists from India is full of apprehensions about the colonial way of 'the colonised's depersonalisation': "The colonised is never characterised in an individual manner; he is entitled only to drown in an anonymous collectivity; 'They are this'"; 'They are all the same' (Albert Memmi 1967, 88 as in Loomba 2001,137). Till today India does not know what happened to its Netaji and in the same token Kunal's disappearance during the war makes every conjecture about seeing him and his whereabouts explicitly vague. The suggestion is that Cesaire's equation: 'colonialism'= 'thingification' (1972, 21 as in Loomba 2001,133) is patently true to explain that it does not make any difference if either a family in the colonised land or a whole colony grieves over someone close to it, whereas for the coloniser the loss is absolutely meaningless.

The only difference is that when Bose worked for the fascists in the hope of getting early independence, Kunal of Samarendra

Basu's family, his son, fought for the British and was equally hopeful like the leaders then in India that the colonisers would leave India on the war being won by them with Indian assistance and support.

Bhabani Bhattacharya, by drawing such a wonderful parallel, invokes a nightmarish national loss of one of the worthiest sons of India through Kunal's loss. History as the archive of all the coloniser's basest and cruellest of designs floats to the fore with Bhattacharya so successfully introducing Kunal's missing episode into his work. Alongside being a sardonic commentary against the colonialist war project, Bhattacharya's *So Many Hungers* in its treatment of Kunal's dislocation invites a fitting comparison with Conrad's *Heart of Darkness* which in its treatment of Kurtz's dislocation assumes the status of a powerful 'critique of imperialism' (Loomba 2001,136). Marlow, the narrator in Conrad's novel describes Kurtz as having his "intelligence... perfectly clear when 'his' soul was mad. Being alone in the wilderness, it had looked within itself, and by heavens! I tell you it had gone mad" (Conrad 1975, 95 as in Loomba 2001: 136).

A similar analogy in application of madness might also explain Kunal's case that his passion for war, and freedom for which war was just a temporary plea, was not any whit below madness. Whereas the warm-ongering attitude of the British as colonisers in itself is madness supreme, explaining Kunal's case in terms of madness is to agree with Loomba that "In this novel (Conrad's) as in much colonialist fiction, Africa is a place where the European mind disintegrates and regresses into a primitive state. Africa, India, China and other alien lands induce madness, they are madness itself." (2001, 136).

Chinua Achebe's (1989) reaction that "Conrad's novel presents a story in which the very humanity of black people is called into question"(quoted in Loomba 2001,136) is pertinent to Bhattacharya's story which equally begs for a reaction tempered with fury and earnestness of concern for a fellow Indian whose disappearance, in whose *thingified* neglect and rejection, in whose practical condemnation as being mad, the novelist actually points out with utmost ire that India as whole is castigated and condemned inconceivably. Projecting this troubled psyche of a wounded nation Bhattacharya seems to be making a passionate plea demanding an explanation from the colonisers for taking the *Indianness* issue so lightly and casually.

In deeply dwelling on the meaning of freedom right from how the colonised have to wrest it from the colonisers; how freedom needs be effectively managed, so that so many hungers suppressed for centuries could be satisfied, Bhattacharya has exhibited exemplary craftsmanship with concern and compassion for the suffering and destitute in a language that resonates with layers of meaning splendidly. When all men's hungers are satisfied happiness results and madness vanishes, and if all those hungers with a maddening and saddening and a shattering potential could be adequately addressed by freedom, literature that attempts to explain the meaning of freedom and also educates on how to steadfastly hold on to it, lest it slip away though sheer carelessness and overconfidence brought in by a new-found power. The novel on its own merit deserves the postcolonial tag. Bhabani Bhattacharya's *So Many Hungers* may be acclaimed as a postcolonial text par excellence.

POSTCOLONIALITY TAG FOR THE NOVEL *SO MANY HUNGERS*

Bhattacharya is profoundly concerned with the appropriate human role in the making of a society. He is for pro-life, pro-freedom and pro-happiness. He is thus temperamentally averse to the practices that fall under the sphere of colonial Manichean dichotomy. The dehumanising and degrading aspects of colonial designs immensely pain him. Cruelty against humanity is unacceptable to him. Human dignity as a theme appeals to him immensely. Colonialism as uniquely striking at it is thus a matter of revulsion for them. He believes in the goodness of man everywhere like his Gandhian character in the novel *Devesh Basu* or *Devata*. However, the scene of debasement of human character in the wake of colonialist rule in India puts a question mark on his optimism about human progress. However, knowing the Indian society, its needs, its people, its culture well, he considers Gandhism is quite capable of curing the ills that have been plaguing the Indian society since ages.

In *So Many Hungers*, his very first novel, he dwells on the theme of hungers in their astounding multiplicity but dealing in a realistic vein with many aspects of human hungers he appears convinced that freedom is an answer to almost all of them. However, on India getting freedom, his encounter of the new reality baffled him so much that freedom's meaning is not translated into action first. For him thus it appears quite urgent to depict the Indian reality against the backdrop of its new- found liberty and its unprecedented list of problems and aspirations emerging on account of this freedom. The question that confronts him is how to accommodate them. And Gandhi and Tagore instantly come to his rescue. He sees that the path to success lies in turning to the villages, in spreading education among the children (Devata teaches village children in his retirement years), and in the effective public distribution system. Side by side he wants to have people's participation in fighting all kinds of activities that may be still following colonial pattern of loot-and-rule.

The role of the elite of the civil society in the reconstruction project in new India, among other things, is his major concern. The *karmayoga* spirit unique to Indian culture and thought appears to be beckoning him from afar because that alone is the sound road to self-reliance and a life of true dignity. To enable our freedom achieve that, *So Many Hungers* presents practical apprehensions. To heed his words of wisdom is to be on the path to progress and light. India in 2003, in echoing his concerns, only vindicates the profound and pragmatic vision of Bhattacharya. To preach is what he is out to do through his art. Consciously then he knows that his art is going to play a religious role – the religion being the rediscovery of the self and freeing it from being used/abused as a slave under the colonial masters. Perhaps he wants to rechristen the colonised Indian people into the new religion of free and dignified life of plenty and pride in every respect.

He also wishes to preach the colonial West to desist from embarking on the path of oppression through its capitalism and racism. He means to preach the religion of new humanity that seeks love, concern and cooperation on an equal footing and not as poor slaves or beggars. He understands the 'self' and its 'other' so that an effective and lasting mutually invigorating kind of relationship may be nurtured. Bhattacharya in a speculative mood appears thus to be talking of effecting *Atma-sakshatkar* (know thyself and know thy neighbour) or self-encounter implying the end of the power imbalance regime and participation in a new order.

India will be 'different' after August as Rahoul Basu previsions in his Gandhian optimistic approval of the war project despite its demand for a million young men to sacrifice their lives. If a new order is to be born to benefit humanity as a whole, this sacrifice will have its definite meaning. Rahoul's concept goes well with the Hindu *Bhagavad Gita's* stress on the universal welfare motive through its justification of the *Kurukshetra* war and in its teaching/preaching by Lord Krishna to Arjuna about why he finally should come out of the trappings of the self (*moha*) and think in terms of mankind as a whole. Bhattacharya's adoption of the Gandhian approach in the novel finds its justification in this welfare motive that extends prominence to the individual and the local.

The postcolonial situation is basically a situation that warrants peaceful co-existence of all irrespective of the past dichotomy and Manichean manifestations and their unsavoury results involving the relationships among the colonisers and the colonised. The process of continuous and constant self-expansion through embracing all in a bond of love sanctified by mature understanding of the essentially good human nature is the way to forget the past, move towards a future brightened with the hope of new possibilities of dynamic relationships, to create a new history of mankind where the past and the memories of it would be contributing positively towards the enrichment of the global human culture without any *malafide* intention of civilising the 'Other' as under the colonial regimes. That would be globalisation of the right order where the self, the local and the global share their mutually enriching responsibilities to their best. The Oriental view of V*asudhaivakutumbakam* (one world-one family) will then be possible in its grand manifestation.

The notion of social purpose is linked to the relationship between art and society. Art is developed in a society, in its language, incorporating its culture and worldview and it is primarily for the society—for its consumption and for its appreciation. In this relational nature art seeks to depend much on society while in certain terms moulding its spirit and mien to face the challenges of ever unpredicted manner and magnitude.

In preparing the society art follows a vision that evolves from the experience of a writer. But in infusing a new spirit into the society, art has to count on ethics in a big way (Mahapatra, 2001). Mahapatra holds: "Ethics (in relation to literature) is thus very relevant—ethics in the sense of an autonomous vision that fashions a creator's approach to reality. Ethics becomes reliant more particularly at our time when life and literature tend to retreat face with an incomprehensible horror. Comprehending an incomprehensible horror was always a challenge to creative writing. But the kind of horror our times have unfolded is perhaps unprecedented in human history" (JCT 2001, 8).

Mahapatra continues: "Like Jesus, literature does not and should not address either the accusing crowd or the helpless accused through rhetoric." For its function is, in the word that Derek Walcott has put beautifully, "to hold a little space and function not for diversion or destruction but for pure concentration." Its attempt is to hold, in a single thought, reality and justice. And that can be possible not by proposing to be instrumental or effective, but to hold attention for some space. And function not as distraction or rhetoric but as pure concentration conceived and nurtured in silence. In an age of speed, Pasternak said long back, "We must think slowly. And judge things, respond to reality and look at relationships also slowly."

The postcoloniality of *So Many Hungers* is an establisned fact as the novel analyses a colonial situation by a writer who was severely exposed to the exploiting side of colonialism and wrote at a time when his nation was thrown off the colonial yoke. The writer addresses both the people of his own country now coming to use freedom in all its promising ways on the one hand and the English-knowing outside ex-colonisers to tell each of them what best may be done by them in order to block the de-humanising potential of colonialism from resurrecting itself anymore.

Works Cited

Bhattacharya, Bhabani, *So Many Hungers,* Bombay,Jaico Publishing House, 1964.

Gandhi, Leela, *Postcolonial Theory-A critical Introduction.*New Delhi, OUP, 2002.

Jha, Rama, *Gandhian thought & Indo-anglian novelists*. Delhi, Chanakya Publications, 1983.

Kunjo Singh, Kh., *The Fiction of Bhabani Bhattacharya*, New Delhi,Atlantic Publishers, 2002.

Loomba, Ania, *Colonialism/Postcolonialism*, London, Routledge, 2001.

Naik, M. K., 1999. *Aspects of Indian Writing in English*. New Delhi, Macmillan.

Sharma, K. K., *Bhabani Bhattacharya-His Vision and Themes*, New Delhi, Abhinav Publications, 1979.

Srivasatava, Ramesh K., *Colonial Consciousness in Black American, African and Indian Fiction in English*. Jalandar, ABS Publications, 1991.

11

The Veil of Irony in Narayan's *Financial Expert*

—*P. Gopichand & P. Nagasuseela*

Malgudi, the home of many lively characters, such as Swami and his friends, Margayya, Raju, Mr. Sampath and Nataraj, is a small fictional town in Mysore. The town was immortalised by the master narrator, R.K.Narayan. The city of Malgudi was born out of the pen of R.K Narayan, considered as one of the pioneers of Indian Writing in English.

It is generally agreed that *The Financial Expert, The Guide* and *The Man-Eater of Malgudi* contain the cream of Narayan's fiction. This is because in these novels, irony so far circumscribed in conception and consequently restricted in its operation, develops from only a useful technique into an all-embracing vision in life.

Human life is overflowing with irony. Margayya, an obscure middle-class man, ekes out his livelihood by sitting in front of the Cooperative Land Mortgage Bank and by helping poor rustics in filling up their forms for loans.

One day he is humiliated by the bank official. This goads him to take a firm decision to grow rich. Under the guidance of a priest he performs a ritual to Goddess Lakshmi for forty days. The old priest, even without a name in the novel, never demands or receives any money for his advice. The description of the manner of the pooja performed is devoid of irony:

> Each day it took him eight hours of repetition to complete the thousand, and then he reverently put the black paste on

> his forehead, lit the camphor, called in his wife and child and sprinkled the holy water on them. His jaws ached his tongue has become dry... he felt faint with hunger, since he had to fast completely while praying.[1]

He accidentally meets Dr Paul and through him gets hold of a pornographic book *Bed Life*. He changes the name of the book to *Domestic Harmony* and prints the book. This is an instant success. Now the flow of money makes him plan for a money deposit scheme. He flourishes beyond his imagination. His plan is to seek Dr Paul's help in implementing the money deposit scheme. He wants to take advantage of the money boom triggered by the war economy. The *Domestic Harmony* paves the way for his financial career but it does not improve his own domestic life at all; moreover the author of the book himself is a bachelor. Though Dr Paul helps Margayya financially, the latter desires that his son should be away from him:

> Margayya didn't like a man who could write domestic harmony to associate with young, impressionable minds; he would probably recite passages from it; talk over further projects with his son; and he could not say why Balu might or might not do under those circumstances.[2]

Thinking that he needs divine grace to be rid from the clutches of poverty Margayya performs Lakshmi pooja. But at the time of the settlement of Balu's marriage, he consults an astrologer. And there the influence of planets on human beings is ironical.:

> It seems necessary as first step to dictate to the planets what they should do. Margayya had made up his mind that he was going to take no non sense from the planets, and he was going to tell them how to dispose their position in order to meet his requirement. These were not days when he had to wait anxiously on a verdict of the stars: he could afford to ask for his own set of conditions and get them. He no longer believed that man was a victim of circumstances or fate. But that man was a creature who could make his present and future provided he worked hard and remained watchful.[3]

But Margayya fails to be watchful of Balu's movements and his actions. Without any premeditation, he assaults Dr Paul as he meets him while leaving Balu's house. Here chance plays a vital role in reversing the position of Margayya:

> Later in life Margayya often speculated what would have become of him if he had started back home after speaking with his daughter-in-law a little earlier and missed Dr Paul's Austin that night or if he had remained in the shadows and allowed Paul to go off after dropping Balu, whom he might probably have tackled with more circumspection and diplomacy; he might even have shared his property with him as he demanded; that would have saved him at least the rest of it and prevented the doctor from what he did.[4]

Dr Paul, with a vengeance, spreads the rumours about Margayya's fictitious financial problems and ultimately leads to a great crash. Is it not ironical to call Margayya, an ordinary literate man, a financial expert? His business crashes suddenly and leaves him penniless. How can he be a financial expert? Probably his concentration is on acquiring wealth but not on holding to it.

> His heart on reaching the summit of Everest.[5]

Some people acquire wealth suddenly in life. We hear many stories of rags to riches. One must be a specialist in differentiating different forms of wealth. Margayya can see the difference:

> With great subtlety between money, riches, wealth and fortune.[6]

In spite of many handicaps Margayya, a puny little man, by sheer luck becomes a financial expert but by a small error he returns to his previous puny state. His original name was Krishna. As he is the one to show the path to many he is called Margayya.

> He showed the way out to those in financial trouble. And in all those villages that lay within a hundred-mile radius of Malgudi, was there anyone who could honestly declare that he was not in financial difficulties?[7]

This very name Margayya is also ironical. He cannot show the way to others but he loses his way and comes to his original place, that is, eking out his livelihood by sitting in front of the Cooperative Land Mortgage Bank. Even after the crash ironically he says to his son:

> I am showing you a way. Will you follow it?[8]

The modern world is peopled with Margayyas. Harshad Mehta, Satyanarayana Raju and many more to fulfil their fancies toyed with the economic status of many commoners and climbed the ladder to run from rags to riches. Many people belonging to the middle class want to become rich and satisfy their desires. In this process they may run for Lakshmi poojas, lottery tickets, share markets and races. When their dreams come true, their success stories will be in print; and their names will be dancing on the tips of tongues. But when their wheel of fortune turns a full circle again they will be in the news. But how many will stay away from the Margayyas and shun to be Margayyas? This is the real irony of life.

References

1. R.K. Narayan, *The Financial Expert*, Indian Thoughts Publication, Mysore, 56.
2. Ibid., p. 157.
3. Ibid., p.152.
4. Ibid., pp. 173-174.
5. Ibid., p. 158.
6. Ibid., p. 110.
7. Ibid., p.1.
8. Ibid., p.118.

12

The Novels of Ruth Prawer Jhabvala and the Problem of Survival in Postcolonial India

—*Pragyasa H. Upadhyaya*

The theme of survival has been very dominant among Indian women novelists. More so with Ruth Pravar Jhabvala. Her novels are important landmarks, as a woman protagonist in each of her novels has been involved with survival motif in mind. It is another thing that some come out of the difficulties successfully whereas the others are weak and succumb to the external pressures.

Among the characters in Jhabvala's fiction are those men and women of the West who try to identify themselves with India and Indian civilisation. However, they fail in this trial. This is the crisis of identity as the process is very painful because in identifying themselves with the Indian culture they lose their original roots and belong neither to India nor to their own country.

Jhabvala herself admits that she has shown herself through her Western characters. The views of Esmond Stillwood and Etta towards India are seen as the views of Ruth Jhabvala herself, and the characters like Judy (*A Backward Place*) and Olivia Rivers (*Heat and Dust*) who show a personal bondage to India also give us the views of Jhabvala herself who tried to reconcile with the Indian atmosphere but could not. Through Esmond, Raymond, Major Minnies and others Ruth Jhabvala has tried to show the Indian culture and appreciate Indian art and music.

Jhabvala being a European by descent is first an individual and a part of society later. After getting married to an Indian she feels enthusiastic to accept Indian society as her future as a futuristic society but she does so much against her abil. y to identify with alien social culture. However, she does so unknowingly because she has never tested her physical and mental limits to accept. In the Western culture human society is composed of individuals who have the willingness to survive only as individuals. If they survive, society will flourish automatically; whereas in India it is the society which takes precedence to individual existence. This has been the phenomenon with the Indian ethos ever since Rama organised Indian society and culture on the basis of a socialist society that the Indian social thought acquired quite significance through all the centuries that followed the reign of mythological or legendary Rama. The Western individual appears to be selfish in nature. In fact, he is more arrogant, factual and instinctive in feeling and action.

The Indian, on the contrary, hides his individual feelings behind the social nomenclature but he works towards fulfilling his personal aspirations under the cover of main social ethos. This basic dichotomy of Indian social content confuses any alien, therefore he or she is almost bewildered and unable to acclimatise himself or herself to the basic accommodation in society. The Europeans are more direct and pointed in purpose, which is mostly obvious, therefore their approach to life becomes specified, one-sided and utility-oriented. It comes in sharp contrast with the Indian. So they fail to conform, and learn and survive in India.

The raw material of a literary work is generally drawn from myths, stories and other written sources, travels, life around the writer, his impressions of reality, the fantastic inventions of the author's imagination, and so on. But the devices, which transmute the raw material into meaningful content, are finite in number, although the individual writer can always effect necessary permutations and combinations of these devices in order to suit his particular inclination and needs.

The fact is that a literary work is not only the material in the raw but also the material as shaped and structured by the writer. A distinction of this kind is particularly important in approach. A realistic fictional work uses the contemporary socio-cultural environment as its content.

It is precisely due to a failure to make the primary distinctions between the various formal structures of the narratives, as well as between the raw materials of life and the content of a fictional work, that several critics of Ruth Prawer Jhabvala have not been able to see the essential nature of her fiction and their judgments seem to be unjust. Most of her critics have liked or disliked her for the aspects of contemporary social life she has presented in her fiction. Again some of her critics have praised or blamed her for her giving them a living or dead picture of India. Man and society in India today are changing. She portrays this change with an acute awareness and sensitivity.

Jhabvala tries to bring out her characters vividly in their own aspirations in adverse atmosphere. She herself has said about her art of characterisation, "I use one character and split that character up. I have certain leading figures in my life and I seem to use them again and again, presenting different facets of their personality so one person can play the role of fifty."[1]

Her splitting of character can be attributed to her attempt at a finer and subtler analysis of the human psyche than hitherto, a literal " taking apart" of what requires further investigation.

But Jhabvala's method of character analysis doesn't pose any challenge to Sigmond Freud and Alder Jung. Characters are not so much analysed as satirically assessed according with some private authorial code of values as to what constitutes the ridiculous. What is evident in this manifold replication of character is that the author's own divided identity is presented. Lee, Evie, Margaret, each individual is affilicted with the same malaise; so are Raymond and Gopi, and Asha and Banubai, and so on. So each of Jhabvala's characters attempts to explain the one before. For example, "sick" Etta of *A Backward Place* is reconstituted in "sick" Asha of *A New Dominion.*

Jhabvala's characters can be grouped into two parts: Indian characters and European characters. Her European characters are more impressive than the Indian ones. She has a deep understanding of European life whereas 'she has only outer knowledge of Indian characters'.[2] Ramesh Chaddha has rightly said, "Herself a European, She cannot probe the Indian psyche as deeply as she can do the European one."[3]

Through all types of characters Jhabvala tries to bring the problems of Indians as well as Europeans. She tries to categorise the characters in rational and intuitive ways. On the one hand we see Esmond and Hardayal's family and their Englishness, while on the other we have Ramnath and Gulab. Male-female and even hermaphrodite find place in her novels. Kent, of *In Search of Love and Beauty* is a typical hermaphrodite... male in physical appearance and female in temperament.

Ruth Jhabvala's women characters may broadly be placed in four major categories. First, there are women who accept with unquestioning resignation the dictates of the society. They adjust to the texture of personal life, no matter what it would be. They are patient, self-sacrificing and modest. In other words, they are passive or submissive characters. Judy of *A Backward Place* and Indu of *The House Holder* are such characters. They are presented by Jhabvala as restless, dissatisfied and rebellious. For example, Etta in *A Backward Place*, Kusum in *Get Ready for Battle* and Olivia and the narrator in *Heat and Dust* are aggressive characters. Submissive and idealistic qualities of an individual character are dealt with in her novels. Indu, in *The House Holder*, is submissive and passive by nature. She tries to follow the conventional ways but she has the ideal of individual freedom. When Prem wants to dominate her, Indu defies him for the sake of her idea. Then there is the fourth category of women who are aggressive but at the same time idealistic. They can take any drastic step to realise their idea, as Sarla Devi in *Get Ready for Battle.*

Jhabvala's understanding of Indian women is greater than her understanding of Indian men. The women of Jhabvala are seen to run after money, position and fashion. In *To Whom She will* Amrita dreams of a romantic love marriage. Nimmi's newly rich father in *The Nature of Passion* wants his daughters to enter the fashionable society. Shakuntala, of *Esmond in India,* like Nimmi and other young girls in rich families in Jhabvala's fiction, runs after the thrill of romance for a while but ultimately reconciles herself to the idea of settling down to a comfortable and arranged marriage.

The indolence of the wives, their habits of over-eating, and over-sleeping, their sentimentality, their lack of practical point of view, their habit of gossiping, their inability to be a worthy companions of their husbands, their over-petting of the children etc., are some of the aspects of the lives of the female characters that have been discussed by Jhabvala in her novels.

In order to make her portraits of Indian life more realistic, Jhabvala presents a series of photographic pictures of the detestable habits of her characters. Gulzari Lal, in *Get Ready for Battle,* has a Western type of house, but he retains his most characteristic Indian habit of sitting on the floor. The unhygienic habit of Joginder spitting all the time red betel juice is again an example of it. We have also a picture of Bundi Basti in *Get Ready for Battle,* who is always ready to squash a house with her murderous finger. Lalaji's character is brought up with a very fine art. Jhabvala glorifies him as an individual though at times she is against his views of giving gifts to officers in order to make his work done. She has captured a view not only of a depressing low life of some members of the lower classes at one end, she has also shown the contrast by presenting other characteristic habits of Indians which are pleasant and wholesome at the other hand—the Punjabi taste and temperament, the Punjabi dish, the humbler women tying honey to their dhotis, of the commonplace consumption of betel leaf, ladies applying red dye to the soles of their feet, arranged marriages, the respectful distance maintained by the daughters-in-law towards their parents-in-law etc.

Jhabvala's novels are full of the individuals blighted by some form of binary opposition of conflicting emotions and appetites. Each of her individual characters is driven by an obsession, a desire, which is a desire to appropriate the superior assests of strengths of another person. Even the masochistic display of her various female questers is itself a perverse means to an act of would-be appropriation. Lee's willingness, of rather absolute need, to be abused by Swamiji in *A New Dominion* has a convoluted logic where suffering is gratefully accepted as a part of a sublime course. In the emotionally void, traumatised conditions of many of Jhabvala's quitters the desire for escape, for a messianic solution, looms overwhelmingly.

In fact, many of her novels and short stories are primarily concerned with portraying either the fulfilment or the frustration of the individual in society. She takes up a couple of families to bring out the scare and fatuity of life, especially of memsahibs.

Mrs. Saunders is almost broken down in the Indian atmosphere while Olivia insists on the realisation of a fuller life. As she is feeling bored and lonely, she meets the Nawab, an extremely handsome and vital man, who overwhelms her. The Nawab, a native ruler, feels helpless and desperate, as he cannot fight out the British who have usurped his rights with cunningness and force. The initiation of her relationship with the Nawab accelerates the process of her estrangement with her husband, Douglas, which results in her complete disillusionment with the life of the Britishers.

Struggles and sufferings of an English girl, Judy, married to an Indian actor, Bal, are described in *A Backward Place*. The author's handling of the clash of backgrounds and her satire, sharp yet never deadly, makes it a brilliant picture of life in Delhi. Among other interesting characters are Etta, a middle-aged Hungarian beauty, who has had a number of Indian husbands and lovers, and Clarissa, another English woman who is a great devotee of Indian spiritualism.

In *Nature of Passion* one is delighted by the attempt of Nimmi for eve's emancipation and modernity against a background of powerful criticism in the women's quarter. The gracious material out look of Lalaji is contrasted with the more revolting type of Chandra Prakash and his educated wife Kanta. Lalaji becomes an unforgettable figure.

The Householder expounds the comic possibilities of the human situation in which the individual always falls short of his expected stature in life. Prem discovers that the newly acquired dignity of a householder is mocked at on one side by his wife and the servant boy and on the other by a disobedient student. He always approaches his boss for a salary or his land-lord for a reduction in the house rent. Jhabvala has portrayed the trials and tribulations of Prem's domestic life effectively.

Her interest in the individual is more markedly revealed with exactness in her short stories entitled *Like birds like fishes and other stories*. They make an absorbing picture of Indian city life today. There are fascinating plots spiced with suspense and romance of day-to-day life, peopled with credible men and women.

Jhabvala makes fun of the young generation who, while thinking themselves to be modern and Westernised, try to do things which the traditional Hindu society would not accept, that is, falling in love with a boy (or a girl) outside one's own caste, community and social status. They face a vehement opposition and the irony is that tradition wins over modernisation. D.C. Agrawal in one of his articles analysing the situation writes:

> The traditionalists achieve much by hypothecating their individuality and freedom. They achieve a sense of security and belonging. The non-traditionalists, on the contrary have to pay the price to their identity and 'Lassaiz faire', even so it is questionable whether they will succeed in the bargain.[4]

The feeling for self-apprehension and identity and a fear of survival makes Hari exclaim, "Who am I? Hari Sahni, an announcer in Hindi section. I draw only Rupees 300/- a month. I live in a rented house paying Rupees 50/- rent. I am nobody. I, am nothing."[5] And this feeling reveals his character. He has been described as a weak character as compared to Amrita. He lacks manners and sophistication; the feeling of being nothing haunts him constantly. Though Hari, portrayed as a weak character, declares his love for Amrita, he is not able to face the opposition of his family. His family naturally does not approve his marriage to Amrita, who is a Bengali girl and thus cannot fit into their family. It is here that Jhabvala brings in the issue of caste and community. Punjabis and Bengalis are considered to be poles apart. Their dress, food, language and social customs, everything is different and hence they find a nice girl, Sushia Anand, a girl from their own caste and community for him. Jhabvala tries to bring out the conception of love in India and she very aptly proves the victory of tradition over modernity. She proves that India is still a backward place, no matter how much its younger generation strives to break the shackles of old traditions and customs. Hari's mother concludes the entire matter by saying:

> He is a good son, he will marry a nice girl, you will see, one of our girls whom his family chooses for him.[6]

Besides the social activities, like marriage, death and engagements, Jhabvala also tackles an important problem of the post-independence Indian society through the character of

Krishna Sen Gupta, describing the plight of those young Indians who go to foreign countries. Their exposure to the Western world is good for them in one way, but when they come back they are in a peculiar situation. They know they cannot change the Indian society, and at the same time they find it very diffcult to merge themselves in it. This predicament leads them to dejection and frustration, and in this mood they become so bitter that they start hating everything Indian. Krishna Sen Gupta, a Bengali youth, highly educated, goes to England for higher studies and on his return finds it impossible to merge in this society and he hates everything around him. At this point, it will not be irrelevant to say that Krishna is only her mouthpiece to speak them out aloud. Jhabvala writes:

> So he had come back, and he hated it at first. He hated the uncomplaining poverty, the apathy he saw all around him, in the streets, the bazaars, on the steps of the temples. He hated the servants... he hated the frank immortality of business and the unashamed dishonesty of shopkeepers. He hated the women because they were ignorant, innocent and submiseive. He hated the heat which under-mined and insulted his vigour. He hated everything, even his parents because it was they who made him come back."[7]

And we wonder, is it possible that Krishna being an Indian should hate everything around him? Often it is the parents who call their sons back, with nothing to offer them and, if at that moment, the sons hate their parents, it is not unreasonable. The entire description is bitter and in no way shows Jhabvala's enthusiasm for this enchanted land.

The entire episode appears to be ironical when Jhabvala writes that Krishna soon forgets the 'West", and merges himself in the Indian society. The fact that the Indian society is too strong for European nerves and one has to drown himself in this society if one wants to live here, has often been repeated in her later novels also. In *A Backward Place*, Mr. Hochstadt, a visiting professor in Delhi, remarks: "It is fatal to come to India and expect to be able to live a western rhythm." The same idea has been expressed in *Heat and Dust* where the narrator makes this remark in the very beginning of the novel, "...India always changes people and I have been no exception." (22)

It is interesting to note that the same idea runs through all her novels. What she writes in her first novel is repeated in her last one also. Krishna, who initially hated everything Indian, soon forgets his sufferings and Jhabvala writes:

> Krishna thought he could never get used to it again.... He talked cynically and bitterly. Then a little work started to drift his way, a newspaper article here and a lecture there... He began not to notice the services done for him by the servants, to accept the beggars at their own valuation, to regard the girls as members of the other species. By the time he got his appointment of Delhi University, he had almost got used to the heat. (59-60)

When Jhabvala wrote her first novel, she was essentially an outsider, viewing this unknown society with awe and wonder, and passing through the first stage of the cycle when there is tremendous enthusiasm and everything Indian is marvellous. She describes in detail the Indian railway stations, bazaars and many social customs like 'mundan', name-giving ceremony and most of all the arranged marriage system in India, which is something entirely new and intriguing to Jhabvala's Western mind.

After assessing the whole scenario of the time when Jhabvala was writing and after taking account of the novels she wrote, we can come to the point in relation to the problem of survival that she surely is individualistic in approach and this shows her European sensibility. She believes in glorifying those of her characters who are European and also those who follow the Western ideas, being Indian.

Jhabvala tries to bring out significantly the social ethos of that time. She takes delight in discussing the society very closely with minor effects. She has not left out even small factors of the Indians to be discussed. She has a European eye and so her characters that are Europeans do not survive in this atmosphere while the Indians in their attempt of modernisation fail and go towards traditionalistic society. She admits:

> She includes herself among her western characters; her critics sometimes see the contempt and revulsion displayed by such characters as Esmond Stillwood and Etta towards

> India as reflecting her permanent point of view. It is not often kept in mind that by the same token, such characters as Judy (*A Backward Place*) and Olivia Rivers (*Heat and Dust*) almost certainly reflect something of Ruth Jhabvala's own commitment, through bonds of personal affection, to India. In Esmond, Raymond (*A New Dominion*), Major Minnes (*Heat and Dust*) and others could be traced some of the approaches she has made herself, through the exploration and enjoyment of Indian art, music and literature, to a better understanding of the country of her adoption.[8]

Jhabvala uses Etta to criticise India, and on many occasions who appears to be her mouthpiece. Etta criticises Judy who has submitted herself to the Indian culture and society, and she also criticises the Indian hairstyle and dress. We come to understand that Jhabvala herself did not like the Indian dress and according to her the last limit of submission is to give up one's dress and to lose your identity forever. Through Etta she tries to criticise the Indian atmosphere, mainly the heat, and says that the Indian sun has been put there to ruin their complexion.

At the beginning Jhabvala is like Judy who has come to India as a bride and through her novel we come to mark that she identifies herself with Judy in the beginning, but after some time she realises that she cannot reconcile with Indian culture.

Miss Charlette is a Western woman, a missionary who has dedicated more than thirty years of her life doing charitable work in India. She is happy to know that she has to go back to England for good. She tells Raymond about going back to her country, "still home is home." This statement reminds us of Jhabvala herself who leaves India and goes back to her own country leaving her family and the primitive society.

Ruth Jhabvala has revealed her deepest sentiments through the character Esmond who comes to India, marries an Indian girl and teaches Indian culture and history to the foreigners coming to India. Although a lover of Indian culture and life, he is unable to understand it completely and cope with its oddities. Although teaching Indian culture he does not imbibe any of it himself. He misses his home country England and after sometime goes back, leaving India. The same situation happens with Jhabvala. She came to India, lived here for twenty-five years and after that went back to her own country.

Vasant A. Shahane writes, "Esmond Stillwood is, of course, not dead wood. His problem is however, similar to the problem of Jhabvala herself:

> Should one want to try and become something other than what one is? It is essentially a problem of identity. Can Esmond in relation to India allow himself to be crushed by the environment?[9]

The following passage from her autobiography beautifully highlights her inner conflict:

> Should one try and become something other than what one is? It doesn't always say no to this question. Sometimes it seems to me how pleasant it would be to say yes and give in and wear a sari and be weak and accepting and see God in a cow. Other times it seems worthwhile to be defiant and European and all right be crushed by one's environment; but all the same have made sure attempt to remain standing. Of course this can't go on indefinitely and in the end I am bound to lose if only at the point where my ashes are immersed in the Ganges to the accompaniment of Vedic hymns, and then who will say that I have not truly merged with India.[10]

References

1. Anna Rutherford and Kristen Holst Peterson, Heat and Dust: Ruth Prawer Jhabvala's Experience of India, *World Literature Written in English,* 15, No. 11, No. 1976, 373.
2. Chaddha, Ramesh, Image of women in the fiction of Jhabvala, *Indian Women Novelists,* Set 11, vol. V, ed. R. K. Dhawan, Prestige, 1993, 207.
3. Ibid.
4. D.C. Agarwal, To whom she will: exploration in Modern Indo-English fiction'. in R.K. Dhawan ed. *Common Wealth Fiction,* New Delhi: Bahri Publication Pvt. Ltd., 1982, 125.
5. R.P. Jhabvala, *To Whom She Will,* George Allen and Unwin, London, 1955, 92-93.
6. *Ibid.,* p. 15.
7. *Ibid.,* pp. 28–29.

8. Yasmine Gooneratne, *Silence, Exile and Cunning,* Orient Longman Ltd. 1991, pp. 12-13.
9. Vasant A. Shahane, *Ruth Prawer Jhabvala,* Arnold-Heinemann Publishers, New Delhi 1976, 102.
10. Ruth Prawar Jhabvala, *An Experience of India,* London: John Murray, 1967.

13

Postcolonial Traits in Bapsi Sidhwa's *Ice-Candy-Man*

—*Jaukkalkar Sd. Imtiaz*

The term 'postcolonial' is used to "cover all the cultures affected by the imperial process from the moment of colonisation to the present day."[1] It is universally acknowledged that the British adopted a 'divide and rule' policy in India to maintain their dominance. India is a multi-religious country. It was easy for them to make Indians fight with each other on the basis of religion. Partition of India and creation of Pakistan is the result of the British policy of divide and rule. The partition resulted in permanent enmity between the two countries.

After Attia Hossain's *Sunlight on a Broken Column*, Sidhwa is the second Pakistani woman writer to write a novel dealing with partition and its aftermath. The novel *Ice-Candy-Man*[2] captures the dispirited effects of communal frenzy that follows partition through the innocent eyes of Lenny, the child narrator of the novel, much more like her creator, polio-ridden, precocious and a keen observer of the happenings around. She is looked after by her Hindu Ayah, "chocolate-brown and short. Everything about her is eighteen years old ana round and plump"(03). Among her admirers Ayah has Ice-candy-man, Masseur, Imam Din, Hari and many more. It is through Lenny, we get glimpse of life of the cross-section of Pakistani society. The Pakistanis feed and cater to her idyllic world of romances. "They are what they are to her-human beings, full of human strengths and weaknesses".[3] This doesn't remain the same as this news spreads like a bush fire in the town. Her idyllic world of childhood innocence gives way to the tormenting adult world of partition riots. The individual identities merge with the identities of the community and soon the society is sharply divided on communal lines.

The news of atrocities on Muslims near Amritsar and Jullundhar are heard in Lahore. The details are so brutal and bizarre that is hard to believe. Lenny has a bitter realisation by now: "One man's religion is another man's poison"(117). Suddenly, the whole atmosphere is charged with religious slogans. The Sikhs are wielding their kirpans shouting "Sat Siri Akal! Bolay se Nihaal!" (134). And the Muslims are roaring: "Allah–O- Akbar! Yaaa Ali!" (135).

Lahore is seething with aliens who have lost their settled homes in India and have been forced to go to Pakistan. Having lost their property, prestige and their nearest and dearest ones in this riot, they are struggling hard to recover from this sudden jolt. People are being butchered—men, women, children, old, young handicapped, diseased—indiscriminately on either side. Houses are set on fire and looted. Women are the worst sufferers as they have been raped brutally and their limbs amputated. 'Ice-candy-man', the protagonist of the novel, doesn't remain the admirer of Ayah. He becomes an extremist fighting for the cause of his faith and land.

One day he becomes breathless in sweat and dust to announce the worst outcome of these communal riots:

> 'A train from Gurdaspur has just come in, he announces, panting. 'Everyone in it is dead. Butchered. They are all Muslims. There are no young women among the dead. Only two gunny-bags full of women's breasts.' (135)

Even though Sidhwa tries to depict the atrocities committed by Hindus, Muslims and Sikhs without partiality, being a Pakistani writer she makes it obvious that her sympathies are with the Muslim victims. Not only are the Sikh's attacks on Muslim villages in Punjab described vividly, but also it is seen through the eyes of the Muslim child Ranna, which shifts the reader's sympathy towards the Muslims.

Sidhwa's re-writing of history in *Ice-Candy-Man* is far more complex than it appears to be, since she rewrites history not just from the Pakistani but also from the Parsi point of view.

After the publication of *Midnights' Children*, many writers showed their interest in history, and tried to capture the changing reality into their narrative. As a result, their works become reflections of the concerned society. "These writers have, quite often, countered the given versions of history, offering their own interpretations of events."[4] Sidhwa, in order to highlight the Parsi dilemma at the time of the partition, goes back thirteen hundred years to the significant moment in Parsi history, when they "were kicked out of Persia by the Arabs"(37) and "sailed to India" (37). After waiting four days on the Indian coast they were visited by the Grand Vazir, with a glass of milk filled to the brim, symbolising that his land is full and prosperous and in no need of "outsiders with a different religion and alien ways to disturb the harmony". (38). However, the Parsi forefathers, intelligently, "stirred a teaspoon of sugar into the milk and sent it back," (39) symbolising that the Parsis "would get absorbed into his country like sugar into the milk. And with their decency and industry sweeten the lives of his subjects." (39).

Sidhwa contradicts the recovered discourses that the Parsis took a neutral position in the consequences of the Partition, by showing the silent but positively active role played by Lenny's parents and her grandmother. They help the affected Hindus as well as the Muslims. It suggests that "the Parsis too were involved in their own ways in the events of the time and they were not just indifferent and passive onlookers to the awful human tragedy."[5] Since the received histories, in their virtual silence regarding the role of the Parsis in the events of the partition, project and perpetuate a misconception of the Parsi, Sidhwa's contradiction provides us with a revision of the Parsis and highlights the unacknowledged nobility and courage of a community that is normally looked upon as remaining apart and indifferent in matters that concern other communities. In this revision and construction, Sidhwa makes us see that side of the Parsis that others have not shown us.

To counter the British and Indian version of the partition, Sidhwa in *Ice-Candy-Man*, not only tries to resurrect the image of Jinnah but also demystifies the image of Gandhi and Nehru. Jinnah, in the novel, is highlighted as an ambassador of Hindu-Muslim unity. She writes: "Forty years later, in films of Gandhi's and Mountbatten's lives, in books by British and Indian scholars, Jinnah, who for a decade was known as Ambassador of Hindu-Muslim unity, is caricatured, and portrayed as a monster" (160). To substantiate this image of Jinnah, Sidhwa quotes the Indian poetess Sarojini Naidu:

> The calm hauteur of his accustomed reserve masks, for those who knew him, a naïve and eager humanity, an intuition quick and tender as a woman's, a humour gay and winning as a child's—pre-eminently rational and practical, discreet and dispassionate in his estimate and acceptance of life, the obvious sanity and serenity of his worldly wisdom effectively disguise a shy and splendid idealism which is of the very essence of the man. (161)

The sublime image of Gandhi constructed by British and Indian historians is totally undercut when he is seen through the eyes of the seven-year-old narrator, Lenny: "He [Gandhi] is small, dark, shriveled, and old. He looks just like Hari, our gardener, except he has a disgruntled, disgusted and irritable look, and no one'd dare to pull off his dhoti! He wears only the loincloth and his black and thin torso is naked" (86). Unlike most of the Indian historians who credit Gandhi for single-handedly ousting the British from India, in *Ice-Candy-Man*, Sidhwa reduces him to the role of an eccentric dietician, who advises every woman to "flush" (87) their system with enemas. According to Masseur Gandhi "is a politician" and "it's his business to suit his tongue to the moment."(91) Similarly Nehru is a shrewd politician who in spite of all the efforts of Jinnah "will take off with the lion's share." (131). Nehru, according to the Ice-candy-man is "a sly one—He's got Mountbatten eating out of his one hand and the English's wife out of his other what not—He's the one to watch"(20).

Another interesting feature of Sidhwa writing from the postcolonial perspective is her use of the English language. In fact the language is a major preoccupation of the postcolonial writer. Sidhwa gives us a new version of English which is full of Urdu words. She makes the English language suitable to carry the burden of her experience. The following Urdu words are used by the novelist in *Ice-Candy-Man*: "*pahilwan*, a wrestler" (27),"*choorail*, witches" (21), "*Shabash*, Well said !" (245), "*Ghar ki Murgi dal barabar*, A neighbour's beans are tastier than household chickens." (232), "*Khut putli*, puppets" (222), "*Mamajee uncle*" (77).

Sidhwa highlights Muslim culture by using Urdu poetry in her novel. *Ice-Candy-Man* opens with Iqbal's poem 'Complaint to God. At the beginning of chapter 13, the quote from Iqbal's poetry is a good example of the poet's anti-colonial stance.

> The times have changed; the world has changed its mind.
> The European's mystery is erased.
> The secrets of his conjuring tricks is known.
> The Frankish wizard stands and looks amazed. (111)

Iqbal demystifies the notion of the white as a superior race by exposing the secrets of its 'conjuring tricks'.

To conclude, Sidhwa's *Ice-Candy-Man* successfully questions the British and Indian versions of the subcontinent's history, and provides an alternative version of history based on Pakistan point of view.

References

1. Ashcroft, Bill, et. al, *The Empire Writes Back*, Routledge (2nd Edition), London and New York, 2002, 02.
2. Sidhwa, Bapsi, *Ice-Candy-Man*, Penguin, New Delhi, 1989.
3. Kumar, Narendra, *Ice-Candy-Man*: The Dehumanising Effects of Communalism, *Bapsi Sidhwa's Ice-Candy-Man, A Reader's Companion*, ed. Gaur, Rashmi, Asia Book Club, New Delhi, 2004, 190.

4. Shah, Nila, 'Yoking of Myth to History: Shashi Tharour's *The Great Indian Novel*', *Novel As History*. Creative Books, New Delhi, 2003, 80.
5. Salat, M. F., 'Magic Writings of Bapsi Sidhwa', *The Parsis, Madhyan to Sanjan,* Ed. Kapala Novy, Khan, A. G., Creative Books, New Delhi, 1997, p.102.

14

Bharati Mukherjee: A Post-colonial Indian English Diaspora Novelist

—Sunita S. Gharge

Bharati Mukherjee is a postcolonial Indian English diaspora novelist and non-fiction writer. To posit her within the larger Indian diaspora, it is necessary to begin with her biography. She is Indian (Calcutta)-born American mainstream writer of fiction and non-fiction. So she asserted in an interview with Ron Hogan,"I am an American writer of Indian origin." America has transformed her and she is transforming America being a writer. The transformation is a two-way process—it affects both the individual and the national and cultural identity. She doesn't talk of loss but that her migration has been a gain.

Studied in India, England and America Bharati Mukherjee has lived in many countries like India, England, Canada, and America. When she was in Canada, she married a Canadian novelist in America. This resulted in her first two novels—*The Tiger's Daughter* (1971) and *Wife* (1975). She found herself discriminated against and treated as a member of "visible minority". So she had taken a bold decision to move along with her two sons and husband to America. They migrated to USA in 1980; since then they have been living as US citizens. From 1966 to 1980 her position was an expatriate's position. Due to this she was writing in the manner of V.S. Naipaul. But then her literary models are Bernard Malamud, Henry Roth and Isaac Babel. It is her transformation from an expatriate writer into a writer of immigrant fiction. Because her displacement is not forced, it is her own choice for career. She struggles for equal rights and status in USA. So she rejects her hyphenated identity.

She asserts:

> Why is it that hyphenation is imposed only on non-white Americans ? Rejecting hyphenation is my refusal to categorise the cultural landscape into a centre and its peripheries; it is to demand that the American nation delivered the promises of its dream (ed. Bart Schneider, Race: Anthology in the First Person, *American Dreamer,* New York, 1997.)

She is the voice of immigrants from all over the world, writing about them in tradition of immigrant experience rather than expatriation and nostalgia. To avoid "otherisation" she strongly opposes hyphenation in her national identity as Indo-American or Asian-American writer. Hence it is necessary to interrogate the nature of her work. It is for her to examine the strategies she adopts in order to negotiate the cultural space of USA. She has contributed seven full-length novels, two collections of short stories, literary essays and books of non-fiction. It tells us how she negotiates the boundaries. She focuses on the immigrants' true search for empowerment, dignity, their identity and a successful survival in the settled country. Bharati Mukherjee is an award winning cross-cultural writer. She has won the National Magazine Award for *Invisible Woman* in 1981 and the National Book Critics Circle Award for *The Middleman and Other Stories* in 1988. It received the national attention.

Like Dalit Literature in Marathi language, Mukherjee in her fiction offers justice to the immigrants from all over the world in USA. She is a born writer with extraordinary ability to communicate different aspects of an immigrant's life. Her staying on in America and cherishing the "melting pot" of America, made her a writer of immigrant literature and a writer of Indian diaspora literature. Her pendulum swings to and fro between the extremes—India and America. "She doesn't discard her Indianness, though she rejects hyphenated identity as Indo-American. She focuses on Indian women and their struggle" (Fakrul Alam, p.7). But due to this it makes us difficult to label her as an American writer or Indo-American or Asian– American or Indian English diaspora writer.

In her first phase of literary career, being an expatriate writer, Bharati Mukherjee tries to find her identity in her Indian heritage. It is due to her nostalgia. The very first novel *The Tiger's Daughter* is the exposure of her own married life and with her husband returning home (India). Tara Banerjee's, the heroine's returning to India, exposes Bharati's personal difficulties, who is caught into two cultures, races and countries. She tries to establish her own identity, but is confused due to her "Trishanku" position. Tara is an outsider in her own country. She feels alienated in Calcutta and doesn't seem to be a part of her Bengali family.

The Tiger's Daughter tells us the theme of expatriation, alienation and isolation. The story revolves around Tara Banerjee. She is raised in Calcutta, educated at Vassar College in New York and married to an American fellow. The novel explores her sense of culture shock when she travels back to India; it is intertwined with political situation. Her father is called the Bengal Tiger and is a Brahmin, an extremely wealthy industrialist. She is the only child of her parents. When she returns to India, she expects India as she had left seven years ago. But she is shocked at the present condition. How can she expect the same India while she is drastically changed with Americanness?

Her second novel *Wife* (1975) is also a novel of expatriation. But it deals with the psychological problem of an immigrant woman, Dimple. She migrates from India to USA with her husband, Amit Basu, who doesn't satisfy her dreamy desires. She has drawn her husband's image from TV ads and magazines:

> In those ..... magazines ... she borrowed a forehead from an aspirin ad, the lips eyes and chin from a body builder ... and put the ideal man herself in a restaurant." (130)

It doesn't exist in him. It turns her into a neurotic. It is the by-product of her expatriation and her failure to assimilate into American culture. It makes her murder her own husband.

"Though the setting of the novel is New York, America, it reflects Bharati's life in Toronto, Canada. Dimple's problem lies within her. She suffers frome psychic disorder. It seems that she is running away from the life. She is an escapist" (Sushma Tandon, *Bharati Mukherjee's Fiction: A Perspective*).

Jasmine, Bharati's magnum opus, came out in 1989. It is the expansion of her short story *Jasmine* from *The Middleman and Other Stories* (1988). Jasmine, in contrast to Dimple, is a widow who gets uprooted and re-rooted thrice in a new world and establishes a new identity. So it is the story of Jyoti who becomes Jasmine, then Jase and finally Jane.

Jyoti is from Hasnapur, Punjab, India who seeks a US-based modern husband, Amit Basu. He renames her Jasmine. But their happy married life is very short-lived. Before her migration she turns into widow due to her husband's death in a terrorists' attack. Yet to fulfil her husband's desire she sets off on a trip to Florida, USA. Here begins the transformation of an individual, her displacement, and quest for identity. Actually it is the phase of Bharati's transformation from expatriation to immigration.

Jasmine is an illegal immigrant in USA, where she is raped by Captain Half Face who has brought her. So to avenge, she murders him and changes her names i.e. identities. As a caretaker of Mr. Taylor's baby, she is Jase, with Bud in Iowa, she is Jane. She has tried new identities to survive in the new country. She was foretold ...'would be a widow'. But she has repositioned the stars of her life. It is the gain of her migration to USA.

Bharati Mukherjee's other fictional works are *The Holder of the World* (1993), *Leave to Me* (1997), *Desirable Daughters* (2002), and *The Tree Bride* (2004), *Darkness* (1985), and *The Middleman and Other Stories* (1988). In these works also she shows the search of her roots. In the process of re-rooting, an individual turns into nothing. But he/she is entitled to everything.

Bharati Mukherjee has discussed in her works the problems of identity of the expatriates and immigrants. They have to create their own new identity in the settled country with their own abilities. In this process they have to face social, cultural, political and economic difficulties, out of which they can create a transnational identity in the process of globalisation.

Works Cited

Alam, Fakrul, *Bharati Mukherjee,* Twaynei's Publishers, New York, 1996.

Dhawan: R.K & L.S.R. Krishna Sastry, ed., *Commonwealth Writing: A Study in Expatriate Experience,* Presitge Books, New Delhi, 1994.

_______________ ed., *The Fiction of Bharati Mukherjee: A Critical Symposium,* Prestige Books, New Delhi, 1996.

_______________ The Tiger's Daughter, *Boston, Houghton Mifflin, 1971-72.*

Wife, Boston; Houghton Mifflin, 1975.

Jasmine, New York, Grove Weidenfeld, 1989.

Nagendra, Kumar, *The Fiction of Bharati Mukherjee: A Cultural Perspective,* Atlantic Publishers & Distributors, New Delhi, 2001.

Tandon, Sushma, *Bharati Mukherjee's Fiction,* Sarup and Sons, New Delhi, 2004.

15

Caste, Exile and Identity: An Intercultural Reading of Bharati Mukherjee's *Desirable Daughters*

—Pratima Das

Bharati Mukherjee is a representative writer of Asian immigrants. Even as an Indian, her plurality of a Bengali Brahmin with an English education makes her identity very unique. Therefore, the question of her identity within an ever-shifting centre becomes a vexed issue in her works. All her narratives have an inherent urge to reveal caste, identity and exile locations of identity wherein definitions merge and collapse. Further, she has chosen fiction as a medium of expression to help her readers locate her position at the intersections of cultures in the traditions of East and West. In the margins between America and India, she certainly occupies an ambiguous position. Duality and conflict are at crossroads and feature in immigrant life in America and Mukherjee's novels dramatise these traits very effectively.

Identity forms a significant axis of self-definition for Bharati Mukherjee in a transnational cultural context. Caste and religion often become the identity deciders in India whereas they play a secondary role in the identity of an Indian subject in diaspora. This paper is an attempt to see the changing connotations of caste and religion in the writing from exile. Nothing about identity can be more authentic than what Mukherjee feels and expresses in her work *Desirable Daughters*. Caste often becomes a mark of identity for a subject of Indian origin and hence it is preserved and problematised in her novels. She writes, explaining how it is a privilege to be a Bengali Brahmin in India:

> To be Calcutta bhadra lok, as we Bhattacharjees were, was to share a tradition of leadership, of sensitivity, of achievement, refinement, and beauty that was the envy of the world. (22)

This kind of feeling assumes a different ethnic significance in diasporic communities as it is indicated in the title, *Desirable Daughters*. The title ironically reveals a sensibility that would look at desirable daughters as native stereotypes: "Bhattacharjee sisters of Ballygunge Park Road, three virgins in pastel saris, three unfurling buds on a massive tropical tree" (53).

Desirable Daughters is also an attack on families, marriages, secrets, social position and the so called spiritual struggles. Yet another issue which keeps surfacing in the novel is that the three sisters are not as close as they think they are; says Tara the protagonist of the novel. "Sisters three are we....as like as blossoms on a tree. But we are not" (21). Their identity has been thwarted by parental repressions as in the case of their love lives and career. Added to this dilemma is the pressure to preserve family peace through silence.

Desirable Daughters is all about the three sisters Padma, Parvati and Tara. They are born exactly three years apart and so incidentally share the same birthday. Naming them after goddesses, the family feels they will survive and prosper, which they all do eventually. Bharati Mukherjee is herself with Tara. On the other hand she makes her position clear when *Desirable Daughters* compellingly argues how Indian women are culturally constructed and sketches the chances for the Indian woman to change her destiny.

This way Mukherjee's writing is always a conscious one. As a formidable writer she has a specific agenda, voicing for the changes taking place among South Asian women in America. Of the three sisters, Padma is completely Indian though she lives in New Jersey as an anchor of an Indian television programme. Parvati is Indian to the core, living with her husband in Mumbai. The most 'un-indian' of the three is Tara who lives in San Francisco, divorced from an Indian.

The novel's most remarkable journey is Tara's desire to trace her ancestry. In the process she unravels the source of her name which was Tara Lata, a five-year-old girl in her family who was a victim of child marriage. What unfolds later is a mythic story of degradation, widowhood and shame. She gives snapshots of the place of ancestral birth, captivating historic details of Bengal, the seat of British power; Calcutta its capital, its cultural and economic centre. Calcutta was endowed with instruments of Western knowledge, museums, colleges, newspapers and the Asiatic Society. The Bengali Hindus were the first ones to master the English language.

Tara is divorced, a teacher in California with her teenage son and her Hungarian boyfriend. She was once married to a millionaire entrepreneur, Bishwapriya Chatterjee. Memory to Tara is only rage and bitterness. Her happiest wedding night becomes a lifetime nightmare reminding her only of how the youngest, rich and decked bride is stripped of a life meant to be happy. Even the solicitous father is helpless to protect his daughter.

From here on, Bharati Mukherjee uses the cultural implication of caste against the backdrop of diaspora and exile. In the most articulate manner, Tara the protagonist talks about what she means being born in an upper-class Brahmin family and the ways caste is located in Calcutta and America. She says: "We are Bengali Brahmins from Calcutta and nothing can touch us" (44).

Even Padma is plagued by caste. She is forced to hide her relation with Dr Swarup Dey who is a Bengali Christian. She hides this link for fear of the disgrace it can bring to a Brahmin Bengali family. Such marriages were not encouraged then, because society would think that the family has not been able to manage their daughters well. In this context even thinking of a marriage beyond their caste was unimaginable and if it was a different religion, the repercussions are even more serious. It is Padma's past that fuels Tara's realisation that she knows very little about life and its complications. When this young stranger appears claiming to be one of some Christopher Dey, Padma's long-lost son, questions arise about family secrets, implications of community and what it means being an Indian in a foreign country. The investigation into Christopher proves to be the central journey in the novel. Tara says:

> Everyone knew the rules and the rules stated caste and community narrowed the range of intimate contact. The Deys, as their names proclaimed, were not only Christian today, but had sprung from a Hindu caste that was not even Brahmin. Friendship, yes; marriage, never. (32)

This paper is an attempt to locate the East in the West, the residual caste marks that help and haunt an Indian subject in her state of exile. The novel also makes an indepth study from the cultural vantage points of both India and America to explain how a diasporic subject negotiates her identity in a distinct postcolonial society.

By writing the diasporic subject, Bharati Mukherjee deploys one of the many survival strategies to resist any attempts of being overpowered. She makes an attempt to bring caste, religion and orthodox rituals as a part of defence mechanism to outlive the pangs of alienation.

Lisa Lowe in her article, "Heterogenity, Hybridity, Multiplicity: Marking Asian American Differences" in *Theorising Diaspora* is of the opinion that Asian Americans are materially, socially, culturally and economically noticeable. She thinks just as Bharati Mukherjee expresses in her novel a glimpse of California, Asian American settlement:

> In California, for example, it has become common place for residents to consider themselves as part of a "multicultural" state as embodying a new phenomenon of cultural adjacency and admixture; this "multiculturalism" is at once an index of the changing demographics and differences of community in California and a pluralist attempt at containtment of those differences.[1]

C. Vijayshree in her article, "Survival as an Ethic: South Asian Immigrant Women's Writing" in *In Diaspora* expresses the feeling of being exiled in the host nation. She states:

> There is yet another variation on the theme of exile in women's writing. Exile is viewed as an escape from the strangehold tradition, orthodoxy of religion and oppression of the societal system of the land of their birth.[2]

Bharati Mukherjee's *Desirable Daughters* testifies a kind of uneasy coexistence of double consciousness and a tendency to ethnicise and privatise other aspects of their lives, and all other relationships among the Indian community. In *Desirable Daughters,* Tara, Bharati Mukherjee's focal character, who she so much identifies with, expresses the same paradox:

> It's one of those San Francisco things I can't begin to explain in India, just like I can't explain my Indian life to the women I know in California. (25-26)

So, crucial to the survival of Asian American immigrant women is ethnicity which gives them a locational status among the Americans. Tara is fiercely protective about her own territory, Calcutta, which gives her an ethnic identity among her American friends. In an unforgiving tone she critiques the way in which they reduce Calcutta to a few appealing images. Her lived experience of Calcutta challenges these stereotypes:

> The city was Calcutta in late fifties and early sixties. My American friends in California say God, Tara, Calcutta! as

> though to suggest I have returned to earth after a journey to one of the outer planets. It's one of those cities in the world with negative cachet, a city to escape, one of those hellholes made famous by Mother Teresa and mindless comparisons in the American press: Dirtier than Calcutta. Crueler than Calcutta. Poorer than Calcutta. I grew up in city that never pitied itself, a city that deflected all the abuse. Insults were the badge of our superiority, proof of others' ignorance. (21)

Writings of the subjects of diaspora are mostly autobiographical and ethnographic projects. Mukherjee's novel too is not an exception. In *Desirable Daughters* one also gets to understand the dynamics of shifting personal and ethnic implications. Pramila Venkateshwaran in her article, "Bahrati Mukherjee as Autobiographier", amplifies this issue:

> Mukherjee combines autobiography with ethnography; her personal story is relevant only insofar as it relates to the outer set of events and the collective identity of Calcutta women. The world outside the self takes on an importance as it would to a novelist or a journalist, such that it provides an area for the narrator to either participate in or observe from the fringes. Her alienation or involvement is contextual; therefore, the centre of the narrative constantly shifts according to the context, from the collective to the individual, from the socio-historical reconstruction of women to individual and personal revelation.[3]

Mukherjee facilitates a cross-cultural understanding of issues like caste, exile and identity by constantly shuttling her setting between Calcutta and Jackson Heights. In Jackson Heights the Asian migrants are forced to consider themselves as a monolithic ethnic group. In this context, caste is only a part of one's memory. More than the caste, nationality becomes the marker of one's ethnicity. In Calcutta, in contrast, caste is still an issue. Tara moves between these two cultural locations and her mobility eventually proves that caste and nationality have to be contested on the basis of personal experiences of living in and moving through different cultural spaces.

So, an intercultural reading of Bharati Mukherjee's novel *Desirable Daughters* reveals survival strategies at various fronts ranging from physical, social, psychological to spiritual levels. Bharati Mukherjee, by way of writing as a subject of diaspora, tries to retain her identity in a pluralistic society by not assimilating but by devising her own ways to articulate her immigrant conditions. Her condition is not exilic and India is a place where she may not be comfortable, but emotional strings with relations is something she cannot shake off. Therefore, her stories set in India shall at least continue to fascinate the enclave of North Americans and Indians if not all Americans. In this context, she expresses, "I have told my Calcutta stories many times, and Americans seem to find them endlessly amusing, and appaling." (26)

Works Cited

Alam, Fakrul, *Bharati Mukherjee,* New York: Twayne Publishers, 1996.

Jans Evans Braziel and Anita Manur (Ed.), *Theorising Diaspora: A Reader.* Massachusetts: Blackwell Publishing Ltd, 2003.

Lowe, Lisa, "Heterogenity, Hybridity, Multiplicity: Marking Asian-American Differences", Jans Evans Braziel and Anita Mannur op.cit.

Makrand, Paranjape (Ed.), *In Diaspora: Theories, Histories, Texts.* New Delhi: India Log Publications Pvt. Ltd, 2001.

Mukherjee, Bharati, *Desirable Daughters,* New Delhi: Rupa. Co, 2002.

Nelson, S. Emmanuel (Ed), *Bharati Mukherjee: Critical Perspectives,* New York: Garland Publishing. Inc., 1993.

Venkateshwaran, Pramila, "Bharati Mukherjee as Autobiographer", Nelson Emmanuel, op.cit., pp. 23-42.

Vijayshree C., "Survival as an Ethic: south Asian Immigrant Women's Writing". Makarand Paranjape, op.cit., 30-139.

16

Worldliness without World, Homelessness as Home: A Study of Amitav Ghosh's *The Glass Palace*

—Prantik Banerjee

If transnational migration and cultural rootlessness have become the essential signifiers for the postcolonial condition, then the work of Amitav Ghosh may be considered both a serious engagement with and a critical inquiry of this phenomenon. The postcolonial writer is the postmodern *Trishanku,* suspended in the interstitial space of 'home' and 'world', 'exile' and 'native', 'East' and 'West'. The peculiar circumstances of history and geography compel him to grapple simultaneously with the contingencies of change and continuity.

Rukmini Bhaya Nair pinpoints the dilemma of the postcolonial literary migrant by arguing that "the existential angst of modernist fiction is replaced in the postcolonial novel by a phenomenon one might call 'exit-ential anxiety'. Diaspora takes the place of doubt and homelessness becomes the principal trope, typifying a historical condition as well as a state of mind".

Amitav Ghosh's novel *The Glass Palace* meditates on large historical and nationalist issues such as diaspora, migration, refugees, anti- colonial resistance, and the economic and cultural subjugation of countries by the Imperial West. Colonial oppression and capitalist exploitation are shown to be perverse instigators of a new politics of 'un-homeliness'—the condition of extra-territorial and cross-cultural mutant. Diaspora finds its apotheosis in the borderline figure of the exile, caught in a historical limbo between home and the world.

The book's narrative traverses across several geographical boundaries, displacing characters and locale back and forth in India, Burma, Malaysia and Singapore. A span of over a hundred years frames the story, beginning in 1857-58 and ending in 1996. While the historical events of British Imperialism and the Second World War propel the narrative action in the book, Ghosh is more interested in tracing their disjunctive impact on the lives of his characters: the severance of filial, racial and national ties; the fragmentation of personal identity; and the migration of labour, force and capital. Ghosh's preoccupation with these issues enables him to expose the disastrous consequences of Imperialism over the lives of individuals 'handcuffed to history'.

Almost all the characters in the story lead lives of rootlessness and displacement. Ghosh seems to suggest that migration is the overwhelming metaphor that shapes, guides and refigures not only the lives of his people but also the destinies of nations. Travelling is both a search for 'roots' as well as a 'route' for the postcolonial 'other' to forge its protean identity. Both his Burmese and Indian characters are caught in the cross-current of political events that make them embattled with the pressures of oppression and resistance on a historical level, and also forever entwined with each other on a personal level. Thus, the book narrates the saga of Rajkumar and his children as they pit themselves against the quirks of historical events.

Beginning his life's bewildering journey as a child worker in Ma Cho's tea stall in Mandalay, Rajkumar sets about with only his wits and acumen as his natural allies to become eventually a prosperous timber plantation owner in Rangoon. Meanwhile, like the African slave-hunter, he has crossed over several times to India to indenture cheap labour from the villages down south to work in Burma. With his newfound affluence he next proceeds to

Ratnagiri to win over Dolly, the girl nurse of the second princess, with whom he had had a brief encounter on that fateful day when British soldiers had marched into the Royal palace in Mandalay, dispatching the King and his family to exile in India.

The novel envisages movement at two levels: ROUTES- the outer migrations of peoples determined by history and circumstance across boundaries and barriers of geographical locations and of race and culture, and ROOTS- the inner movement of the individual on their quest for self-determination and identity. Both journeys, however, are without final destinations; the former without the finality of a settled place called 'home' in a transcultural, globalised world, and the latter, without the fixity of a completely individuated consciousness named 'self' in a milieu of polarity and hybridity.

The movement on the first level, i.e., 'routes', entails the migration of people across national borders in the form of refugees, exiles and indentured labour. The principal characters in the book undertake several crossings wherein their affiliations to notions of community, nation and culture get constantly modified and altered. Deposed by British imperial troops in a short and swift operation, King Thebaw and his royal family are forced to evacuate the Glass Palace in Mandalay and exiled to Ratnagiri in India. Stripped of his crown and glory, the King is treated pathetically by the British. He and his family are dispossessed of all their royal belongings, including the family jewels, and are allowed to retain only a few servants.

In Ratnagiri they are forced to live as commoners divested of power and glory that once held their subjects in awe and reverence. It is Queen Supalayat who provides us with the most scathing indictment of the British: "Yes, we who ruled the richest land in Asia are now reduced to this. This is what they have done to us; this is what they will do to all of Burma. They took our kingdom, promising roads and railways and ports..." (88).

Colonialism which often sneaked in the garb of commercial enterprise promising progress and profit to the locals, only to wrest away their land and wealth, is operational in the book at several levels. While the British master and subjugate this vast populous region, the opening up of Burma to European capitalism creates opportunities for Indians like Rajkumar and Baburao to take advantage of the situation. With the rise in demand for timber and rubber in the European market, the Indians like their colonial masters profiteer from the rapidly escalating traffic of labour and capital between Burma and India. Both Indians and Europeans aggrandise their own interests at the expense of the locals. No wonder, that the local populace turns hostile against the Indians, viewing them as rapacious outsiders and base slaves of the English.

What makes the contestation for power and place among the natives, the Indians and the British interesting is the complexity of their many-stranded relationship. On the one hand, the Indians work together with the Burmese locals and contribute to their common weal. On the other hand, as soldiers in the British army, they also act as instruments of torture and oppression. Ironically, the British invasion of Burma is carried out largely by Indian troops from the same regiment "who had stood steadfastly by their masters even through the uprising of 1857"(26). Already, European imperialism had thrown open the Far East to capital and investment. Rangoon in the 1850s resembled a global hub with its banks and hotels, wharfs and warehouses and timber mills, and populated with "Englishmen, Cooringhese, Tamils, Americans, Malays, Bengalis, Chinese"(49).

A structural ploy Ghosh uses to mesh the narratives of the principal characters traversing space and time is the remarkable device of coincidences. One crucial coincidence among the several that Ghosh employs in the novel, one that he means us to take as paradigmatic of transnational crossings, is the strange parallel between the fortunes of two monarchs, both of whom are deposed by a common foe, the British. While Bahadur Shah Zafar, the last Mughal emperor in India, was exiled to Rangoon after the Sepoy mutiny, King Thebaw is shipped to Ratnagiri following his capitulation in Burma. King Thebaw reflects on his humiliating exile: "What vast, what incomprehensible power, to move people in such huge numbers from one place to another—emperors, kings, farmers, dockworkers, soldiers, coolies, policemen" (50). Capitalistic greed is shown to be the driving force behind Imperialism to expand its dominion in a global sprawl of hubris.

While the politics of economics propels imperial power to global expansion, in Ghosh's novel characters also undertake crossings to forge and reestablish human ties that transcend race, ethnicity, culture and language. Rajkumar takes the route from Rangoon to Calcutta and then to Ratnagiri to seek and bind Dolly to a lifetime relationship. He finds her in the house of Beni Prasad Dey, the Collector of Ratnagiri, and Uma, his wife. It is Uma who encourages Dolly to slough away the dead skin of royal duty and start a new life with Rajkumar. Uma, after her husband's death and after several years of European wanderings, makes a stop at Morningside and at Rangoon to be with her friend Dolly. Then, during the Japanese invasion of Burma, Rajkumar and his family make the long march by land, joining others in an exodus stupendous in sheer size and number rarely witnessed in history. Famished and fatigued, and bearing the loss of Manju, their daughter-in-law, Rajkumar and Dolly with their granddaughter, find themselves knocking at the gate of Uma's house in Calcutta. Many decades later in the story, Jaya, the granddaughter of Rajkumar, journeys from Calcutta to Myanmar in search of Dinu, her uncle.

In all his works, Ghosh grapples with the question of whether one 'goes home' or 'comes home'. The paradox of 'going' or 'coming' is suspended by Ghosh in the indeterminacy of interstitial space, as though it is the movement and not the final destination that defines and constitutes the subjectivity of diasporic people. Rajkumar's long stay in Burma, his marriage to Dolly, a Burmese, does not give him a Burmese identity. Calcutta is the final place of his 'enigma of arrival', of his 'background, casually'. Yet his return to roots makes him feel more alienated, a stranger among his own, who only finds himself 'at home' in the Buddhist temple in the centre of the city, where the expatriate

Burmese community gather on festival days. Rajkumar, then, is the prototype of Homi K. Bhabha's "a chiasmatic figure of cultural difference", whose mobility makes the slippages between places, cultures and languages, the defining characteristic of diasporic people.

The operation of both colonialism and capitalism perpetuates a new politics of "un-homeliness"—the condition of extra-territorial and cross-cultural initiation. In a significant way the dilemma of displacement confronted by Raj Kumar is emblematic of any postcolonial writer who is forced to engage with transitions of national identity and family genealogy. Straddling New York and New Delhi, First World and Third World, metropole and margin, Ghosh finds a pattern of his own migratory self in the narratives of his culturally contaminated exiles. His characters are irresistibly caught in a historical limbo between home and the world.

Like Rajkumar's fluid and free position, Ghosh the writer is necessitated by his location of 'being-in-between' to experiment and evolve a literary form that cross-fertilises across several genres—travel writing, autobiography, anthropology, journalism and fiction. His *In an Antique Land, Dancing in Cambodia, At Large in Burma* and *Countdown* authenticate this argument. Other Indian writers in English subject to similar urges and a comparable geographical displacement include both Vikram Seth (*From Heaven Lake*) and Salman Rushdie (*The Jaguar Smile*).

One of his most ardent admirers, the anthropologist, James Clifford, associates Ghosh's work with the idea of 'transit lounge of culture', a conception of 'identity' which lives with and through, not despite, difference. In *The Glass Palace,* even where separatist barriers of colonialism and racism most drastically assert cultural differences, Ghosh shows the redemptive possibility of establishing ties and connections. Several of his characters may be seen to epitomise this idea. In a defining moment early in the novel, when the audience with the Burmese King and Queen seem to go disastrously for the new District Collector of Ratnagiri, it is his wife Uma's cry on recognising a picture of Pagan that breaks the ice. She informs the Queen that although she has never been to Burma, her uncle in Rangoon had sent her a picture of Pagan. In an instant, the gap between monarch and commoner, between jailor and prisoner, between native and exile is bridged, barriers are broken and ties get established. Among all the characters it is Dinu who best exemplifies the complexity of transnational cultural identity. While the major Indian characters in the book return to India, Dinu entrenches himself firmly in the land of his birth, Burma. He is, paradoxically, both an insider and an outsider, for he becomes U Tun Pe, marries a Burmese writer, and opens a photo studio, significantly called, 'The Glass Palace'.

The psychological effects of imperialism and colonialism on the mind of the individual is brought out most forcefully in the depiction of all the principal characters in the book, but it is most notably felt as individualised consciousness in the figure of Arjun. Meeting him halfway in the novel, we see him being selected in the Indian Military Academy at Dehra Dun as a gentleman-cadet. His entry into Imperial service is a momentous event, a major achievement, for the British after years of racial discrimination had only recently opened up some of its seats to the natives. Trained in the best military tradition of valour and honour, Arjun is proud to be among the first Indian officers in the 1/1 Jat regiment, a regiment that not only stayed loyal to the British during the Sepoy Mutiny of 1857 but also captured the Mughal emperor, Bahadur Shah Zafar. Yet in the thick of World War action when the British are forced to retreat from Malaya in the face of Japanese assault, Arjun finds his notions of duty and loyalty constantly challenged and questioned. Rebuffed by members of the Indian National Army, bewildered by the increasing desertions of Indian soldiers from the British army, Arjun is buffeted by self-doubt and identity crisis. He is no longer sure where his loyalties should lie, and is besieged by the thought that perhaps he is nothing more than a lump of clay moulded by the British to serve them unquestioningly: "He, Arjun, was the first to have been touched by the unseen potter; a hand had come down on him, touched him, passed over to another; he had been formed, shaped—he had become a thing unto itself—no longer aware of the pressure of the potter's hand, unconscious even that it had come his way"(430-431).

Arjun's internalisation of the coloniser's discriminatory structures of knowledge is crucial to the process of colonial subject formation. It cannot simply be erased and shrugged off as a kind of false consciousness. That, after all, is the burden of Frantz Fanon's *Black Skin, White Masks* (1952). Arjun's crisis is the result of the coloniser-colonised encounter, his subjectivity is produced in response to the contingencies of a traumatic and disruptive breach in history and culture. The same doubts afflict even his aunt Uma, the wife of the District Collector of Ratnagiri.

A unique literary device that Ghosh has employed in several of his books is the use of certain objects as coordinates of his narrative space and as metonymic equivalents of thematic ideas. If in *The Shadow Lines*, maps and compasses are the tools to imaginatively coalesce distance and time, then in *The Glass Palace*, Ghosh utilises cameras and binoculars to capture geography and memory through the concavity of lenses. In Ratnagiri, the exiled king Thebaw is gradually taken by the locals to be an all-seeing protector for his ability to announce first the daily return of the fishermen as well as the arrival of monsoons with the help of his binoculars. The ocular makes the king oracular.

Later in the novel, Dinu's camera shop in Yangon, significantly called 'The Glass Palace', becomes a meeting place for students, artists and aspiring photographers. Photography lessons become incidental as Dinu encourages his listeners to talk freely about politics, government and democracy. He transforms his studio into a place of resistance and insurgency, lending support and strength to the pro-democracy movement in Myanmar spearheaded by its charismatic leader, Aung San Suu Kyi.

In Dinu's sessions, even photography becomes a secret language, a demotic medium of revolution: "And when we talk of politics it is in such ways that they (spies) cannot follow ... we don't say things they can pin down... in Myanmar nothing that is worth saying can be spoken in ordinary language... everyone learns other means of communication, secret languages"(509). In fact, Ghosh carefully positions the narrative, stops within the reflecting lenses of King Thebaw's binoculars in the beginning and Dinu's camera in the end, giving structural unity to the many-episodic novel.

In *Author's Notes* appended to the book, Amitav Ghosh emphatically states that *The Glass Palace* is a work of fiction and except for King Thebaw, Queen Supalayat and their daughters, none of its principal characters are to be taken as real. He also acknowledges the help of people he cannot name for fear of their facing reprisal, his numerous friends in Myanmar who provided him with details that helped him with his work. However, he hopes that "*should any of them ever happen to read this, they will know who they are*"(italics mine). One of the empowering positions of the migrant intellectual is to be able to resist political and cultural authoritarianism by substituting the notion of history as a single, normative text of indubitable facts with the notion of history as a text ridden with gaps and enclosures that admit the possibility of recovery of silenced voices.

Ghosh's cultural dislocation and his subversive blending of autobiography, history and fiction in his work, make him a leading exponent of this project. His refusal to have *The Glass Palace* short-listed for the Commonwealth Writers Prize is a quiet confirmation of his oppositional stance to the politics of Western hegemony. The book transmutes the historian's documentation of incontrovertible facts into the apocryphal tale of the raconteur's imagination. At the same time, this technique becomes a subversive method of 'writing back' to the master discourse of Imperialism by adopting the subaltern view of the 'coolie', of the Indian administrator in colonial garb, and of the Indian soldier in English jack straps.

Works Cited

Ghosh, Amitav, *The Glass Palace,* Ravi Dayal and Permanent Black, Delhi, 2000.

Nair, Rukmini Bhaya, 'The Road from Mandalay: Reflections on Amitav Ghosh's *The Glass Palace*', Tabish Khair (ed.), *Amitav Ghosh: A Critical Companion,* Ravi Dayal and Permanent Black, Delhi, 2000.

17

Interpreting the Dilemmas of Diasporic Identity and Culture: Jhumpa Lahiri's *Interptreter of Maladies* and *Unaccustomed Earth*

—*Soma Banerjee*

The diasporic condition, the voluntary or forcible movement of people from their homelands into new regions, is a central historical fact of colonisation. Colonialism itself was a radically diasporic movement, involving the temporary or permanent dispersion and settlement of millions of peoples over the entire world. The widespread effects of these migrations continue on a global scale even in our contemporary times. However, what has made this continuum of migrant histories is the complex nature of the intersection of diverse cultures and value systems. The enormous machinery of globalisation, the transnationalism of labour and capital, the porosity of borders, and the celebration of the truly cosmopolitan citizen, all these and more are redefining the structure of traditional societies and the attributes of the individual. Within the ambit of postcolonialism, the issues of multiculturalism have almost gained notoriety for constant reconfigurations and revaluations.

However, the transglobal movement of labour, intellect and capital in the past few decades has signaled a new phenomenon within the study of postcolonialism. This new movement is of people from former colonies to the land of their former colonial masters. This 'reverse colonialism' has given rise to a range of fascinating issues of conflict and cohesion, of attrition and assimilation that are experienced by immigrants. My paper therefore, seeks to highlight the diasporic dilemma of Indians who have relocated themselves in the land of their erstwhile colonisers and who try to become one with the alien culture, but yet remain distinct and reclusive.

According to Amartya Sen, there are two distinct approaches to deal with multiculturalism: one which promotes "diversity' as a value in itself and the other approach focuses on the freedom of the individual in decisionmaking, and celebrates "cultural diversity" to the extent that it is as freely chosen as possible by the persons involved. But this approach falls into the category of "social progress" and might be difficult to emulate.

When we speak of multicultural or polyethnic societies, it denotes societies wherein several cultures exist, each having its distinctive features. It represents about citizens coming in from all four corners of the world and settling in one place. In the global scenario the term is in vogue. The analogy used to take cognisance of the new circumstances is the 'salad bowl' theory. Different constituents retain their distinctive flavours and forms, but the dish as a whole is recognisably "sui generic", having its own distinctive character as a result of its unique blending.

Over the past decade or more many Indian writers who were born in India and write in English have begun living in the U.S. or Canada: Anita Desai, Amitav Ghosh, Rohinton Mistry, Vikram Chandra, Bharati Mukherjee and of late Jhumpa Lahiri and Kiran Desai. Amongst them I have chosen to deal with Jhumpa Lahiri and two of her works, namely, *Interpreter of Maladies* and *The Unaccustomed Earth*. My paper attempts to explore some of the diasporic maladies, namely, a feeling of rootlessness, alienation, displacement and isolation that are highlighted in both the works.

Diaspora is a term that implies traditional talks about the 'Jewish exile'. But during the last decade, diasporic discourses have emerged in relation to postcolonial migration, resulting in the shifting definition. The classic definition of diaspora based on the Jewish model presumes that dispersal is a 'forced exile' from homeland to which people desire to return eventually. Recent usages of diaspora, far from being eternally fixed to some essentialised past, are subject to continuous play of history, culture and power. The diasporic groups are also connected in a network of family ties, manners and traditions to a homeland (i.e., an idea of a homeland).

Jhumpa Lahiri's *Interpreter of Maladies* which won her the Pulitser Prize for fiction in the year 2000 is a collection of nine short stories, of which three are set in India and six in the US. *Unaccustomed Earth* is a collection of eight short stories where the intricacies of family life of Indians in the US is explored with sensitivity and maturity.

In an interview when she was asked how she had come upon the title of the book *Interpreter of Maladies* Jhumpa Lahiri said that once an acquaintance of hers was asked what he was doing with himself. He said he was working at a doctor's office, interpreting for him, because he had a number of Russian patients and it was a problem for them to explain their ailments in English. She was thus struck with the phrase 'interpreter of ailments', i.e. maladies.

The title is apt because she has assumed the role of an interpreter of maladies, of stifled emotions of the characters in the book. In her own words, "the title best expresses the predicament at the heart of the book—the dilemma, the difficulty and often the impossibility of communicating emotional pain and affliction to others." Through the stories she interprets the maladies of Indian immigrants, of people navigating between strict traditions they have inherited and the baffling new world they encounter every day. At a press conference in Calcutta in January 2001, she disclosed that she suffers from an absence of belonging. She said that no country is her motherland. And she always found herself in exile in whichever country she travelled to, and that's why she was tempted to write something about those living their lives in exile. This idea of exile runs consistently throughout her stories in *Interpreter of Maladies.*

In both her works Jhumpa Lahiri tries to decipher and put across the pain of alienation and dislocation of immigrants. By interpreting the maladies of those created characters living a 'diasporic' life, she at the same time camouflages the undercurrents of her own emotional pain. As a child of immigrant parents she has borne the brunt of living two lives, one in India and the other in the States. She feels strong ties to her parents' homeland as well the States and England. Growing up in all the three countries created in her a sense of homelessness and an inability to feel accepted. Like all ABCDs she too suffered from the effects of Diaspora.

This feeling of rootlessness crept in because she says of her inheritance of her parents' ties to India. As she says, "It's hard to have parents who consider another place as home even after living abroad for thirty years. India is home for them. We were always looking back so I never felt fully at home here. India was different. Our extended family offered real connections." Yet her familial ties to India were not enough to make India 'home' for her, as she says, "I didn't grow up there and wasn't a part of things."

The title story 'Interpreter of Maladies' is about a second-generation Indian-American couple caught too early in the tangle of matrimony and parenting. Mr. and Mrs. Das along with their children are visiting India and hire a tour-guide to see the famous Sun Temple at Konarak. Mr. Kapasi who is their tour-guide marvels at the couple who look like Indians but dress like Americans and speak with an American accent he had heard many times on American T.V. Shows (Dallas). Mr. Kapasi is intrigued by the fact that Mr. Das has a paperback tour book, which reads "India' and looks as if it had been published abroad! The boys Bobby and Ronny are in turn fascinated by the goat tied to a stake, the monkey (whom Mr. Kapasi points out to them as Lord Hanuman) and also the statue of the Elephant God taped to the glove compartment. Everything Indian looks exotic and strange. But Mrs. Das is totally disinterested in her surroundings and finally the children too seem bored. The children are confused and ask their father why Mr. Kapasi sat on the wrong side of the car. Mr. Das seems apologetic when he explains to Mr. Kapasi, "in America you know .... It confuses them."

Mr. Kapasi wonders at the modern concept of parenting; he realises that Mr. and Mrs. Das behave like an elder brother and sister to the children, not parents. They are too casual in their attitude. Once Mr. Kapasi has to pull over since Mr. Das wants to snap a picture of a barefooted man, his head wrapped in a dirty turban, seated atop a cart of grain sacks pulled by a pair of bullocks. Both men and bullocks are emaciated. This fascinates Mr.Das but Mrs. Das looks the other way. She cannot stomach the harsh ground realities of her country, alienating herself emotionally from anything ugly and trying to create a new identity of the adopted country. Here the author depicts the struggles between the two worlds—not just Asian and Western, but inner and outer, tradition and modernity and one of, I would like to add, the real and the make believe.

The story takes a turn when Mrs. Das getting an opportunity, discloses to Mr. Kapasi that one of the couple's two boys was illegitimately fathered by her husband's Punjabi friend during a brief visit and that Mr. Das does not know about this. After disclosing she says to Mr. Kapasi, "I was hoping you could help me feel better, say the right thing. Suggest some kind of remedy." As if expecting the land of magic and sages and yoga to come with instantaneous remedies! Mr. Kapasi feels depressed and insulted at the same time that Mrs. Das has the temerity to ask him to interpret her common trivial malady. A malady begotten on foreign shores! He is unable to decide as to why of all people she should confide in him. He aptly asks, "Is it really pain you feel Mrs. Das, or is it guilt?" She feels that his question needs no answer and walks away. Jhumpa Lahiri uses her silence to indicate the dilemma of the deracinated Indian, caught between the tug of her native tradition and the pull of her foreign modernity.

Seen from the perspective of multi-ethnic or poly-ethnic groups, the offsprings of the immigrants come under the slot of ABCDs—American Born Confused Desi. They are unable to identify with anything Indian. They are either delighted or quizzical at the whole scenario. Reality sinks in only when they grow up. The parents themselves ABCDs are in no better position. Mrs. Das for one falls into the temptation of an extra-marital liaison, but being Indian at heart seeks a readymade remedy for her guilt, affliction that too from India.

In another story, 'Mrs.Sen', Lahiri narrates the loneliness of a woman who knows that there is only one Sen in the telephone directory in her small East Coast Town of America. To fill in the empty hours when her husband is at work, she takes up a babysitting job to an eleven-year-old American boy, Eliot. When Eliot's mother interviews her and asks who is there in India, Mrs.Sen goes into a nostalgic trip, automatically touches the border of her sari (a link to homeland) and says rather sadly, "everything is there."

Eliot enjoys Mrs. Sen's company, especially watching her chop things using "a blade that curved like a prow of a Viking ship, sailing to battle in distant sea", i.e. in Bengali a 'boti'. He is fascinated by the fact that she splits things in half, and then quarters speedily producing cubes, slices, shreds, that too never keeping an eye on the blade. She elaborates that the blade is from India and a must in every household. She says that whenever there is a wedding in the family, the neighborhood women come with their 'botis' and chop 50 kilos of vegetables while chatting, laughing at the same time through the night. She becomes nostalgic and confesses, staring unblinkingly at some point outside the window, "When Mr. Sen brought me here I couldn't sleep in so much silence."

She questions Eliot if anyone would come if suddenly she screamed loudly. She explains to the perplexed boy that at home, in Calcutta, if you raised your voice to express joy or grief the whole neighbourhood would show up at the door in a gesture of genuine sharing. The boy is thoughtful about this and replies that if Mrs. Sen were to scream, her neighbours "might complain that you were making too much noise."

In another incident when Eliot questions her about the crushed vermilion on her forehead thinking that she has cut herself there, she explains she has to wear that for the rest of her married life. She compares it to a wedding ring but with no fear of losing it in the dishwater.

Two things Mrs.Sen's charge realises make her happy—one is the arrival of a letter from India, and the other is the fish from the seaside. She lets Eliot know that in Calcutta people eat fish first thing in the morning and the last thing before bed. She loves to buy fish and the fish becomes a sort of talisman, a charm which will link her to her roots. She clings to this small replica of a homeland.

One day she asks Eliot, "Do you miss your mother, Eliot, these afternoons with me?" This surprises Eliot because it never occurs to him to 'miss his mother in her absence' and she admonishes him by saying, "You must miss her. When I think of you only a boy separated from your mother for so much of the day, I am ashamed." Mrs. Sen, deeply entrenched in her own traditional culture of family ties can't seem to come to terms with the 'alien' one, which lacks in a sense of belonging. Thus in these two stories, laced with the intensity of felt-experiences, Jhumpa Lahiri makes the reader join her in her discovery of what it means to be an Indian in America.

In 'Interpreter of Maladies' Lahiri evaluates the scene through the two protagonists—Mrs. Das and Mrs. Sen. Through both the characters Lahiri tries to commute between cultures and writes from a space of "in-betweenness". A hybrid soul herself, she tries to give voice to hyphenated identities. Between the stories, Lahiri has finely balanced the issues and problems of diaspora, and it is left to us to think of solutions.

Mrs. Das, hardly 28 years, suffers from the ambivalent consciousness rising from bicultural identities. Nearly 30, she suffers the same problem related to diaspora, i.e., a feeling of rootlessness, alienation and homesickness. C.W. Watson says that immigrants, though committed to the laws and norms of 'alien' society, see no need to abandon their religious traditions, cuisines or languages. Thus one realises that assimilation is not the only means of incorporating immigrants into the society but that integration is also necessary. Integration might be a plausible solution on the grounds of what Amartya Sen has said, i.e., promoting diversity as a value itself.

And when we are unable to both 'absorb' or 'unite' with the alien culture, like Mrs. Das, one is left standing at the crossroad, i.e., developing ambivalent consciousness, or like Mrs. Sen suffer from a feeling of alienation. Prof. Bikhu Parekh says, "No culture is perfect or represents the best life and that it can therefore benefit from a critical dialogue with other cultures." Thus, in this age of mass migration, cultural plurality is an irreversible fact, and from the angle of 'diaspora', since of late it is 'willing exile', I believe the answers may lie with the individuals themselves.

In *Unaccustomed Earth* Jhumpa Lahiri returns to the familiar terrain—the theme she expresses best, that of displaced immigrants. The only difference is that here the characters are offsprings of immigrants who non the less face similar problems of displacement. In various stages of setting up home, these young settlers feel adrift—unfamiliar with their parents' world and still young to assimilate the new adopted one.

Thus these second generation immigrants try to traverse a path bymaintaining a balance between retaining the traditional values of the mother country and adopting the mainstream American values. As Jhumpa Lahiri herself expressed, there is "intense pressure to be two things, loyal to the old world and fluent in the new." She excels in depicting the lives of these alienated second generation children. For example, in the title story, 'Unaccustomed Earth', Ruma nervously awaits the arrival of her father from Pennsylvania and is distressed with the fact that her parent might decide to settle with her. She also suffers from a sense of dislocation moving into a new house shortly after the death of her beloved mother. She is not only on unfamiliar ground geographically because she has moved to the lonely suburbs of Seattle with her workaholic white husband and son Akash but she also feels alienated from her filial connection. She is unable to relate to her father and share her innermost thoughts with him. This communication gap arises between the first and second generation immigrants because the parents create small Indias abroad which the offsprings are unable to relate to. They try to locate a comfort zone in the adopted land. The tentative interactions between the characters show how circumstances and situations can lead the most familiar relationships into unfamiliar territory. Ruma, a second generation immigrant is unable to locate and find solace in the new world, and at the same time faces sociocultural crises when she is uncomfortable with her old one where children care for their parents in their old age.

In the story 'Hell-Heaven', Usha looking back on her Boston childhood, interprets and understands as an adult the sociocultural and psychological alienation her mother was burdened with. Usha's mother, a typical Bengali housewife, falls in love with a young Bengali immigrant, a bachelor studying at MIT. That almost leads to a crisis in the family. The pain and loneliness felt by her in alien surroundings is depicted in various nuances. Her workaholic husband doesn't have much time for her and her isolation is complete living in foreign locales. Thus, she falls in love with a young fellow countryman though he addresses her as 'Boudi.' The alien territory, and immigrants suffering from a sense of dislocation, develop strain in familiar relationships between husband and wives and parents and children. Each strives for survival not in the material sense because Jhumpa Lahiri's immigrants are all well placed in life but crave for attention and affection, identity and solace for their bruised souls.

The aching loneliness the immigrants face in a foreign land is poignant and Jhumpa Lahiri is a master weaver when she depicts their grief with sensitivity. The characters find themselves alienated not just from their homeland but also alienated from their own flesh and blood, that is the second generation immigrants. The after effects of diaspora still continue and will do so till the immigrants find roots that are 'Accustomed Earth'.

Works Cited

Lahiri, Jhumpa, *Interpreter of Maladies,* Harper Collins, India, 1999.

_______________, Unaccustomed Earth, *Random House, India,* 2008.

Loomba, Ania, *Colonialism/Postcolonialism,* Routledge, London, 1998.

Ashcroft, Bill, Griffiths Gareth & Tiffin, Helen, *Key Concepts in Post-Colonial Studies.*Routledge, London, 2004.

18

The White Tiger: A True Manifestation of Indian Society

—Beena Lad

Arvind Adiga, the winner of Man Booker Prize of 2008, for his debut novel, *The White Tiger*, is the first novelist who has taken an exhilarating ride through the darkest alleys of modern India. *The White Tiger* published in India by Harper Collins, is born out of an India of paradoxes: an India of Light and an India of Darkness. India of Light presents the picture of Shining India which is advancing day by day as a global economy embracing new technologies, new gadgets, and going in a big way for huge apartments, malls, PVR, etc., and on the other hand, India of Darkness tells the story of crushing rural poverty, peasants drivers, servants, struggling middle class, and the nation which has still not been able to provide safe drinking water, enough electricity and a good sewage system and public transport. Adiga has made a daring attempt to focus on the dark side of India, by lifting the veil of India's superficial success. He launches a scathing attack on the present systems in India, be they health, hygiene, education, politics, police, bureaucracy or judiciary.

Adiga is a writer with commitment and has glaringly exposed the pains of the poor. Having keenly observed the world of the low profile people, he successfully and strikingly presents their sufferings. This was the world with which he first came in contact as a journalist, but at the same time he realised it was a world that could not be captured in its entirety, in all its moral and political ambiguities in a reporter's notebook. Always taking bold decisions in life, he left his Time job and became a full-time writer and this is how: *The White Tiger* was born.

The White Tiger is the name given to the protagonist Balram Halwai who is a man from Gaya in Bihar. Balram, the narrator of the story, is the servant, chauffeur, philosopher, entrepreneur, murderer—a composite of various men we find around us. He is the voice of India's silent underclass who resides in slums, railway platforms, bus-stands, servants' quarters and in every city in India. There is always a kind of murmur or growl beneath low and middle class life in India, but this murmur is never heard or recorded. About giving literary voice to India's silent underclass Adiga himself comments:

> *The White Tiger* tries to give literary voice to a man from our gigantic underclass, which is over 400 million strong, according to recent estimates.... "The portrait of Balram Halwai may challenge the deeply held, if not always openly stated, assumptions that many in the middle class hold about the poor: that they are stupid, easily manipulated, excessively religious and bound by caste and family. It is an attack on a rotten political system that is stopping half of this country from achieving its potential."[1]

Throughout the narrative, Balram sits for seven nights beneath a prosperous chandelier and narrates his story to Jiabao, Premier of China, on the subject of Indian entrepreneur. He begins his story at the very bottom; without so much as a name his family called him only "Munna" which means 'a boy.' His mother might have named him but she was very ill and suffered from tuberculosis. His father was too busy pulling a rickshaw, weakening himself and later died of the same disease. The novel is built on a substratum of Indian reality where we can find thousands of people dying every day from some disease or due to the lack of proper medical aid. This happens because neither the doctors nor the authorities are honest towards their duties. Adiga has ironically pointed out the condition of hospitals and doctors in the following lines:

> The Great Socialist lets all the big doctors know that he's having an open auction for that post. The going rate for this

> post is about four hundred thousand rupees these days.... I beg and borrow the money and give it to the Great Socialist. He gives me the job.... Next I call all the junior government doctors whom I'm supposed to supervise, into my office.
>
> Now Dr. Ram Pandey—will kindly put one third of your salary in my palm... you can keep the rest of your government salary and go work in some private hospital for the rest of the week.[2]

The Great Socialist is the name given to our political leaders. So in the government hospitals poor people go for treatment and come back untreated or face death like Balram's father. But in the ledgers of doctors the patients are cured and treated well.

The villages in India are called paradise on earth. But the irony is that on official records these Indian village paradises are adequately supplied with electricity, running water, working telephones and the village children are raised on proper nutritious diet. For these government gets aid from United Nations and other organisations. But in reality Adiga says:

> Electricity poles—defunct.
> Water tap—broken.
>
> Children—too lean and short for their age, and with oversized heads from which vivid eyes shine, like the guilty conscience of the government of India."[3]

In the Darkness, that is in villages, Adiga gives new terminology to these landlords; he calls them Buffalo, Wild Boar, Raven and Stork. These animals (landlords), the narrator says, are the greediest, and eat up the rickshaws and the roads. These landlords live in big mansions in towns and their families too live there. But they come to the village only to receive their share in produce.

Balram as a boy is sent to school. Like every parent his father also has a dream for him. He wants him to read and write and become a 'man' one day. His father says:

> My whole life, I have been treated like a donkey. All I want is that one son of mine- at least one should live like a man.[4]

Adiga, with irony and humour, describes the schools in rural India, or we can say government schools all over the country. As per the government programmes the students should be given mid-day meals, free uniforms and books. But these things never reach them. The following lines aptly give the picture of education system in Darkness:

> But we never ever saw rotis, or yellow dal or pickles and everyone knew why: the school master had stolen our lunch money.
>
> The teacher had a legitimate excuse to steal the money—he said he hadn't been paid his salary in six month. He was going to undertake a Gandhian protest to retrieve his missing wages; he was going to do nothing in class until his pay cheque arrived in the mail. Yet he was terrified of losing his job because though the pay of any government job in India is poor, the incidental advantages are numerous. Once, a truck came into the school with uniforms that the government had sent for us; we never saw them, but a week later they turned up for sale in the neighbouring village.[5]

Balram wants to continue his studies. He is intelligent, honest and vivacious fellow, a white tiger in the crowd of idiots. But soon he is taken out of school by his family and put to work in a teashop. He crushes coal and wipes tables and nurses a dream to escape—of breaking away from the banks of Mother Ganga. Adiga in an interview says:

> Too many people in this country have no access to proper education, health care or employment opportunities. They share the same dreams that we do: of succeeding as entrepreneurs or businessmen, but they don't get the same solid foundation that we do. For such poor people there are only two real outlets for their entrepreneurial drive : crime or politics. Balram Halwai is one such man, and he (luckily for us) chooses only to become a criminal entrepreneur. Many others like him become political entrepreneurs and become far more dangerous."[6]

The novel is rich in details from the (often corrupt) workings of the force of the political system—from the servant class of Delhi to the businessmen of Bangalore. The past fifty years have seen great changes in Indian societies. The traditional hierarchies have been overturned for the betterment of the new Shining India. But the lot of poorer Indians are left confused and perplexed by the new India that is formed around them. Adiga wanted to bring this invisible lot of men and women on the literary scene. Old traditions, old values, cultures are things of the past. Commenting on caste system Adiga says:

> To sum up in the old days here were one thousand castes and destinies in India. These days there are just two castes : Men with Big Bellies and men with small Bellies.[7]

The men with big bellies are eating up the men with small bellies. The servants who serve their masters in any field are the world's most honest people. The trustworthiness of these servants is the basis of the entire Indian economy. A handful of men in this country have trained the remaining ninety-nine per cent as strong, talented and intelligent in every field—to exist in perpetual servitude. This is the story of the millions in India who wake up at dawn and rush towards their master's posh houses to work. But we see that this extreme inequality is stabilised by some strong bond.

Adiga says that advancement can be achieved only by patronage and corruption. If you make friends with the local political thugs you might get a job. If one wants to be successful one has to step outside the 'coop' of conventional morality. Balram's big chance comes when a rich village lord hires him as a chauffeur for his son. The city is a revelation to him; he learns a new morality at the heart of new India. Getting a job in the 'Light' of New Delhi, must bring an end to the darkness in his life, but ironically the moral darkness only increases.

The White Tiger is a furious and brutally effective counterblast to "India is shining" slogan and exposes its rotting heart. It is certain of its mission and pursues it with an undeviating determination that one cannot expect in the first novel. It is a novel whose architectural cleverness is matched by its inherent humanism. Adiga never misses the stirrings of denial and dispossession beneath the sheen of India Shining. "It is not the sociology of his narrative alone that makes Adiga, 33, one of the most distinctive voices in fiction today even though the sociology is steeped in anger and wit, satire and scatology,"[8] says S. Prasannarajan.

Its caricatures are sharply and confidently drawn. He attempts to highlight the brutal injustices of the Indian society and says that it is not an attack but it's about the greater process of self-examination.

We see that criticism by writers like Flaubert, Balzac and Dickens of the nineteenth century helped England and France become better societies. We can call him a writer with social conscience, but he says that he is just a novelist, a writer and his purpose is to entertain his readers and keep them hooked to the end. He says that he is not an activist or a socialist, but a writer writing about the India he knows and the one in which he resides. In the postcolonial Indian literary scene he is the fourth Indian author to win the prize. With the sensational triumph of Adiga, who is brainy as well as funny, India has again regained its supremacy in the international lit mart.

References

1) *The Times of India,* New Delhi, Wednesday September, 2008, p. 14.
2) Adiga, Arvind, *The White Tiger,* NewDelhi, HarperCollins Publishers India, 2008, 49-501.
3) Ibid., p. 20.
4) Ibid., p. 30.
5) Ibid., p. 33.
6) *The Times of India,* New Delhi, Wednesday September, 2008, p. 14.
7) Adiga, Arvind, op.cit., p. 72.

19

Postcolonial Cartography of an Indian Town: A Study of Class, Community and Cultural Spaces in Aravind Adiga's *Between the Assassinations*

—Dinesh Kumar

Postcolonial societies in countries of South Asia and Africa reveal the symptoms of both colonial and neocolonial practices. These symptoms indicate an enormously complex machinery dedicated to the ideology of imperialism, exploitation of the weak, of natural resources, and the continued subordination of certain sections of the society. This machinery also points to the instabilities in the systems, both social and political. Literary texts and art forms churned out of such a society capture moral, political and cultural maps of the society. Such maps project the tectonic drifts of the inhumanity of colonisation and the images of people who are consumed, exhausted, deadened and robbed of meaning. Map topos also figure prominently in the de/reconstructive readings of contemporary postcolonial texts as they are loaded with ironic and parodic use of texts and images. David Punter amplifies the political significance of postcolonial cartography:

> One of the phenomena with which we are presented in the postcolonial writing is, then, a whole panoply of maps, a treasure chest of charts, piled in heaps, lapped one over another, imaginary geographies, but one in which the root of power that has nourished them is in the slow process of being exposed (Punter, 2000, 33).

Novels which become cultural materials in postcolonial societies capture images and instances of cultural and social trauma by interweaving history, geography and memory. They also configure imaginings of locations and cultures that mark the changing faces of world orders.

The moral cartography of a postcolonial society is landmarked with a phony rhetoric of law that mantles criminality and perpetuates itself in a ghostly fashion above rules and ethics. It also highlights patterns of local dominations. Further, it shows how the concept of a place changes with changes in communal relations and the relations between the exploiter and the exploited.

Third World spaces, both geographical and cultural, are contaminated with words and signs which mirror the legacy of colonialism. Postcolonial writers make the readers aware that the spaces and their verbal projections have to be cleansed of imperialist motives before describing them. Hence, such writers draw maps which articulate native realities in imaginary narratives.

Aravind Adiga has made his appearance on the Indian literary map with his Booker Prize winning *The White Tiger* (2008) which sketches the political and economic map of India. His second novel, *Between the Assassinations* (2008), is also concerned with a postcolonial cartography though its projections are more local and culture-specific.

Between the Assassinations chronicles seven days and each day transforms into a narrative unit. Further, these seven days bring out a kaleidoscope of lives which bring to the fore the landscape of Kittur, the setting of the novel. Adiga also prefixes each narrative unit with passages which remind certain sections from tourist guides. These prefatory, expository notes remind the language and tones of master texts. They are given in italics and certain expressions within them are in upper case to indicate the emphasis and impact.

The narrative begins with an apparently benign road map to Kittur:

> Kittur is on India's South-Western coast, in between Goa and Calicut, an almost equidistant from the two. The Arabian Sea

> is to its west, and the Kaliamma river to its east....Given the town's richness of history and scenic beauty, and diversity of religion, race and language, a minimum stay of a week is recommended. (2)

Though this passage maintains the factual tone of verbal map-making, its promotional subtext reminds one of the orientalist's exoticised projection of a landscape. It also appears that the text creates the place as the pseudo-factual tone gives way to the capitalist rhetoric made of "richness", "diversity" and "scenic". These expressions indeed promise Kittur as a tableau, a spectacle for the visitors.

Life in Kittur proves otherwise. Underneath the assured richness, diversity and scenic landscape, Kittur proves a backdrop for communal hatred, casteism, corruption and hate-crimes of the colonial vestiges.

The first section of the novel is titled "Day One: The Train Station." By doing so Adiga combines a temporal marker with a spatial marker with a colon in between. This remains a pattern throughout the novel. The second section, "Day Two (Afternoon): Lighthouse Hill", too implies the author's move from time to terrain, the Lighthouse Hill. "Day Three: Angel Talkies" signposts another landmark of Kittur. "Day Four: The Cool-Water Well Junction", takes the reader to another corner of Kittur which is named after a water body of that place.

"Day One: The Train Station" however begins with a near factual description of Kittur station in a viewpoint of a passenger who moves into Kittur for the first time:

> The arches of the train frame your first view of Kittur as you come in as a passenger on the Madras Mail (arrival early morning) or the West Coast Express (arrival afternoon). The station is dim, dirty, and littered with discarded lunch bags that dogs poke their nose into: in the evening, the rats came out. (3)

This expository note acts as a master text that would just manage to scratch the surface of the cultural realities of a place. It fails to reveal Kittur in its living details, what it is notorious for. Communal intolerance that plagues Kittur and, by extension, the whole Indian cultural spaces, surfaces in the very first sentence of the narrative that follows the introductory note:

> None of the other shopkeepers near the railway station would hire a Muslim, but Ramanna Shetty, who ran the Ideal Store, a tea-and-samosa place, told Ziauddin it was okay for him to stay. (3)

Ziauddin, the protagonist of the first story, lives under typical self-delusion of the colonised. Despite having a dark skin tone he believes that he is a Pathan. He also lives with a distorted sense of place. In Kittur, he is a misfit because he believes that he is from the North. Hence, his moral commitment to Kittur gets distorted and subsequently he believes that all the people of the place which he hates are his enemies. He picks quarrels with both Hindus and Muslims, even as a boy. Eventually, he plays into the hands of a terrorist who plans to attack the trains that carry soldiers. Ziauddin is drawn towards this visitor mainly for his fair skin and the belief that the visitor is a Pathan. The visitor plants in the mind of Ziauddin the vicious map of communal hatred. He instigates Ziauddin by thrusting upon him the same colonial cartography based on communal divide:

> The Indian army is setting up a base somewhere between Kittur and Calicut. For one and one reason only he held up a thick finger. To do to the Muslims of South India what they are doing to Muslims in Kashmir. (20)

Most of the time, Ziauddin hovers around Kittur railway station. The station for him is a location of arrival and departure. By placing himself in such a location, he tries to nourish the dream of connecting himself with the North, the land of the Pathans. This dream at once makes him a native and a visitor in Kittur evoking the colonial pattern of making the natives alien to their own land.

Ziauddin also behaves like an Anglophile. He worships English and believes that by speaking English, he will be able to cloak his local identity. He rattles off borrowed expressions in English: "Sunday-Monday, Goodbye, sexy!" (4). Elsewhere he says, when he is tipped in the teastall: "Thanks you, sir!" (5). These expressions clearly indicate his dependence complex—a mindset of the colonial subject who looks up to the master and master's language.

Streets of Kittur are signposted with billboards, names and announcements in English. These scattered expressions in English convert the topography of Kittur into a microscopic colony which echoes the colonial vestiges in the form of scribbling in a leftover language. Ziauddin takes the visitor to a hotel that displays the use of English in a funny flavour of the natives. Besides, it also reveals the neocolonial attitude that what is advertised in English has more credibility:

> Hotel Decent
> Boarding and Lodging
> very high quality
> North Indian South Indian Chinese Western Tibetan Dishes
> Taxi passport visa xerox trunk call for all countries

The absence of punctuation in this signboard indicates a shoddy use of English; it is also a reminder of the Babu English which even the so-called postcolonial societies are not able to get rid off. Further, the signboard has a spatial significance as it occupies the public domain in Kittur. By being in the public domain it becomes a landmark in Kittur's geography.

The narrative voice in *Between the Assassinations* enacts a playful hide and seek in its alternative stands of familiarity and distance. "Day One: The Train Station" is narrated by an objective, omniscient point of view which maintains a degree of distance from the reader. However, the epilogue to this chapter converts the narrator to an involved insider who owns up Kittur altogether. Here the narrative voice also captures the moral geography of Kittur with an unabashed honesty that reveals geographical projections of corruption, vanity and capitalism—all the colonial, imperial tendencies.

In the geographical centre of Kittur stands the peeling stucco façade of Angel Talkies, a pornographic cinema theatre. When townsfolk give directions, they use Angel Talkies as a reference point. The theatre divides Umbrella Street, the commercial district. A significant chunk of Kittur's economy consists of the manufacture of handrolled beedies; no wonder then that the tallest building in town is the Engineer Beedi Building, also on Umbrella Street owned by Mabroor Engineer, the town's richest man. Not far from it sits Kittur's most famous ice-cream shop, the Ideal Traders Ice-cream and Fresh Fruit Juice Parlour. (22)

This description also shows that Adiga's narrative is a geonarrative, a narrative that gives birth to a place, legitimises its existence and highlights its familiar spots in the process of telling. Further, it shows the incongruities of postcolonial spaces which are hijacked by the forces of capitalism and corruption. Angel Talkies, the pornographic film hall, coexists with the benign ice-cream shop. Engineer Beedi Building amplifies the colonial tendency to hybridise languages and metaphors, with "engineer" and "Beedi" going together.

The second story is titled "Day Two: The Bunder." It also begins with a perspective that moves along the roads of Kittur to reach the Bunder. Here the narrative brings the olfactory experience of Kittur:

> You have walked down the Cool-Water Well road past Masjid Road, and you have begun to smell the salt in the air and note the profusion of open-air fish stalls, full of prawns, mussels, shrimp and oysters; you are not far from the Arabian Sea. (24)

This journey into Kittur soon leads to another picture of its landscape, torn with communal hatred and violence. This part of Kittur is remembered for the stabbings and crimes that had happened there. It also reveals the tone of a colonial master text which exoticises the past, even its human plight into a verbal spectacle. Adiga uses this tone to parody both colonial and neocolonial texts which rolls place history and culture together into certain labels and foreshortened marks of memory:

> If you walk to the other end of the Bunder, you find the industrial area, where dozens of textile sweat shop operate in dingy old buildings. The Bunder has the highest crime rates in Kittur, and is the scene of frequent stabbings, police raids and arrests. In 1987, riots broke out near the Durgah between Hindus and Muslims, and the Bunder was shut down for six days. The Hindus have since been moving out to Bajpe and Salt Market Village. (24)

The Bunder which holds great economic and cultural significance in the topography of Kittur is rather remembered more for the Hindu-Muslim riots of 1987. Ironically, it is the history of this human tragedy that adds to the tourist's interest in the Bunder. It is in this geographical setting that Abbasi, a garment manufacturer has to revive his factory, negotiating with the corrupt officials of the State electricity board and the revenue department who demand Johnnie Walker Red Label whisky and money as bribe. Eventually, Abbasi's factory is closed, which adds another dead, desperate monument to Kittur's geography.

Kittur's walls are stuck with hand-painted posters that announce the titles of spicy movies such as "Her Nights", "Wine and Women", Mysteries of Growth", "Uncle's Fault". To these titles, the expression, "Adults Only" is attached prominently. These cheap pornographic amusements are counterbalanced with the propaganda of higher class amusement in the Hotel Woodside that is famous for Paris Cabaret. The same hotel displays the propaganda for "Dr. Kuruvilla, MBBS, MD, Mch, MS, DDBS, PCDB." Thus roads, walls and street corners of Kittur hold visible markers of immature sex, another symptom of a sex-starved community that finds a pervert projection in public spaces.

Kittur that has memorials of riots, violence, corruption and psychological repression, is the site of resistance and defiance too. When it becomes a site of resistance, Kittur becomes a postcolonial space. This is evident in the story of Xerox, a Dalit subject who makes his living by selling pirated copies of books. Xerox manages to sell the pirated copies by greasing the hands of the police quietly now and then. His blue bedsheet near the Lighthouse Hill is another spatial marker in Kittur. He displays his photocopied books on a bedsheet and sells anything from Karl Marx to Advanced Obstetrics. However, his space in Kittur is threatened with the arrival of Salman Rushdie's *The Satanic Verses*. He is taken into custody for selling the pirated copies of the banned book. He is bashed up badly by the police who break his leg. Eventually, when he is released, he heads in the direction of the hill only to get back to his space in Kittur and to sell more copies of *The Satanic Verses*. Xerox defies the coercive forces of the society which remind us of imperialism. He also reclaims his space in Kittur though it is just a corner in the street. Adiga implies in the act of

Xerox, the personal politics of a postcolonial subject which connects him to the geographical and cultural realities in a sensible way:

> Xerox turned around on his crutches and walked out of the station. His daughter came behind him. They went in the direction of the hill. The climb took two hours and a half, and they stopped six times to drink tea, or a glass of sugarcane juice. Then his daughter spread down the blue sheet in front of Desh Premi Hemachandra Rao Park, and Xerox lowered himself. He sat on the sheet, stuck his legs out slowly, and put a large paperback down next to him. His daughter sat down too, keeping watch over the book with a stiff upright back. The book was banned throughout the Republic of India and it was the only thing that Xerox intended to sell that day: *The Satanic Verses,* by Salman Rushdie. (51)

One's social class decides the access to public places in Kittur. The lighthouse of Kittur is open only for the rich visitors:

> An old guard in a blue uniform sits at the base of the lighthouse. If the visitors are poorly dressed, or speak to him in Tulu or Kannada, he will say, 'Can't you see it's closed?' If the visitors are well-dressed or speak English, he will say: 'Welcome'. He will take them into the lighthouse, and up the spiral staircase to the top, which affords a spectacular view of the Arabian Sea. (43)

Adiga's narrative moves from the centre to the margins of Kittur as it takes the readers progressively from the locations that hold tourist interest to the outskirts and to the dwelling places of the less fortunate ones. The narrative begins in places of importance like the Train Station and the Bunder, and slowly moves to seedy places like the Angel Talkies and eventually in the last segment, "Day Seven" to the Salt Market Village. This village is rural and poorer than the rest of the town. If Kittur is in the margin of the grand national map, economically and politically, Salt Market Village is the margin within the marginalised space. This segment of the narrative also dramatises the political hypocrisy of Kittur. Murali, a budding writer who functions as an assistant to the town's communist volunteer, Thimma Swami learns that the classes in Kittur are not just two but many because in a Third World situation, caste and gender can fragment the class structure further. This chapter also carries visible spatial markers as Murali discovers them in his location in the Comrade's house. The Comrade, Thimma Swami with an appendage, B. A. Kittur, M. A. Mysore prefers to hold his talks with visitors in the best space of the house while Murali is relegated to the kitchen, to make tea or under the kitchen sink, cleaning the place. The Comrade's house is at once a site of market and labour and it is also a site that locates the centre and the margin. Into that space moves in an illiterate widow of a farmer who commits suicide under duress. This hapless woman believes that the Communist Party of Thimma Swami (Marxist-Maoist) would enable her get her pensions and allowances from the Government. She explains how her caste makes her situation more pathetic, to which the Comrade who still basks in the days of Lenin, Stalin and Trotsky remarks: "I refuse to accept the category of 'caste' in our discussion" (255). Here one finds political activist who wishes the caste system away without even bothering to visit the Salt Market Village where the widow stays. Murali, eventually, visits the widow and his journey takes the readers to the margin within the margins:

> Murali got off the no. 67C bus at the Salt Market Village stop, and walked down the main road, picking his way through a bed of muck, while hogs sniffed the earth around him. (256)

Ironically, Murali, who himself struggles under the kitchen sink most of the time is looked upon as a deliverer in the Salt Market Village. People crowd around him, asking for assistance, narrating their misfortunes. This brings out the classic dependence syndrome of the colonial subjects who look up to masters. What happens in Murali's case is that a shift in geographical segment creates a shift in his class-identity. While he is only a helper in the Comrade's residence, he is made to feel as a potent politician in the Salt Market Village. This postcolonial irony reaches its peak in the conversation between the widow and the Comrade. The widow reveals her dependence on the Communist party whereas the Comrade gives her a lecture on resistance.

Thus, Adiga converts Kittur into a cultural topography wherein usury, duress and coercion coexist with minor acts of resistance. What he invokes in this work is a spirit to observe one's own immediate surroundings minutely. In this novel, this spirit marks the beginning of decolonisation, a decolonisation of mind than that of the space.

Works Cited

Adiga, Aravind, *Between the Assassinations*, New Delhi, Picador, 2008.

Punter, David, *Postcolonial Imaginings: Fictions of a New World Order*, New Delhi: Atlantic, 2000.

20

Feminine Bonds of Harmony in *The Binding Vine*

—B. Kavya

> Desire, says the Buddha, is the cause of grief;
> But how escape this cord.
> This binding vine of love?
> fear lies coiled within this womb-piercing joy (1)

Woman in the traditional oriented Indian society is bound by 'Gender' like an anaconda. The suffocation of women in such a fatal binding, restrains their advancement. Shashi Deshpande has voiced against such oppression in all her novels. *The Binding Vine* unveils the reality of modern Indian women who are still deprived of their rights in love, marriage and sex. The title *The Binding Vine* is a representation or metaphor, which is as imaginatively real as its liberal and metaphorical meaning.

Perhaps Shashi Despande's faultless work uses the symbolism of the Binding Vine. It has allegorical significance and becomes the central metaphor for the great story saga of an Indian working woman. At several levels it embodies the contrary meanings. The vine cannot be torn from the tree, the vine has no existence outside the tree. Shashi Deshpande brings to the novel a rare splendour in the delineation of Indian society through such homespun metaphor. Perhaps she extends a psychological insight to the character of Urmi.

In this novel Shashi Deshpande succeeds in portraying the miracle of love generated by a victim of patriarchal society, plumbing psychological death where other novelists skim surfaces. Urmi's early reaction "Appears obviously sinful" but as the novel moves on we see her underlining them of redemption for her incapacity for penitence is a sin. For that sin she goes a penance as it were by helping Shakutai. Her character grows in nobility. The whole process of getting justice to her daughter is filled with penance and at the end of the novel it is the love that binds her to women like her, like the binding vine going round and round but hugging the tree tenderly unlike anaconda; that is why Urmi even grows spiritually. Even the reader feels that she has done enough penance and deserves redemption through exemplary deeds of self-sacrifice she has performed.

The story of *The Binding Vine* revolves round the protagonist Urmi, who is caught in the battle of selfhood. She is not only a narrator but even acts as a buffer and gets linked with all the other characters. She is a lecturer in college, the wife of a Merchant Navy officer Kishore. She is shaken by a recent bereavement in the family and is mourning for her dead daughter Anu. She fights within herself to get relief from her distress. She has kept everything bottled within herself. She is haunted by a sense of fault: 'To forget is to betray' so wants to linger in the memories of her dead daughter.

Her meeting with Shakutai in the hospital where her friend and sister-in-law Vanna works changes the course of her life. Shakutai's daughter Kalpana is a victim of rape fighting between life and death in a hospital ward and Urmi fights for justice for her. Thus, a mother's anguish is subsided by helping an anguished mother. Kalpana's tragedy is compared with Urmi's mother-in-law's tragedy. "What has happened to Kalpana happened to Mira too"(3). Urmila decides to publish. Mira's poem, which was neglected, sets as a mirror to her unhappy married life. Urmi's tale of woe is balanced with Mira and Kalpana's tales of woe.

The Binding Vine is a saga of three generations of women under suppression, depression and oppression in the patriarchal society. The 'Binding Vine' of feelings and emotions connects all the three generations women. In the first generation we have Mira's mother, Vanna's mother and Urmi's mother. In the second generation it is Mira, Vanna, Urmi, Shakutai and Sulu. In the third generation are Mira's son Kishore, Vanna's daughter Mandira, Urmi's daughter Anu, Shakutai's daughter Kalpana. Protaganist Urmi is connected to all the three-generation women. Urmi has fallen in love with her closet friend Vanna's brother Kishore at the very young age of 15. She marries Kishore, the boy next door. Though she marries a man of her choice, her imagination of a happy family is broken by the hard reality—that he "flits into her life a few months in a year and flits out again leaving nothing of him." (21)

On their wedding night Urmi is able to read Kishore's face that looks 'trapped'. After learning the truth on his face she just walks out of the room. He never asks the reason. She wants to pour her feeling out; "Each time you leave me, the parting is like death, she tries to tell him twice but fails". Kishore, a typical Indian guy, misses the mark to understand his wife's tender feelings. Urmi knows sex is only a temporary answer and she knows the big problem that Kishore will never remove his armour, there is something in him she will never reach. She yearns for mental and emotional bond with her husband but she is utterly disappointed. Marriage in our Indian context is so sacred, uniting two persons. Shashi Deshpande condemns the institution, which just binds two bodies that fails to blend the two hearts and minds.

The Binding Vine can also be seen as a novel, which lights up sisterhood and upholds humanitarianism. Urmi and Vanna are good friends and sisters-in-law. They help each other in their problems. Vanna tries her best to console Urmi when her little baby daughter is dead. When Vanna's daughter Pallavi is sick it's Urmi who rushes immediately when Mandira calls her. Urmi is always there to help Vanna and vice versa. There is greater ease between them. Vanna's mother Akka is very happy with Urmi who plays the role of a sister to Vanna. According to Indira Nityanandan, the step forward, achieved in this novel, is the introduction of female bonding, the desire of one woman to help another less fortunate one. Urmila draws a society's attention to the plight of the rape victim and is determined to get Mira's poems published. "This is a positive development in the protagonist, for Sarita, Jaya and Indu were involved in fighting their own battles."(2)

It is Akka, who tells Mira's story where even her story lies. That is, Akka, a stepmother to Kishore, and his mother Mira died in her childbed. Mira's husband married Akka. What really made him to marry was for his son's sake. What he really wants now is a mother for that motherless child. The enormous cruelty behind this silences all the three—Akka, Vanna and Urmi. Then they are pained even more by Mira's poetry. It is through Mira's poetry they learn the truth of her married life. After reading Mira's writing Akka and Vanna break down and cry inconsolably. It serves as a beacon light to Urmi who is on the ship of questions in a sea of despair. Mira's husband loves her at first sight. Mira is just eighteen when a man who is crazy about her marries her. But Mira rejects his obsessive love. He is a man who tries to possess another human being against her will and Mira is led into a marital rape. It is through her writings Urmi discovers that Mira has intense dislike of sexual act with her husband, a physical repulsion from the man she marries. Mira who hates shis lovemaking says, "What is it he wants from me? I look at myself in the mirror and wonder, what is there in me? Why does it have to be me? Why can't he leave me alone?" (67). Mira's husband is an insensitive man whose love is based on sexual level. She never talks to him though he gets irritated. He pleads with her and says he loves her. Though Mira says no it doesn't make any difference to him. He always forces himself on her and as a result of this Kishore is born. Mira is subjected to marital rape in a society where marriage is a divine bond of life. Barb Kiffe says: "Marital rape is seldom given the legitimacy or validity of other forms of sexual violence, but it can be just as devastating. What sets marital rape apart is that the victim has to live with her rapist"(3).

Urmi is very fascinated with Mira's writing. Her thoughts are in English but her creative writing is in Kannada. That dairy is not an account of her routine life but a "Communion with herself". Mira's poetry reveals her potential as a writer and she means to assert herself and even find a way out of her frustrating married life. The silent effort of Mira to use language as a means of her redemption may be treated as "a demand for access to and parity within the law and myth making groups in society." (4) Mira dies at the age of twenty-two, leads a lonely, choiceless life without any freedom in her in-laws' house. They call her mad and are indifferent to her. She is cloistered in a home, living with a man she cannot love, surrounded by people she has nothing in common with (127).

Mira knows love makes vulnerable and one always fears to lose it. Urmi sees this fear in the eyes of Shakutai when she meets her in a hospital where Vanna works. Urmi is moved by Shakutai's overwhelming anxiety towards her daughter Kalpana. Earlier Shakutai assumes that her daughter who is now unconscious has been injured in a car accident. But later she is flabbergasted when the doctor, after an examination, declares that she has been raped. The immediate reaction of Shakutai is: "It's not true; your people are trying to blacken my daughter's name." Shakutai is scared of her society, which would be very cruel to them henceforth. She thinks death is the only thing which can help Kalpana. In the eyes of society, regardless of her fault, she would remain guilty and invalid for marriage as she has lost her virginity and lifelong she has to bear the burden of impurity. Shakutai is more worried about her daughter's marriage. She is agonised with the fear of society and cries not to publicise the issue. "I will never be able to hold up my head again! Who will marry the girl? We were decent people."

Urmi who is caught in the web of grief is ready to give her time and consoles Shakutai. She becomes a regular visitor to the hospital to inquire about Kalpana. She is empathetic towards her and patiently hears her story.

The truth is that she was married to an irresponsible, lazy man who never wanted to work at all and used to quit his job quite often. He left her alone with three children for another woman. Shakutaj then did all sorts of work for their livelihood and finally settled in a girls' school. Shakutai was very thankful to her sister Sulu who was beside her to help in troubled days. Sulu loved Kalpana very much and she had brought frocks, pins, ribbons etc., when she started earning money. Shakutai and Sulu were also good sisters who helped each other and loved each other.

Whenever Shakutai talks about Sulu to Urmi the words are dipped in love and affection. Sulu was a good Maushi to Shakutai's daughter. But she changed after marriage and lacked the courage to face the reality and lead her life. As Sulu was childless and suffered with white patches on her body she was frightened that her husband would leave her, send her out of the house and have another woman in her place. Finally she commited suicide, just increasing the pain of Shakutai after Kalpana's plight. Bell Hooks writes in her essay "Sisterhood", "...Sexism is perpetrated by institutional and social structures, by the individuals who dominate, exploit, or oppress, and by the victims themselves, who are socialised to behave in ways that make them act in complicity with the status quo".(5) She called women to bond with one another to counter male dominancy. Kalpana was always reluctant towards her mother's warning. Kalpana who was proud of her adulthood flaunted wearing good dresses, painting her lips. Now Shakutai felt it was all her fault that she didn't cover herself decently and went her way with her head in the air, caring for nobody. Its unfortunate woman is always expected to act according to the will of the society. She has to follow the norms set by it, but men without caring breaks them and lead a guilt-free life and a woman being innocent is made to feel guilty.

As Vikas Malik says: "Shakutai who keeps meandering between praising have daughter and criticising or blaming her is a victim of her own values. Yet she wasn't born with these values embedded within her mother's womb someone had to shape their values, make her believe that they were her own who? Her mother,her mother's mother, her mother's mother's mother? Not at all. It was her father, her father's father, her father's father's father, ad nauseasm." (6)

It's Urmila who makes her understand that it was not Kalpana's fault. She was injured, wronged by a man and she didn't do anything wrong. But Shakutai feels Kalpana has shamed her as people are talking about her as a woman who has left her husband. So women are always blamed for no mistake of theirs, unfortunately nobody blames Kalpana's irresponsible father.

The words of Shakutai, "men are like animals, these are always people waiting to throw stone at us, our people first of all, women must know fear" (148) depicts her fear regarding the safety of her daughters. Overburdened by her responsibility and sensing the victimised state of women she asks Urmi, "Why does God give us daughters?"(60). Urmi remains a mute spectator until the hospital authorities decide to shift her to a suburban hospital. For four months Kalpana has been lying in a bed and there is demand for bed in their crowded hospital. Urmila understand Shakutai's pain in coming to this hospital and how inconvenient it will be for her to go to the suburban hospital. She takes the help of Malcolm, a journalist who was her classmate at one time. He contributes his share of help by publishing it in his paper. Urmi spends her time with Shakutai, into her house and when Sulu is dead stays at her house. Though Shakutai belongs to a working class Urmi helps her to get justice which is a victory of humanitarianism. It's Urmila who is very kind and gentle towards each and everyone, after learning the truth about her mother. She changes her rude behaviour towards her. She is kind towards her servants Rekha or Balakaka of Ranidurg. She is friendly with Priti, a filmmaker, and is able to judge her. Priti is a modern lady brought up abroad by working parents. Urmi understands her very much and pities her lonely childhood.

Inni tells Urmila that she never liked to send her child to Ranidurg but it was her father's decision. Urmi was not easy to handle as she used to be crying all the time. Inni as a girl—mother had no idea how to sooth her. So she had taken the help of Diwakar who was there with them since Inni was a child. But Inni's husband was angry that she had left the child with a man. Even though Inni begged him and promised him that she would not leave her child alone yet there was no use. He did not understand her feelings nor forgave her. Urmi was left in the care of his parents. Urmi, after hearing the truth (from her mother), was able to forgive her mother. It was a new morning in her new life, as she became a new person after reading Mira's poem, sharing Shakutai's agony and getting justice for Kalpana.

Now she decides to publish Mira's poem who doesn't have a chance to express her poetic talent. It would be a tribute to her mother-in-law who died in pain and sorrow. Each and every character in the novel is craving for love, caring, emotional support which is the spring of life. Urmi loved her daughter very much, and thinks that forgetting her is to betray. But she can't wrong her living son Karthik in the thoughts of her dead daughter. She loves her husband very much and hopes he would shed his armour one day and be very close to her. She gets a chance to recover from her agony only through her bonding with Shakutai, Mira, Vanna and Inna. The caring, sharing and empathy with these female characters act as a redemptive power and it leads to her personal development. The feminine bonding leads her to harmony and peace of mind.

WORKS CITED

Koplan, Cora, *Changes, Culture and Feminism*, London, Verso, 1986, p. 71.

Deshpande, Shashi, *The Binding Vine*, New Delhi: Penguin India, 1992.

Hooks, Bell, *Feminist Theory; from Margin to Center*. London, Pluto Press, 2000, p. 45.

Nityanandam, Indira, "Shashi Deshpande's *The Binding Vine* : 'Silent No More', *Indian Women Novelists*, III, Vol., R.K. Dhawan Ed., New Delhi, Prestige Books, 1995, p. 66.

Malik, Vikas, "My Son You Rape Some Girls—But Marry a Nice Girl", Rev. of The *Binding Vine, Asian Times*, No. 29, June 1993, p. 9.

http: //www.esap.org/advocacy/PDF/*marital rape* dekota. P.d.f.

21

Feminism in Shobha De's *Socialite Evenings*

—Ram Sharma

The quest for feminine identity is largely a post-independence social phenomenon in India, a phenomenon influenced by various changing forces of reality—the freedom movement, progressive education, social reforms, increasing contacts with the West, urban growth, etc.

The emergence of women writers in the last quarter of the nineteenth century carried with it a double significance. It bore testimony to the birth of a new era of emancipation for the Indian women, an era of increased opportunities and a more dynamic participation in the social and intellectual life of the country ushered in by the great social reorientations which came at the turn of the century. Secondly, it was also a commentary on the rise of individualism in the life and letters of the age, an individualism which is closely associated with the rise of the novel in India in the same way in which it was associated with the rise of the English novel.

Feminism emerged as a worldwide movement to secure women's rights on the one hand and love, respect, sympathy and understanding from men on the other. It focused on women's struggle for recognition and survival and made them realise that the time has come when they should stop suffering silently in helplessness. Shobha De, an eminent modern novelist and journalist has presented feminism in her novels, like *Socialite Evenings, Strange Obsession, Sisters, Sultry Days* and *Starry Nights*.

Gayatri Chakravorty Spivak writes in her article "Can, the Subaltern speak?"

> Between patriarchy and imperialism subject constitution and object formation the figure of woman disappears not into a pristine nothingness, but into a violent shuttling which is the displaced figuration of the 'Third-World Woman' caught between tradition and modernisation. (80)

Simone de Beauvoir has very precisely exposed the condition of woman in her most famous book *The Second Sex*. Of course, the miserable condition of women all over the world inspired the women of talent like Virginia Woolf to do something in this field and the result was the emergence of *Feminism*, a great movement in the Western world in 1960. It is a movement for the emancipation of women and their fight for equal rights. The condition of woman is equally miserable in Indian society. The Indian society is basically patriarchal where a woman is given the secondary role. Even in *Anushashan Parva* it is said.

> All her glorification, all her fulfillment lies in sacrificing her life and happiness for the sake of man in different forms father, husband and the son.

The modern woman does not find any sense in such self-sacrifice and yearns for self-expression, individuality and self-identity. She is trying to free herself of the dependence syndrome as Chaman Nahal says:

> I define Feminism as a mode of existence in which the woman is free of the dependence syndrome. There is a dependence syndrome, where it is the husband or the father or the community or whether it is a religious group or ethnic group when women free themselves of the dependence syndrome and lead a normal life, my idea of feminism materialises. (30)

Socialite Evenings gives us the picture of the marginalisation of Indian women at the hands of their husbands. Simone de Beauvoir expresses her own views on the man-woman nexus: "Man represents both the positive and the neutral, as is indicated by the common use of man to designate human beings in general, whereas woman represents only the negative, defined by limiting criteria without reciprocity."

A woman is never regarded as an autonomous being since she has always been assigned a subordinate and relative position. As Simone de Beauvoir says, "Man can think of himself without woman. She cannot think of herself without man. And she is simply what man decrees. She appears essentially to the male as a sexual being. For him she is sex.... absolute sex, no less. She is defined and differentiated with reference to man and not he with reference to man and not he with reference to her, she is the incidental, the inessential as opposed to the essential."

Shobha's is the picture of woman not only as protagonist but also as motivating factor in society. Karuna's marriage is a failure since it is loveless, joyless and bridgeless. She hates the stand-offish and cruel behaviour of the husbands who often kept themselves busy in drab monotonous activities like reading the business pages of the *Times of India*. Karuna says:

> We were reduced to being marginal people. Everything that mattered to us was trivialised. The message was "you don't really count, except in the context my priorities." It was taken for granted that our needs were secondary to their. And that in some way we ought to be grateful for having a roof over our head and four square meals a day. (69)

Karuna, the main character and narrator of Shobha De's *Socialite Evenings*, is not concerned with the lot of women. But here that concern changes to 'I am the good thing' and even this 'I' does not stand for any commitment to spiritual and moral values but it is 'a good thing' because it can be dressed up and presented as an extremely marketable product over the media. Karuna's pre-occupation with 'I' and 'the good thing is me' becomes clear when the journalist of a foreign magazines comes up with a proposal to make a documentary with Karuna's experiences as the focal point of such a film. Karuna's reply to such an idea is:

> I think it's a great idea. Infact; I think I'll steal it. There may be a documentary in it but I'm going to give a book, a shot. I've always wanted to write one—so you can take a walk, Yankee agent. I know when I'm on to a good thing and the

> good thing is me. If anyone is going to cash in on this, baby, it isn't going to be you.... (306)

Even during the period when she has been divorced by her husband and has to move from place to place in search of job. Her sole concern during this stage, too, is how she can shake off her middle-class background.

> And I hated the poverty, this meager income forced on me. I suppose I was a bit too old for the drastic changes I had to adjust to or perhaps I just wasn't cut out to be middle class, lower middle class. For a start, there was the matter of transport. I'd never travelled by bus since my school days. Or waited in queues for anything. Getting into a local train and commuting to town was a major trauma. I could not relate to the other women in my compartment. I felt revolted by their small concerns. I'd watch with horror as they squabbled over small change and petty issues. Their conversations depressed me. It was all so much stomach... their talk of vegetable price and milk strikes. Sometimes I'd over-hear a husband being discussed, but it was invariably in servile terms. Every problem of theirs seemed trivial and insignificant to me. The quotidian detail of their lives– spats with the mother-in-law, a child with mumps, school admissions and donation money, husband's stalled promotions, office gossip, a crisis at the neighborhood crèche, an ailing parent, a relative's hernia operation, saree sales at Kala Niketan, haldi versus cold cream, Garden Vareli at a suburban store, discounts at Sahakari Bhandar. I hated to be in that environment. (240-41)

In a patriarchal male-dominated society, it is the man who abuses and subaltern attitude of woman finds expression in the exclusion of all thoughts of feminine liberty and equality from their minds.

> He brainwashes me constantly. I'm made to feel obliged and indebted. It's awful, but even my insistence on working and contributing to the running expenses of the house has become a battleground. I don't know what to do—either way I'm stuck. (69)

Karuna's husband is inadequate and incomplete since he lacks the traits of an ideal husband. Karuna wonders:

> ... how could we communicate anything at all to men who perpetually sat reading pages of the *Times of India* while concentratedly picking their nose? (68)

Karuna's imaginary craving for the fulfilment of her physical desire finds reflection in her fantasies. Anjali's fancy place in Malabar Hill where Karuna usually goes is symbolically the projection of her fancy, her dream which is reality.

> I think our marriage was over the day our awful honeymoon started. We've got have. As for you—I really don't know to this day why you chose to marry me. I don't think you even know who you married. You don't have a clue what sort of woman I am. (185)

Karuna faces all difficulties but she does not protest but obeys her husband dutifully. Her husband is not a cruel person and he even throws away all her (Karuna's) sins like her affairs with Girish.

Later also when she leaves her husband's house and starts living with Anjali, the idea of keeping the baby does not sink into her system firmly. Once again the consideration is about herself—whether her parents would accept her with the child. She gives an inkling of her thoughts after her husband has talked to her at length about the settlement.

> For a couple of days after his call I actually toyed with the idea of keeping the baby. May be it was just spite, may be I felt 'it was what I needed... someone to call my own as the cliché goes. (222)

But the moment her friend Anjali hears of such an 'idea' germinating in Karuna's mind, she decides to nip it in the bud. She tells Karuna:

> Don't be crazy— A baby is a life-long responsibility... look at me. Are you prepared to tie yourself down for ever? Get a puppy or a kitten if you are feeling all that motherly, forget about a kid. Besides, you won't be able to handle the scene. You aren't cut out for a single parent situation. You can't go around with an orphan Annie — like kid, with no father on the scene. (222)

Women in Shobha's novels symbolise the overpov'ering materialism and the lack of spirituality, that characterises modern age. With the crumbling of moral and ethical values there is an inner conflict which drives the modern Indian women to take shelter in different identities for momentary solace. Girish, the great art film maker, exhorts Karuna to take life more seriously and commit herself to some serious thing like cinema:

> But life is about more than just goofy kids and surf- boards. I want you to get involved. Commit yourself. Get into the mainstream The mainstream of what? Cinema? Life? I find all that very complex. (255)

What Girish implies is that Karuna should take her role of Shakuntala in his film more seriously. Even her intellectual pursuits suggest that she is in capable of involving herself in anything serious, for her preoccupation is with only 'cross- word puzzles' and 'newspaper-chess'.

It appears that Karuna has just a formal relationship with her husband. Intimacy between the husband and wife is lacking for Karuna who never calls her husband by his name but derogatorily as 'Black Label'. Helena Cixous observes:

> A male privilege can be seen in the opposition between activity and passivity. Traditionally, the question of sexual difference is coupled with the same opposition, activity/ passivity. (Lodge 1989, 288)

Anjali throws off the traditional conventions of moral values. She enacts a marriage of her choice with Abe. Karuna too discards conventions and she had extramarital relationship with Krish. Even she dares to restrain her husband from a week long sexual orgy with Krish Kukherjee in Rome. As a housewife. Karuna remembers:

> I felt like an indifferent boarder in the house, going through the motions of the house keeping and playing wife but the resentment and rebellion remained just under the surface, ready to break out at the smallest provocation. (69)

When Karuna's husband comes out with a 'package' /deal containing an assured income and all the luxuries which she had hitherto been enjoying, Karuna's only remark "(the package) sounds sweets." Similar is the case with Anjali. Her second marriage to the homosexual Kumar is nothing but an exchange for "the Porches emeralds, holidays in Biarritz, shipping along the champs—Elysees, a villa in Ooty, parties every night, unlimited champagne and the choice to pick my own bed-mate but only discreetly." (217)

Ritu exploits her sexual breakthrough, her female potentiality to keep her husband within her reach, within her control. Look, what she tells Karuna about her strategy:

> ... make them feel you have done them a favour by marrying them—make them feel insecure. Let them think you'll walk out on them if they don't toe the line. That's what keeps them ir their place. (86)

Even the role of providing security to his wife which the traditional society has assigned to a husband is faulted and the so-called emancipated v. omen in rise revolt. The only thing which these ladies can do in a fit of boldness is abuse the man in words which even coarse, illiterate women would not use in public. We have only to recall what Karuna tells Karan when she meets him in the Oberoi Hotel and enquires about her friend Anjali: "Listen Ass hole —Don't give me your fancy lines. You are nothing but cheap male whore. Why don't you leave Ritu alone?" (SE, 112)

Also, Karuna thinks she has become one-up and vindicates herself as a woman by abusing her husband verbally when he comes with the proposal to remarry her:

> And you waited all this while to tell me. Just get the hell out of my house and life. I don't ever want to see you again. I let you in this time.... but never again I'll call the cops if you try and invade my home in future. You are even more of a worm than I thought. You deserve Winnie — I hope she's got a wax doll of yours. I'll send her some extra pins to stick into it. Now take your frigging pipe and out!! (264)

For the likes of Anjali and company marriage also becomes a necessity because it not only provides them security, status and luxuries, but it also enables them to indulge in adultery, for adultery is possible only within marriage. It might begin as a possible escape from a 'meaningless marriage' as happens in the case of Karuna's affair with Krish but once it is discovered she is advised against going on a 'guilt-trip' by Anjali.

Despite these facets of a woman's personality, *Socialite Evenings* is a success story. Karuna fights her way up after her divorce, gets recognition in advertising and television productions and becomes financially independent. The author also seems to approve of the kind of life Karuna has led which becomes clear in the brief third person one paragraph Epilogue wherein she says:

> It has been very hard work, this packaging of her life, and often it had almost seemed impossible to finish the book. But now that it was over she felt a certain sadness, autumnal in its intensity... she loved this time of the day and she willed herself to relax. Tomorrow's anxieties could be dealt with later, today she would rest. (307)

In the end we can say Shobha's *Socialite Evenings* presents aesthetics of feminism and emancipation of woman.

Works Cited

Anushashan Parva, Chapter 21, Verse 19.

Beauvoir, Simone De, *The Second Sex,* transl and ed. H.M. Parshley, London, Penguin, 1974.

De, Shobha, *Socialite Evenings,* New Delhi, Penguin Books, 1990. (All citations in the paper are from this edition of the text, followed by page numbers in parentheses).

Lodge, D., *Modern Criticism and Theory: A Reader,* London, Longman, 1989.

Nahal, Chaman, Feminism In Indian English Fiction, *Indian Women Novelists,* R.K. Dhawan, ed., New Delhi, Prestige Books, p. 1971, 30.

22

Women's Identity in Post-Colonial Society: A Reading of Imtiaz Dharkar's Purdah Poems

—Mukti B. Shah

Imperial rule in India strategically used instruction in English to reinforce their dominance. Macaulay's infamous minute of 1835 and establishment of the Hindu College had a major impact on the literary scene in India. Under the influence of English language and literature, many poets like Toru Dutt, Sarojini Naidu, M.M. Dutt, Kashiprasad Ghosh, B.M. Malbari, Henry Vivian Dorezio, Rabindranath Tagore, Arvind Ghosh etc. started writing poetry in English in India.

In the pre-independence era we find only two significant women poets writing in English. Toru Dutt (1856-1877) produced two collections of poems: *A Sheaf Gleaned in French Fields* (1876) containing poems about the beauty of nature. *Ancient Ballads and Legends of Hindustan* (1882) contains ballads retelling Indian myths and legends with focus on mythical characters. In Sarojini Naidu's *The Golden Threshold* (1905), *The Bird of Time* (1912) and *The Broken Wing: Scngs of Life, Death and the Spring* (1917), her major concerns are nature, national identity, memory, myths, legends. Naidu's poetry shows influence of Romantic and Victorian poetry. All these figures appearing in the poetry of Toru Dutt and Sarojini Naidu are ideal and angelic.

Women poets of post-independence period, also known as the modernist phase, began to compose a new kind of poetry different from their predecessors. Their poetry has been wide-ranging and close to real-life experience. Our nation was corroded by communalism, linguistic chauvinism and corruption, and these influenced the poets of the post-independence period in a way that it became difficult for a sensitive poet to be sentimental or idealistic like those of pre-independence period. The aspects of modernism could be found in the formal quality of poetry as well as the content too in terms of explicit sexuality, urban angst, existential awareness, confessional element, autobiographical element, self-analysis, quest for identity. In the poetry of pre-independence period, we find mysticism, romanticism, nature description, patriotism and lyrical elements; whereas, in modern poetry we find disillusionment, identity crisis, alienation. The emergence of bilingual poets like Kamala Das, Mamta Kalia, Gauri Deshpande and English translations connected different regional cultures. Nissim Ezekiel seems to be the first poet to exhibit the major aspects of modernity in Indian English Poetry. A.K. Ramanujan, Adil Jassuwala, Dom Moraes, Gieve Patel, A.K. Mehrotra, Jayant Mahpatra, Keki Daruwala are some poets other than women poets who emerged during this postcolonial period.

The poetry of Kamala Das takes up issues like gender, pain, inability to communicate, denial of humanity and the violence of patriarchy. She mapped out the interior landscape of the Indian woman in bold idiom. Gauri Deshpande wrote about the drama of marriage, man-woman relationship and longing for the lost love of man. Mamta Kalia writes about the loss of identity and revolt against patriarchy. Melani Silgardo and Eunice De Souza wrote about the life and problems of the women of Goan community.

Postcolonial awareness exerted a tremendous impact on the artists by upsetting their thematic priorities and also by inculcating new perspectives to comprehend the external realities. The contemporary Indian poetry in English appears to be seriously involved in the power-struggle to dislodge patriarchy. They have responded to the woman-question in accordance with their training, accomplishments, exposures to West and anguish of empowerment.

Imtiaz Dharker (b.1954) introduced a major new voice to the Indian English Poetry. Born in Lahore, he grew up in Glasgow and now divides her time between Wales and Mumbai. *Purdah and other Poems, Postcards from God, I Speak for the Devil, The Terrorists at My Table* are her four books of poetry, conceived as sequences of poems and drawings. In this paper I wish to focus on her first volume *Purdah and Other Poems.*

Using purdah as a metaphor, she brings out the vulnerability of women both at home and outside. As a spatial metaphor, purdah allows us to look at the situation of women both in domestic and public spaces. The idea of travel, journey in these poems metaphorically suggests crossing a line of boundary, a limit that leads to the idea of transgression.

Through the metaphor of purdah, Dharker criticises not just the purdah system but social, religious and moral taboos and repressions that go into the institutionalisation of purdah. Purdah is projected as a symbol of these taboos. It not only excludes her physically but also mentally from the rest of the world. The 'invisible purdah' which operates in the society, religion and culture alienates a woman from her true self. The physical custom and trappings of purdah form not just some components of the subject matter but also via analogy and metaphor most of the themes of Dharker's poems. A close reading of the volume shows that the word 'purdah' is used in its metaphorical sense suggesting conditioning a female child, control over female body, subordination, violence, exclusion of women from the mainstream, creating a line of restriction keeping low the spirit of independence among women in the post-independence period.

Dharker explores the difficult facets of Muslim women's identity in postcolonial Indian society. Her poetry transcends the personal to voice the problems of community, sometimes the diaspora of Muslim women in England. And while exploring this theme through several of her poems, she raises the role of institutions like family, marriage and religion in shaping the woman's identity. Family becomes an immediate social unit where the girl's identity is shaped by training her to exhibit a modest behaviour. She is taught that something is womanly or unwomanly. Simone de Beauvoir's well-known statement that one is not born but rather becomes a woman, is enacted in the society, where the girl learns early that she is *paraya dhan* (another's property) or a plant growing in the neighbour's courtyard, her parents' responsibility till the day she is handed over to her rightful owners. Dharker puts the fact in "*Pur*dah I": "One day they said/she was old enough to learn some shame/she found it came quite naturally" (POP, 3). The girl since her childhood sees the older women of the household behaving in a set pattern and for the girls this pattern becomes the reference model. Right from her adolescence, she carries a sense of guilt of being a woman and learns how to save her from those "eyes aslant" (3). In "Going Home" the girl knows this and says, "Mummy put me in purdah/or he'll see the hair sprout in my lap./ Mummy put me in purdah quick/or he will see" (24). Sexuality and modesty are associated with her existence. Thus right from childhood, she is enveloped by the "purdah of mind" (7) so that her thought process takes a definite shape and contour. Purdah talked with reference to modesty, 'Izzat', 'laaj', 'sharam' is symbolic of conformity, while the concepts of independence, freedom and self are relegated to a world outside. Her body becomes the property of society, religion and the family. Family becomes a patriarchal institution which does not allow her individual choices—choices for education, entertainment, mobility, marriage etc. She is always seen as a second-class citizen in the family, who is bound to support her husband or other males of the house. Thus, family is seen as a purdah obstructing her natural growth. In such a purdah society this modesty goes to the extent of preventing a woman from accepting or refusing a husband.

In this context Dharker raises the question of relationship between the individual and the family. Mothers who underwent a tough fate, who are the sufferers of the marriage still want their daughters to be part of the same process for the sake of protection and security of their daughters. The relationships should sustain her. Instead, her relationship with the male as well as female members of the family becomes a major factor for the denial of her choices and the cause of her victimisation. Poems IV and V of "Purdah II" show that how mothers and "gossip aunts" have become agency and in turn an agent for power application of patriarchy by plotting the wedding of their daughters.

There she goes, your mother,
still plotting at your wedding.
long after she is dead. (POP, 7)

In the name of social wisdom and guardianship, the groom is selected by the parents and she becomes nothing but an object having no identity which can be sold or purchased. Dharker here questions the fruitfulness of the Muslim tribal custom of *mehr*, which is associated with the financial protection of the wives in any problematic situation after marriage. The dictates of the men in the history of their religion, the religious leaders and the elders in their lives act as taboos for controlling girls' desires and temptations.

A horde of dead men
held up your head,
above the mean temptations
of those alien. (7)

In some of the poems Dharker depicts the social reality of a marriage as purdah. Marriage is seen as a social necessity because through marriage, families are established and the family is the fundamental unit of society. To a girl waiting to be married, to a woman after she has gained that state, marriage works as effectively as purdah as though she were indeed swathed in folds of heavy black cloth preventing her from achieving selfhood and individuality, cutting her off from the mainstream of life. It works in fact in a more insidious fashion than an actual purdah since it grants an outward semblance of freedom. Marriage should give a new identity to a woman. But the persona of Poem IV of *Purdah II* only becomes a sex object gratifying sexual urges of her husband. The purdah, hiding the contours of the body, the planes of the face, with only a grid to enable her to see where she is going, is seen by some of the women who wear it as a liberating invention, a kind of safety. Reverberating to the same irony is the concept of marriage as a liberating invention. In Poems IX, X, XI and XII of *Purdah II* Saleema and Naseem's attempts to liberate themselves by marrying the men of their choice brings them to a stage where Saleema becomes "watchful as any creature" (10) and Naseem, who was assured freedom by her English husband, smiles and urges to be accepted. The institution of marriage arranged by parents or even the one which is willingly chosen acts as a kind of prison, a cage where a woman's true self is suffocated. In both these poems Dharker expresses her annoyance against this system as it undermines the woman's identity making her an outcast.

Religion is presented as another taboo in some of the poems. Purdah in both literal and metaphorical sense is legitimised in Muslim religion. For the sake of avoiding deviations from the moral code, women are required to wear veil and hide their bodies, lower their gaze, to get education but separately, marrying under the guardianship of parents, the custom of *mehr*, no marriage with a non-Muslim, not to talk to any other males than her father, brother, husband or other male relatives, Religion severely limits the mobility of women. Poems like *"Grace"* (POP:11), *"Prayer"* (POP:13) question the exclusion of women from the mainstream.

> He does not look at you.
> Instead, 'A woman comes
> with her eyes concealed.
> She trails the month behind her.
> We are defiled'. (11)

She cannot go even to the mosque to pray, and must wear a burkha (veil) whenever she has to go out. If at all they are allowed then a separate, segregated place is reserved for them to say Namaz. Here again the female sexuality plays a major role in her exclusion from the power structure. Legitimisation of Purdah is inbuilt in the life of Muslim women. For avoiding the moral trespassing the victimiser is not punished but the victim is. Such exclusion has its deteriorating effects upon the physical as well as psychological constitution of Muslim women. Dharker, in these poems, questions the religious taboos that exclude a woman, render her anonymous, oppress her identity and controls her body. Religion, places of worship, Holy Scriptures and rituals which should give peace and solace, on the contrary, brings her pain as suggested in poems such as "Grace" (11), "Prayer" (13), "Pariah" (17).

This conflict between her individual self on the one side and family, customs, religion on the other turns her into a victim. Dharker's woman gradually comes to know that she is a bird imprisoned in the cage of traditions, customs, religion and culture whereby she is deprived of opportunities of self-realisation and full development. She becomes the one whose mobility is under other people's control. In "Grace" (11) and "Prayer" (13) she understands that she is an outcast. The girl in Poem V of "Going Home" (23) is aware that she has to hide her from those "eyes aslant". In "Sacrifice" (14) she knows the outcome of her marriage, where she will be nothing more but a production machine: "There will be no rest from harvesting" (14). Zarina's mother in "Zarina's Mother" knows that once Zarina gets married she will meet the same fate of her mother. "Another Woman" (38) significantly emphasizes the powerlessness, fear and plight of a poor a married woman. In "Voice II" she wears false mask on her face, hiding her truthful self: "Usually I smile, to reassure them" (20). Poems I, II and III of "A Woman's Place" (32) reiterate the fact that fear is a woman's place.

> Mouths must be watched, especially,
> if you are a woman. A smile
> should be stifled with the sari-end.
> No one must see your serenity cracked,
> Even with delight. (32)

It is pathetic to note that if a woman wants to purgate her frustration, she has to scream alone in front of a mirror. She can not make her expressions public. She should hide within herself all the pains.

> If occasionally you need to scream, do it
> alone but in front of mirror
> where you can see the strange shape the mouth makes
> before you wipe it off. (32)

There is a constant conflict between what she wants and what she is expected to do. The last line of the poem is:

> Fear, you tell me, is a woman's place. (34)

Poem II of the actually titled poem "The Child Sings" knows that,

> She is nothing but a crack
> Where the light forgot to shine (31)

Geography is the central metaphor Dharker uses in her poetry. These are geographies of brutality, of desire, of repression, of utopian freedom, frequently merging into each other. Such geographies are imaged as houses/homes, mirrors and faces, space and relationships. Purdah, which in its literal and metaphoric sense is based on the principle of inequality and establishes itself on the dual strategy of control and exclusion, itself, is a spatial metaphor that defines space, action and relationships. Thus, the girl growing in the family in *Purdah I* (3), marriage following tribal customs, and her condition after marriage in *Purdah II* (5), masjid in "Grace" (11), place outside the temple in "Prayer" are all scenes of a demarcation lines drawn for women. Body becomes a territory in Dharker's poetry. Body is something which is controlled and possessed by oneself or others.

Another important aspect of Dharker's poetry is that her poems constitute a kind of narrative, a sequence even when they can be read individually. This style of writing allows Dharker to trace the development of self and stages of its development. Poems here are not lyrical but a narrative which allows her to construct a speaking self. These poems are not static. There is progression in the narrative. Poems also have conversational quality, a dialogue like quality that allows one to construct a speaking self which is a searching self that looks for answers in the context of oppression and silence. There is dialogue within the speaking self, with other woman's selves. By identifying herself with these women, the speaking self internalises their trauma within her.

Dharker's significance as a poet today can be traced in the poetry she writes. Her poetry is informed by a deep sensitivity to women's condition in the modern world. She is a socially conscious writer who addresses issues related to women everywhere. Using purdah as a metaphor, she brings out the vulnerability of women both at home and outside. As a spatial metaphor, purdah allows us to look at the situation of women both in domestic and public spaces. The idea of travel, journey in these poems metaphorically suggests crossing a line of boundary, a limit that leads to the idea of transgression. Several of the poems imply the idea of transgression, which is part of the attempt to reinvent herself. When this crossing over is not possible, the oppression breeds morbidity. Satan enters and we have a number of images related to devil, possession and becoming the other.

She also underlines the need to reorient social institutions to bring women into the mainstream. The use of open forms in her poems, particularly her use of sequence where poems can be read individually and also as part of a larger narrative, is indicative of her view of a female self which, even as it remains individualist, flows into other lives and times.

This study is limited to two of Dharker's only one volume of poems. There are further possibilities of extending the present discussion to other volumes of her poems and similar volumes of poems by other women poets. The study of woman's writing in general and poetry in particular helps us to understand the social status of women in a society. The study of women as an emerging discipline, has contributed substantially towards our understanding of women's subordinate status in society.

Wors Cited

Beauvoir, Simone de, *The Second Sex,* Translated and Edited by H. M. Parshley, London: Vintage, 1997.

Bhattacharya, R.D., A New Generation of Indo-English Women Poets, *Poetry Chronicle,* 3, -6, (1991), 161.

Chitnis, Suma, *Violence Against Women-Women against Violence,* Delhi: Pencraft International, 1998.

Dharker, Imtiaz, *Poems Purdah and Others.* Delhi: Oxford University Press, 1989.

Kumar, Hajira, Ed., *Status of Muslim Women in India,* Delhi: Aakar Books, 2002.

Kakar, Sudhir "Feminine Identity in India", *Women in Indian Society: A Reader,* Ed. Rehana Ghadiyali, New Delhi: Sage Publications, 1998.

King, Bruce, *Modern Indian Poetry in English,* Rev. ed., New Delhi: Oxford University Press, 2001.

Nair, Rama, Ed., *Trends and Techniques in Contemporary Indian English Poetry*, New Delhi: Prestige Books, 2001.

Nair, R. P., Ed., *Kavya Bharti:* Special Issue: Poetry Of Indian Women. Madurai: SCILET, American College, No: 12, 200

"What the Koran says about women, Marriage and Divorce". http://www.csmonitor.com/2001/1219/p10s1-wogi.html

"Imtiaz Unbound"- Jerry Pinto's interview with Imtiaz Dharker on August 2, 2004.http://india.poetryinternationalweb.org/piw_cms/cms/cms_module/index.php?obj_id=2686

23

The God of Small Things: A Study in Feminism

—*S.K. Navin*

Precisely speaking, *The Gold of Small Things*, a Booker Prize winning novel, impinges on our imagination at different planes producing different responses just like the responses we receive from plucking the different nodes of a musical instrument. On the one hand it unfolds the vision of a child of the world of much stronger adults, on the other one can find in it a social and political satire, a radical and myth-breaking novel, a story of a family where its members gradually proceed to ignonimous decline or catastrophic disaster. The novel has a religious dimension as well as a racial one which often makes a person its victim at the lowest social hierarchy. However, the present paper concerns a study in feminism brushing aside all other overtones which are equally important stands in the novel.

Feminism, all would agree, concerns women's cause, their subjugation to men folk, their inferior status, their exploitation– physical, social, political, economic. Feminists all over the world have been raising such issues with a pious wish that the women must be considered equal to men. They should not be discriminated because of their sex. Truthfully speaking, whether it be social, political or economic, power has been centred in men and women have been denied access to it. They have been generally forced to feel alienated and depressed. Angela Miles rightly says:

> The domination of women by men precedes the emergence of class domination and is structured deeply into the relations of production and reproduction of almost all known societies. Although understanding of the dynamics of gender oppression across class, culture and time is at an embryonic stage, we know that this oppression is the most profound condition of alienation, the deepest division of humanity within itself and from itself, upon which all other fragmentation and domination has been built.[1]

Feminism is a movement giving voice to women's subordinated position in society and discrimination encountered by them because of their sex. A woman is considered not more than a womb, an ovary. Simone de Beauvoir in *The Second Sex* depicts a woman from the viewpoint of men as:

> In the mouth of man the epithet 'female' has the sound of an insult, yet he is not ashamed of his animal nature, on the contrary, he is proud if someone says of him: 'He is a male !' The term 'female' is derogatory not because it emphasizes women's animality, but because it imprisons her in her sex, and if this sex seems to man to be contemptible and inimical even in harmless dumb animals, it is evidently because of the uneasy hostility stirred up in him by women.[2]

It is true that the bleak status of women mentioned above has improved considerably in the context of Western women. The spread of education and technological advancement have certainly provided them a privilege to be aware of themselves especially of their rights.

However, not much has changed for the women living in the oriental countries. A large chunk of oriental women are still ill-treated, persecuted and tortured. The scenario, indeed, is changing but the pace is too slow. Processions led by them exhibiting solidarity of women are increasingly becoming a common feature. The demand for reservation of seats in the body polity is only to be considered with reference to their awareness of being a class by themselves. Their vision represents a major break with the existing male-defined world and politics. Equality, freedom and justice are central to the movement of feminism for bringing about a radical change in society. Margaret Benston's views are very relevant in this connection. She writes:

> We are feminists because we believe not only that the evidence shows the oppression of women, but further, that such oppression is wrong. We also believe that society should be changed to end all forms of oppression.[3]

Arundhati Roy in her very first hauntingly wonderful novel *The God of Small Things* lays bare abundance of details concerning the problems affecting women in a male-dominated society. She depicts the sad plight of Ammu, the central female character. She gives a moving account of her loneliness, helplessness, agony and affliction through the eyes of her young children—Estha and Rahel.

One encounters in the novel a world which has been cruel and harsh for women. Ammu's tragedy began when she was young. Her father Pappachi thought it unnecessary that she should have college education after finishing schooling as she was only a girl-child. Prospects of education concluded she remained to idle away at Ayemenem to which she came with her retired father. Life, utterly uneventful, appeared to be a burden more that a charming one especially when she realised that nobody there had any concern for her. Her eighteenth birthday went unnoticed.

She felt depressed, lost. Her soul fluttered to fly away from depressing and demoralising Ayemenem which hardly had anything to offer to a world of love and concern.

Ultimately she did get permission to go to Calcutta to join her aunt where she happened to meet her future husband, an assistant manager of a tea-estate in Assam. Just after five days of their first meeting the proposal of marriage came her way. She did not pretend to be in love with him. She just weighed the odds and accepted. She thought that "anything, anyone at all, would be better than returning to Ayemenem."[4]

The marriage that had raised her hopes brought nothing but the birth of unfortunate twins and frustration and disillusionment. Her husband turned out to be "not just a heavy drinker but a full-blown alcoholic with all of an alcoholic's deviousness and tragic charms."[5]

Her husband's persuasion that she should oblige Mr. Hollick by warming his bed in order to retain his job in fact made her dumbfounded and speechless.

Her silence infuriated him and he "lunged at her, grabbed her hair and punched her."[6]

Ammu retaliated and taking down "the heaviest book she could find in the book shelf—*The Reader's Digest World Atlas*—she hit him with it as hard as she could. On his head. His legs. His back and shoulders."[7]

Drunken violence continued. She was repelled by medicinal smell of the stale alcohol. And when his bouts of violence began to extend to her children, she left her husband and returned unwelcomed to her parents in Ayemenem.

The novelist "implicitly advocates greater social reform in the rigid positioning of women. The world of Arundhati's novel is captured in a state of flux where the values of the patriarchal society are under attack from a new world in which self-interest and self-aggrandisements and social equality are forcing their entry. Seen from a feminist point of view, the novel speaks of the violence perpetrated upon women and paternal tyranny engulfing the luckless children."[8]

Her husband's drunken violence reminded Ammu how her mother Mammachi suffered her father's outbursts of physical violence. Her father would hold a brass vase every night and beat her mother. She had left her parents' house in search of a good life. She hardly knew that nothing better was in her fate.

Beauvoir remarks, "There is a unanimous agreement that getting a husband or in some cases a protector is for her (woman) the most important of undertakings. She will free herself from the paternal home, from her mother's hold, she will open up her future not by active conquest but by delivering herself up, passive and docile, into the hands of a new master."[9]

Ammu with her twins in her parents' house was like a fly in the milk detested and despised. Baby Kochamma, her aunt believed that "a divorced woman had no position at all."[10]

It was shocking for Ammu to observe that her children too were neglected and ill-treated. Isolated everywhere, she needed badly the company of someone who would bring some solace. And who else could she have turned to if it was not Velutha, the Paravan (the untouchable)? He would comfort her children as if he were their father. This brought her close to him. And transgressing social and caste bounds, she established a sexual relation with him which resulted in her banishment from Ayemenem house and catastrophic death of Velutha in police custody.

Arundhati Roy seems to imply that a woman's individual identity, her wishes, her desires do not have an honorable place even in the contemporary society which is predominantly caste and tradition bound.

For establishing sexual relationship with Velutha, the untouchable Ammu is convicted and punished but for the same crime Chacko, Ammu's brother, who established the sexual relationship with women labours of his factory, is acquitted. Besides Mammachi makes provision for a secret door in the Ayemenem house for women to enter and gratify Chacko's sexual needs and also paying them secretly. The discrimination surfaces only too glaringly. Roy seems to question Mammachi about her dual moral standards.

Divorced Ammu worked as hard as Chacko in the family factory. However, Chacko always let her feel that the factory really belonged to him and him alone and she didn't have any claim, whatsoever, in it.

Ammu suffered and suffered submissively without raising a banner of protest. It is the novelist who, through her character in the novel, held it against injustice to women throughout the world giving a message to the male dominated society.

She was confined and finally disowned and disinherited. She was forced to leave the house and take shelter in Bharat lodge in Allepy where she breathed her last in utter seclusion. The dignity of a funeral even was denied to her as the church refused to bury her. "Chacko had her wrapped in a dirty bedsheet and laid out on a stretcher."[11] She was reduced to a mere receipt number

Q 498673 in an electric crematorium where she was cremated and attended only by her daughter.

The story of persecution of Ammu under the male hegemony was turned upside down by her own daughter Rahel. Where Ammu was submissive and she accepted her fate as granted, Rahel was rebellious and aggressive. The kind of unkind atmosphere she was brought up in made her a nuisance at school. She was transferred from one school to another on account of her misconduct. She was blacklisted in Nazreth convent. She was caught outside her House mistress's garden gate decorating a knob of fresh cowdung with small flowers. At another time she was expelled on complaints from senior girls. She was accused of hiding behind doors and deliberately colliding with her seniors to know whether breasts hurt.

She could not win friendship with her classmates at the college of Architecture in Delhi and for this none else could be held responsible save herself. She was a depraved child right from the beginning. Her marriage with Larry McCaslin could not last. They were soon divorced. After that she worked as a waitress in an Indian restaurant in New York and later as a night clerk at a gas station outside Washington for several years. Only Rahel with her rebellious spirit could have done all these against overwhelming odds. Unlike her mother, she was rough and immodest. Her perversion and defiance are her own way of working out personal emancipation.

Postcolonial Indian women authors have raised varying ideals of feminist emancipation in relation to the roles that communities play in aiding or obstructing feminist freedom. Anita Desai's women characters valiantly rebel against patriarchal system to explore their own strengths. They do not think of the consequences such a rebellion would have on their lives. They challenge and fight whatever comes in their way of becoming free individuals. However, breaking away from the community makes them realise eventually the futility of such a rebellion which is not enough to make them complete. Very often, the act of running away in the "opposite direction"[12] culminates in their death, physical or metaphysical. What Desai seems to imply is that her women want freedom within the community of men and women. This is what brings fulfilment.

Mannu Bhandari portrays the helplessness of the women between community and freedom. Education and economic independence do help them rid themselves of humiliation issuing from dependent relationships with men. But, at the same time psychological dependence on men, family and the community is also felt. The novel *Bunty* and the play *Bina Diwaron ke Ghar* present the helplessness and confusion in women that arise due to discriminatory patriarchal attitudes towards them.

Ashapurna Devi considers men not just as agents of female oppression. She condemns women more than men. Chhaya Datar flouts all those who consider that the role of scripture is tremendous behind the subordination of women or that there is a flaw in women's nature. She thinks that the real cause behind the subordination is in their innate filial and maternal instincts. According to her a woman's maternal instincts, her spontaneous attachment to the members of her family, her respect for her husband, her natural abilities to manage her house are exploited in such a way that she is virtually made a slave of the man.

Arundhati Roy's *The God of Small Things* seems to convey that women's status in a patriarchal society in spite of all hue and cry for their equality and freedom has not materially changed. Men are still more equal than women.

References

1. Angela Miles & Finn Geraldine (eds), *Feminism, from Pressure to Politics*, Rawat Publications, Jaipur and New Delhi, 17.
2. Simone de Beauvoir, *The Second Sex* (Le deuxieme sexe), Paris trans. and ed. H.M. Parshley, London: Jonathan Cape, 1949.
3. Angela Miles & Finn Geraldine op.cit., p. 18.
4. Arundhati Roy,*The God of Small Things*, 39.
5. Ibid., p. 40.
6. Ibid., p. 42.
7. Ibid., p. 42.
8. Indranil Acharya, *New lights on Indian Women Novelists in English* (ed.), Dr. Amarnath Prasad, Sarup & Sons, New Delhi, 2003, p. 198.

9. Simone de Beauvoir, op.cit, London: Four Square Books, 1961, p. 352.
10. Arundhati Roy, TGOST, 45.
11. Ibid, p. 162.
12. Dr. Amarnath Prasad (ed.), *New lights on Indian Women Novelists in English* (Part I, Part II).

24

Faces of Neocolonialism: A Critique of Anita Nair's *Better Man*

—Sunila Pillai

Anita Nair, an emerging voice in the horizon of Indian English Fiction, echoes the continuum of history by opening up postcolonial concerns in her novels. Her *Better Man* helps the readers analyse the politics of neocolonialism. Kwame Nkrumah, the Ghanaian leader, in *Neocolonialism: The Last Stage of Imperialism* (1965) suggests:

> ...although independence has been achieved, education, economics and power systems have not moved on, in effect the land is still colonised and old values and rules still operate, even if only in the vestiges of colonial laws and in the mindsets of people who find it difficult to shake off colonial views and behaviours so soon. (Gina Wisker)

This notion of Nkrumah can be imported in the reading of *Better Man* to locate new patterns of colonial master-slave equation which have percolated into local culture. This paper is an attempt to analyse the society, culture and politics of Kerala which form the setting of Anita Nair's fictional world that clearly projects the symptoms of being infected with neocolonial viruses.

The setting of the novel, *Kaikurussi,* is a microcosm of India that witnesses the drama of confluence of colonial, postcolonial and neocolonial eras. The very opening of the novel reveals the colonial and neocolonial perspectives by way of the narrator, Bhasi, the painter who introduces himself as an animal, "a human lizard with brushes for claws and a can for a tail" (3), as against the suddenly rich, powerful Power House Ramakrishnan whose house has high brick walls and imposing metal gates in the village of bamboo fences and makeshift gates. The characters like Shankar, the tea club owner, Postman Unni, Barber Nanu, Che Kutty, the toddy seller Kamban, the Post Master Achuthan Nair, all reveal some colonial traits and tendencies at some point in the novel. Kaikurussi, with its innocent wild scenic beauty of mountains, forests, hills and rivers has been housed by the natives who find it hard to shrug off the colonial imperialistic system of existence.

Mukundan, the protagonist of the novel, is on a self-imposed exile from his native home in Kaikurussi to erase the ghost of insecurity and guilt of his mother, Parukkuty's mysterious death and his father, Achuthan Nair's high-handedness. His return to the village as an outsider who longs for a firm footing in the village echoes the ambition of colonial masters. His outsider colonial tag is expressive of the way he sells his ancestral paddy fields to Power House Ramakrishnan to strip himself of his nativity and become the member of the elite class, obsessed with rationality, sophistication and civilised life with no native strings. In response to his caretaker Krishnan Nair's criticism, Mukundan opines: "What am I going to do with all this when I die? Can I take it with me? Do I have children to safeguard my heritage and keep it intact for them?" (39)

Power House Ramakrishnan raises the ugly head of new imperialism by the acquisition of land and property with his newly acquired wealth to buy position and respect in Kaikurussi. From the fringes of poverty and 'marginalisation', he climbs the ladder of money and power to the 'centre' to generate a reversed colonial pattern:

> When a lottery ticket changed him into a rich man, perhaps the richest man in the village, the first thing he decided to do was to acquire land....Moreover, by buying the land that for generations had belonged to Mukundan's family, he would be buying himself a position in the village. (38-39)

Anita Nair's introduction of Achuthan Nair as a domineering father who battered and bruised the spirit of his son, Mukundan as a young boy configures the pattern and image of colonialism taking its first infant step in the four walls of our homes. On his return from serving the white imperialists in Burma, he takes a leaf from their history of domination and dons the garb of a neocoloniser who treats his son and wife as slaves.

This image creates a new pattern of violence and master-slave equation that creates embittered familial relations:

> The cane swished through the air as Mukundan had known it inevitably would....'Paru Kutty!' he hollered at the top of his voice. 'Look at your wonderful son, sniveling and standing in his own piss. He can't even take a few blows on his skin without piddling in his pants' (71).

Further, Achuthan Nair retains the pair of wooden clogs which he had worn in Burma. In Kaikurussi, he wore them as a testimony to who he was—a man who has seen the world, a man who is to be respected, a man whose authority is not to be questioned and who is on a colonial civilising mission.

Whenever postcolonial theory queries what Irene Genzier describes as "the Other directed nature of the reactions of the colonised and the need to struggle to free himself of this externally determined definition of Self" (Gendzier 1973, 23), it evokes categories which are reminiscent of Hegel's paradigms of the master-slave relationship. Hegel believes that human beings acquire identity or self-consciousness only through the recognition of others. Each self has before it another self in and through which it secures its identity but initially there is an enmity between these two confronting selves. Hegel maintains that the master and slave are locked in a compulsive struggle until the slave accepts his subjection to the victorious, recognisable master. The slave then becomes a dependable 'thing' whose very existence and identity is shaped by the master. Anita Nair in *Better Man* attempts to recover this colonial condition by revealing the master-slave relationship in the relationship of Achuthan Nair and Mukundan and Achuthan Nair and Krishnan Nair. The tendency of Mukundan to please and be accepted and recognised by his father by way of offering gifts of his liking highlights the slavish identity in Mukundan: "Nothing Mukundan ever did satisfied his father. He accepted the gift in the manner of God accepting homage to his greatness." (79). Krishnan Nair's adulation and loyalty to Achuthan Nair and the slavish pleasure he derives on being at his beck and call and pleasing him by cooking his favourite chicken curry smack of master-slave pattern of the colonial era.

A discussion on postcolonialism is not complete without a discourse on Orientalism. It becomes a discourse at the point at which it starts systematically, to produce stereotypes about the natives and their culture. These stereotypes confirm the necessity and desirability of colonialists by endlessly confirming their superiority over the positional inferiority of the natives and their practices. Philipose the postmaster, an outsider posted in Kaikurussi, serves as a constant reminder of the historical contents and continuity of oppression, domination and stereotyping of the marginalised. He wears the mantle of a neocoloniser by degrading and demeaning Kamban, the Harijan postmaster. Philipose emphatically challenges Kamban's efficiency and intelligence and leaves no stone unturned to harass and rebuke him in front of his colleagues and villagers. He strips him of all his dignity by commenting on his low status. He believes that as a representative of the marginalised native, Kamban needs corrective study by the master, Philipose. He construes Kamban and his community as a population of degenerate types on the basis of their caste-origin. He takes it upon him the civilising mission of the native Kamban that involves domination, oppression and humiliation. He barks:

> Why can't you do your duties? Why do I have to do everything....You are lazy and irresponsible, you know, that's what you are. This is what happens when you take useless people and give them responsibilities that they are not qualified to handle. But do the department heads realise all this? No, year after year, they give you promotions, special benefits. (162)

Further, apart from stereotyping native servitude, the fantasies of the colonial attitude of stereotyping often finds expression as in the horrifying stereotypes of savagery, mystery, exoticism and cruelty. The incident of a cat attacking and terrorising Philipose and the hammering, rattling sounds in the chilling darkness of the night in and around his house are easily connected to Kamban and his pact with the devil. Philipose tries to identify Kamban with black magic and effectively demonises the Dalit subject as the white master would do of a native Philipose explains these mysterious happenings to Mukundan in language that represents the apprehension of the colonial master of the wild native:

> Last night as the cat sat there staring resentfully, I realised who it reminded me of. Kamban. I tell you, Kamban and the cat are connected in some way. No wonder it hated me so much. (166)

If we accept postcolonial views of imperialism and colonialism, *Better Man* brings in the images of colonised and coloniser binary sets in the relationship between Bhasi and Power House Ramakrishnan. Power House Ramakrishnan's expedition to acquire Bhasi's land for the community hall, which is a symbol of development for the village and his reputation, is an invasion on the peaceful settlement of Bhasi. This expedition contains in it the story of the neocolonialist trying to control and rule over the less privileged native. Further neocolonialism works best with the help of hegemonic and coercive forces which take the mantle of politics, religion, development and class consciousness. When Bhasi resists the colonial attitude by not succumbing to the pressures of selling the land, Power House Ramakrishnan wields the sword of power and influence to warn him:

> Take my advice. Sell me the land. I have the support of all VIPs in the village. The temple board. The masjid committee. The village officer. The political parties. The young Men's Association for Culture. Everyone who is anyone in this village will back me. So if you don't sell me the land, I'll tell them why the community hall can't be built. I don't need to tell you what the consequences will be. All I say is, there will be no more work for you in this village. (288)

Even in the so-called postcolonial societies one can see the legacy of the oppression of the marginalised natives by the dominant power-hungry coloniser. The changing faces of colonialism become overtly clear in the disillusionment of Bhasi at the lack of support and resistance from the villagers, especially Mukundan with whom he bonds well. He introspects his concern:

> In the final reckoning they were all natives of this village, bonded by birth and banded together. "While I was the outsider. The one who could be dispensed with (289).

The transformation of Mukundan from an 'outsider' to the recognisable 'centred' Self of a native indicates once again the emergent trend of neocolonialism. Mukundan is elated at his inclusion in the community hall construction committee, a symbol of recognition among the native neocolonialists. This is where he wants so much to belong to, to feel important and to be appreciated. He wants to prove to his father that he had an identity of his own and that too an identity his father had cherished for him of being dominant and successful. But this new identity of Mukundan cripples the healed, uninhibited, peaceful self that he had attained with the help of Bhasi's alternative medicine, spiritual and psychological healing. He had risen from the deep chasm of a nervous wreck to that of a positive natural self with Bhasi's native wisdom and medicine. By transforming himself to a neocoloniser, he has not only disrespected the native wisdom and healing process but acts as a link in the coercive force that tries to unsettle and displace Bhasi, the subaltern subject who guides him towards a liberated and guilt-free life.

He argues with Bhasi:

> But you are just a settler....If I were you I would accept the offer as quickly as possible and scout for some land to buy somewhere around. (311-312.)

But his new identity in liaison with the hegemonic imperialists freezes and cripples his natural native identity. This forces him to keep his love affair with Anjana, a married woman on the brink of divorce, under wraps from society. His patriarchal-colonial attitude silences their healthy and progressive non-dualistic relationship. Anita Nair here echoes Gayatri Spivak's notion of speaking out against patriarchy's silencing and that of the coloniser. In her essay, "Can the Subaltern Speak?" Spivak elaborates contexts wherein contesting representational systems violently displace/silence the figure of the 'gendered subaltern'. She states:

> Between patriarchy and imperialism, subject-constitution and object-formation, the figure of a woman disappears, not into a pristine nothingness, but a violent shuttling which is the displaced figuration of the 'third-world woman' caught between tradition and modernisation. (*Gayatri Spivak*)

Anita Nair uses the language of the coloniser and of her own traditional and cultural background in new combinations in order to problematise the condition of silence attributed to the colonial subaltern female subject. Anjana's matriarchal background allows her to make choices regarding her life as a form of indigenous resistance and subversion of the colonial patriarchal attitude. Her subtle resistance by distancing herself from Mukundan for his cowardly act of sacrificing her on the altar of his quest for self-worth speaks volumes of the agency of cultural authenticity and native wisdom. Her matrifocal culture helps her choose her subversive act of resistance. She tells Mukundan, exposing his hypocrisy:

> You are a coward. A smug and completely self-absorbed coward who puts himself before anyone else and then uses his own feebleness of character to excuse it. What a great trick that is! To admit to your frailty so no one will condemn you later on. You disgust me. Please leave. (323)

Mukundan's greed for recognition, acceptance, importance and adulation blinds him to everything around him, even his very identity. When realisation dawns on him, he makes amends by embracing activism by gifting a part of his property to Bhasi. He reverses capitalist/coloniser urge of people like Power House Ramakrishnan by donating land instead of acquiring it. Thus, he transforms himself to a better man, by rupturing the class line of Kaikurussi:

> All my life I wanted to be my father's equal. But now I want more. I want to know what it is to love and to give. And, in turn, be loved. I don't want to wake up one morning and discover that I have frittered away my life chasing after ephemeral dreams....But nothing would make me happier than to have you living alongside me. I will wait for you, Bhasi. (354)

In his acceptance of Anjana wholeheartedly and without the fear of sanction of the villagers, he makes his choice and does what his conscience tells him. Nair captures Mukundan's transformation in a piece of free direct discourse:

> I shall let everyone see that I love Anjana, he told himself. But, more important, he would no longer allow his past to damn his passions. (356).

Further, his self-realisation and self identity sparks in the form of resistance backed with ideological thought and courage when feels that he should do something against the community hall, a symbol of colonialism and a statement of his cowardice. But the new Mukundan wants no remnants of his past colonial/feudalist identity. So, he decides to show his resistance by deciding to blow up the symbol of colonialism, the community hall, there by changing the face of life.

> Within everything rests a power to ignite, to explode, and to change the face of life. All that was necessary was to kindle and set it alright. (357)
>
> The edifice to the man he had been would no longer exist. This was the moment that had eluded him all his life. When he would become a man. A better man than he ever had been. (361).

Mukundan, through his psychological resistance, cures the symptoms of a colonial unwholesome alliance between power and money and the residual traces and memories of subordination.

Works Cited

Gandhi, Leela, *Postcolonial Theory: A Critical Introduction*. India: OUP, 1999.

Nair, Anita, *Better Man*.

Nelson, Cary and Grossberg, Lawrence (eds.), *Marxist Interpretations of Culture*, Basingstoke, MacMillan Education, 1988.

Spivak's Gayatri, "Can the Subaltern Speak?" in *Marxist Interpretations of Culture*, eds Cary Nelson and Lawrence Grossberg, Basingstoke.

Wisker, Gina, *Key concepts in Postcolonial Literature*, London: Palgrave Macmillan, 2007.

25

Salman Rushdie's *Shalimar The Clown*: A Trilogy of Innocence, Betrayal and New Beginning.

—Devasree Chakravarti** & **G.A. Ghanshyam

Postcolonialism or postmodernism is the term of reference that has been used to describe and dissect critically the New Literatures of the world. Postcolonialism is but a legacy of our colonial past, a legacy of the subjugation and dominance of the colonised by the coloniser that gave way to de-colonisation after the Second World War. The term 'postcolonialism' is subject to various connotations, however to understand the concept in terms of literary practice it can be referred to as, "... different forms of representations, reading practices and values" (Rai, 2005:1).

Postmodernism is a concept that can be referred to as the direct outcome of this modern postcolonial world, a world that has been a witness to mass migration, cross-cultural encounter and the amalgamation of various cultures into a hybrid multicultural society. This has resulted as Rushdie says in *The Moor's Last Sigh*, "That most profound of our needs, to our need for flowing together, for putting an end to frontiers, for the dropping of the boundaries of the self" (Rushdie, 2006:433).

This postcolonial, postmodern world is one where myriad worlds and experiences flow, seeping into each other as there are no boundaries or barriers anymore. Today the world is a globalised world where borders have ceased to exist. All concepts of conventionality and rules are broken, and new ones created to give expression to this new phenomenon of rule breaking and free world. Art and literature of this modern world also reflects this trend as is evident in the fiction of Salman Rushdie.

Salman Rushdie is an eminent postmodernist. A pioneer in the field of Indian English Diasporic Literature, Rushdie's fiction accurately portrays the complex and confusing postcolonial, postmodern worlds. All his novels represent his interpretation of history and the world, and their influence on life and society.

A postmodern novelist that he is, Rushdie reflects the rebellion from conventionality. Like most postmodern writers his fiction too has a touch of unreality and vastness that is needed to project contemporary reality, a reality devoid of borders.

In his latest novel, *Shalimar the Clown* (Rushdie, 2005), he voices this concept of a borderless world and its implications:

> Everywhere was now a part of everywhere else. Russia, America, London, Kashmir. Our lives, our stories, flowed into one another's, were no longer our own, individual, discrete. This unsettled people. There were collisions and explosions. The world was no longer calm. (37)

So even the idyllic setting of a small remote village of Kashmir is not immune to this effect of different worlds colliding, exploding and unsettling its social and cultural fabric, its identity as well as the identity of its people.

The novel is an ode to the simple, idyllic life of the valley, the land of Rushdie's roots, a land of eternal beauty and charm, that, "... as lost...like paradise, ...Kashmir, in a time before memory" (4). Portrayed as the ideal world with its unique way of life, its 'Kashmiriyat', where differences and divisions were non-existent; a world untouched by hatred and communalism.

Peace, love and brotherhood characterise the Kashmiri way of life. It is a life and world of innocence that is betrayed by its own people, and slowly walks down the path to destruction as embodied in the life of Shalimar, the protagonist and his village, Pachigam. Not only Shalimar, but also the other main characters of the novel are highly symbolical, for Rushdie believes that history and the individual, "... interpenetrate and that is how the writer needs to examine them, the one in the context of the other." (Rushdie, 1984,57)

Pachigam, a small village in Kashmir situated in the serene surroundings beside the river Muskadoon, is a quiet, peaceful village. Happy and contented, the people in the village live their lives in blissful oblivion only to wake up to the harsh realities of life when insurgency first raised its ugly head in the valley in the form of Kabalis from Pakistan. The seed of distrust and hatred sown by the fundamentalists and extremists, the by-products of a savage and cruel dissection of the nation, gradually take enormous forms and engulfs the whole valley in its fire. Partition of the nation did not only carve out two nations out of one but it also created a sharp division between two communities. Geographical as well as psychological partition took place, the echo of which still reverberates in the minds and hearts of two nations, two communities and people.

Through the novel, Rushdie expresses "...sadness for the ideal that has been lost in Kashmir and in so many parts of the Muslim world, the ideal of tolerance and secular pluralism" (Cowley, 2005, 27). The drastic transition from innocence to betrayal has been represented by the author through the character of Shalimar, the clown. Son of the village headman, Shalimar is a sweet innocent boy, "clown prince of the performing troupe." (50); a young boy madly in love with Pandit Kaul's daughter, Bhoomi or Boonyi as she prefers to be called.

Shalimar and Boonyi's love blooms in the beautiful and pristine environs of the Kashmir valley hidden from the eyes of their elders. When people find out, they uphold the values of 'Kahmiriyat' and bless the young couple. But Boonyi is far from happy. Claustrophobia grips her, and she realises rather too late that she wants to escape. "She knew then that she would do anything to get out of Pachigam..." (114) The free unbridled spirit inherited from her mother coupled with her youthfulness ill-marks the love story of Shalimar and Boonyi, giving it a tragic turn.

Increasing influence of alien presence on the Kashmiri landscape slowly starts corroding and degrading the values of the valley, the 'Kashmiriyat'. This influence can be seen in the radical preaching's of Bulbul Fakh, the 'iron mullah'; and in the arrival of Maximilian Ophuls on the scene, the representative American presence in the valley. And thus unfolds the tragic events of the tale.

> ... the story of Max and Boonyi's doomed relationship [which] can be read as a study in human vanity, selfishness and aggressive mutual need, but also as a parable of the carelessness of American intervention on the subcontinent. Beware the return of the repressed, he [Rushdie] seems to be saying, in often unexpected and violent forms. (Cowley, 2005, 27)

Mesmerised by Boonyi's beauty, Max arranges for Boonyi and her friends to give a dance performance in Delhi. The performance is only a pretext for Ophuls to get close to Boonyi. Boonyi had been waiting for this opportunity only. Her father used to say, "The dance of the shadow planets is the dance of the struggle within us, the inner struggle of moral and social choice" (48). And she chooses to transgress the moral and social code, opting to go, "... in search of a future and though she had thought of it as an opening it had been a closing, ..." (367).

Boonyi enters into a relationship with Max in the hope of a better life. As for her heart, she feels that she was, "... tearing it out and breaking it into little bits and throwing it away ..." (194). Though she thought that by her action she had gained release from the village existence that she so detested, yet the stirrings of her heart never let her escape the Kashmir embedded in her very being, her soul. She could not tear out memories of her valley, and her husband who still loved her. As is customary with such superficial relationships the attraction started waning. She became increasingly alienated and depressed in her "liberated captivity" (201), finding solace in drugs and food.

Her desire to excel herself was but a fantasy lived in the shadow of the glamour and glitter of elite society, which was bound to shatter hopelessly one day. She was but a simple, naive village girl with big dreams in her eyes that were terribly misdirected. The path she chose for herself, sooner or later had to lead only to one destination, and that was imminent disaster for its traveler. Like Ila of *The Shadow Lines*, a novel by Amitav

Ghosh, Boonyi, "... desires freedom from a middle class [rustic] orthodoxy, but she discovers that the free world she had tried to build for herself was not free from the squalor of betrayal" (James: 155). Boonyi's disastrous flirtation with desire led to an avalanche of catastrophe not only in her life but also in the lives of the people related to her. She loses her identity and tumbles down the path of complete psychotic degeneration, waiting alone in the wilderness for death to truly free her.

Freedom was what Boonyi desired, "But free isn't free of charge" (253). The freedom that she chooses for herself is 'false freedom', an illusion, a bait to tempt her to sin, which she, "... like Eve, is easily tempted and eagerly accepts the Ambassador's offer of a change...." (Mathur, 2007, 92). In the character of Boonyi we find the eagerness for liberation, lured by which she symbolising Kashmir, loses herself courting ruination as a result.

The innocence of life in the valley gradually transgresses the boundaries of that innocence and simplicity in the name of false hopes and dreams, and is ultimately betrayed in the process. Betrayal leads to a loss, a loss of identity and hopes, leading to a metamorphosis of life and characters. "Self-creation in times of conflict, one of Rushdie's themes ..." (Roth, 2005:19) is represented through all the main characters who undergo and grow as per the changes in circumstances. No doubt, "Metamorphosis was the secret heart of life" (56), but the metamorphosis that occurs in the novel almost but extinguishes the very life, giving place to death instead.

Shalimar, Boonyi's husband, represents this metamorphosis from innocence to betrayal in his transformation from an innocent village boy, an artist into a hardcore killing machine.

> He was as dynamically physical a comedian as ever, but there was a new ferocity in him that could easily frighten people instead of making them laugh. (231)

Leaving his life and family, Shalimar joins the extremists pretending to believe in their cause, but all the while preparing himself for the ultimate aim of his life, to kill Maximilian Ophuls. Listening to the Iron Mullah, he realises that:

> By crossing the mountains they had passed through a curtain and stood now on the threshold of the world of truth, which was invisible to most men. (266)

The 'curtain' is an important symbol that hides as well as separates. A similar curtain or 'membrane' is the dividing factor present in Rushdie's other novel *The Ground Beneath Her Feet*, through which Ormus crosses over to emerge into an alien land and culture. A symbol often used as a metaphor for 'Transculturalism', it is a boundary that separates two worlds or cultures; and here the curtain separates the innocent, beautiful, multicultural and hybrid world of old Kashmir from the violent, betrayed and divided world of the new terror stricken Kashmir. It divides the actual truth from the illusion of misguided ideology.

By crossing over to the other side, Shalimar takes his first step to avenge the betrayal of his wife. A true performer that he is, Shalimar very easily manages to assure his comrades of his affiliation to their ideology:

> Shalimar the clown rose to his feet and tore off his garments. "Take me!" he cried. "Truth, I am ready for you!" He was a trained performer, a leading actor in the leading bhand pather troupe in the valley, and so of course he could make his gestures more convincing. (267-8)

Mindanao, a Filipino Muslim in the group however, sees through Shalimar's pretence when he says, "I see through you like window. You are not man of God." (269)

The fight for a religious cause just provides a platform for Shalimar to cross over to the other side, to reach his target in America and eliminate him. Like the crusades that were undertaken in bygone times, the recent fight is also for power and possession. The author here tries to unearth the hypocrisy of war and bloodshed behind every fight, because violence begets violence. Life can be shaped out of love not violence, irrespective of any kind of faith or religious beliefs.

Here Rushdie is again reinstating the bare truth of modern life wherein, it is the furies that are ruling men and life everywhere, and so he expresses, "An age of fury was dawning and only the enraged could shape it"(272). Today every nook and corner of the world is under the grip of the wrath. Reasons may differ, but the reactions are always one of rage and disaster, be it in Kashmir or in New York, for now, "Everyone's story was a part of everyone else's." (269)

So the story that began in a small remote village of Kashmir progresses to cross half the globe to reach its climax in America. The American presence is the catalyst that escalates this dance of the furies across the globe. Max represents this presence for he is not only a goodwill ambassador but also has a secret identity as well, of being involved in the exchange of weapons between America and extremist groups.

Shalimar is the resultant fury in this case. The degeneration of Boonyi from her pinnacle of beauty to a psychotic figure in the woods does not evoke any sympathy or cool down the embers of rage in Shalimar's heart. Knowledge of the ambassador's secret dealings and his views on Kashmir fuels his rage further and gives new life to his ambition. After killing Boonyi ruthlessly in cold blood, he becomes free to pursue his final target.

The journey from innocence to betrayal reaches its final stages through the pathway of complete destruction. Pachigam ceases to exist. Charged with harbouring extremists, the village bears the full brunt of the atrocities of the armed forces. Everyone is killed, people and life is totally obliterated from the place where love had once bloomed and blossomed. "The village of Pachigam still existed on maps of Kashmir, but that day it ceased to exist anywhere else, except in memory." (309)

The furies thus find a new home in the action of the armed forces meant for protection of people. Rushdie here indicates the pathetic situation of the people of Kashmir who have to bear the atrocities of both the terrorists as well as the forces. Life for them has left no option open for them to live in freedom and without fear:

> undone by the twin forces of nationalism and religious fundamentalism. As usual in Rushdie's novels, these forces are not the enemies of enlightenment as much as they are the enemies of freedom, and that means they are the enemies of the natural. (Roth, 2005,19)

It is not only fundamentalism or extremism, which proves to be detrimental for life and country; nationalism can also endanger life and freedom when taken in the stringent sense concerning itself only with selfish aim of possession and power. Bound in these twin chains, an individual loses all, identity, liberty and life. The fury unleashed by their combined powers creates only havoc and destruction wherever they exist. And these furies find another abode in the heart of India or Kashmir.

Shalimar after finally reaching America moves closer to his target by getting employed as Ophuls's driver. The knife in his hand that had long been thirsty for revenge ultimately finds its target when Shalimar kills Maximilian Ophuls at the doorstep of his daughter.

India is also Kashmira, the daughter of Boonyi and Max. Her existence gives a new twist to the revenge tale of Shalimar, for her presence makes his revenge incomplete, for early in the story Shalimar had vowed that if Boonyi ever betrayed him, he would not only kill her and her lover but also the child if any from the relationship.

The death of her father leaves India shocked and furious:

> Blood called out for blood and she wanted the ancient Furies to descend shrieking from the sky and give her father's unquiet spirit peace. (331)

Like her mother who left home and family for the sake of a false and borrowed identity, India leaves for Kashmir in quest of her true identity. She returns not as India but as Kashmira:

> Kashmir lingered in her, however, and his arrest in America, his disappearance beneath the alien cadences of American speech, created turbulence in her that she did not at first identify as culture shock. She no longer saw this as an American story. It was a Kashmiri story. It was hers. (372)

To avenge the death of her mother and father, Kashmira targets Shalimar not with arrows or knives but with her letters that were her "arrows of hate" (374). She slowly kills Shalimar's ego, which is the real cause of her parents' death. Yet his hurt ego fails to find satisfaction in their death because his efforts to obliterate their presence are negated by Kashmira, a living reminder of both Boonyi and Max.

Hatred can never extinguish the Life Force. It lives on in the hearts of people, like it does in Kashmira. Kashmira embodies the emergence of a new beginning from the chaos and turmoil of betrayal to the arrival of a bright new dawn, full of hope and regeneration. Her presence is an indication by the author that Kashmir will not be lost, it will emerge from the darkness into the light of true freedom and hope for all its people, a new life.

Kashmira symbolises this new beginning in her realisation and acceptance of her true identity, in her love for Yuvraj, and ultimately in her emerging victorious by executing the hatred and violence of Shalimar. She was no longer a prisoner of fury when she lets her arrow find its mark. "She was not fire but ice."(382) She had already killed Shalimar with the glimpse of truth, and the one she kills with her arrow at the end of the novel is but a shadow of that man.

"...grappling imaginatively with the shock of 9/11 and the wars that have followed." (Cowley, 2005, 17), Rushdie has portrayed the recent tragic history of Kashmir with poignancy and sensitivity in the novel. In the story of his characters is intertwined the story of Kashmir, its life and culture, and the degeneration of this Paradise into Hell. Making the 'personal bleed into the political', Rushdie has once again voiced his concern for the modern world at large and Kashmir in particular, lamenting the loss of love, innocence and brotherhood.

Shalimar looks to several beginnings: reflecting on what has been lost in Kashmir, it also looks forward to a time when the words Muslim and Hindu will once more be merely "descriptions" rather than "divisions." (Cowley, 2005, 27)

The novel is not only an odyssey from innocence to betrayal but also an affirmation and belief on the resilience and strength of the human spirit, a belief in the future. Truly a trilogy of innocence, betrayal and new beginning, Shalimar the Clown is a story portraying the lifecycle of death in life and life in death, a perpetual cycle of birth, destruction and regeneration.

It represents a new life, a new beginning with the dissolution of all divisions and segments. Now, "There was no India. There was only Kashmira, and Shalimar the clown." (398) The multicultural, hybrid world is welcomed on the horizon, that has no place for any kind of divisions or borders. All divisions dissolve and disintegrate paving the way for the reign of Humanism, for the victory of the essential Life Force present in all of us.

Works Cited

Cowley, Jason, "From here to Kashmir", Rev. *Of Shalimar the Clown*. The Guardian Weekly, Vol.173 No.14 Sep. 2005, 27.

James, Louis, "Shadow Lines: Cross-Cultural Perspectives in the Fiction of Amitav Ghosh", *Indian Literature Today,* ed. Dhawan, 155.

Mathur, O.P., "Salman Rushdie's Shalimar the Clown: The Enigma of Terrorism", *Points of View,* Vol. XIV, No.1 Summer 2007, 92.

Rai, G., "Postcolonialism: Its Meaning and Significance", *The SPIEL Journal of English Studies,* Vol.1 No.2 July 2005, 1.

Roth, Marco, "Give the People what they want", *Rev. of Shalimar the Clown, The Times Literary Supplement,* No. 5345 Sep. 9, 2005, 19.

Rushdie, Salman, *The Moor's Last Sigh,* London: Vintage Books, 2006, 433.

____________, *Shalimar the Clown,* London: Jonathan Cape, 2005. All Parenthetical references of the text are to this edition.

____________, interview by Gordon Wise, *Gentleman,* Feb.1984, 57

26

J.M. Coetzee's *Disgrace*: A Study in Transformation of Consciousness

—*Madhu Kamra*

Art is something more than transmission of ideas, an imprint of cultural and racial temperaments. It may, as Nietzsche argues, tame man's understanding to the demand of the reality around or it may be an interpretation of "reality to men and men to themselves". Tolstoy in his essay, *What is Art,* declared with profound observations that it is "the transmission of emotions." *Disgrace* affirms in its intellectual depth, Nietzsche and Tolstoy's intellectual and profound truths. Here the aesthetic sensibilities come out fresh and the emotional response embodies the pleasure of reading a genuine book of art. To an intelligent reader the novel holds moral and philosophical debate issues and there is sufficient excitement and compulsion to embrace critical process.

The identity problem is a common probe to most of the African writers of postcolonial period. In a transitional society the advent of technology has led to the movement of the people from villages to cities in search of job opportunities. This social and psychological mobility has affected the tribal or group solidarity, and an individual in this kind of transitional society is divided in his loyalities to himself and his community. Fanon states that postcolonial literature aims at capturing the ills of colonialism which in turn aims at "de-culturation through the process of a systematic elimination of raison d'etre for the colonised."

Coetzee as a novelist of colonial consciousness reveals the hegemonic phase of colonialism. This phase is well described by Jan Mohamed as "By contrast, in the hegemonic phase (or neocolonialism) the natives accept a version of the coloniser's entire system of values, attitudes, morality, institutions, and more important, mode of production." Homi J. Bhabha calls such writings " a mutation, a hyrbrid". Neverthless, Coetzee's *Disgrace* as a postcolonial novel echoes the message that political change can do almost nothing to eliminate human misery. The psychological basement and physical torment endured by David, shows a portrait of the new South Africa, where life is quiet and brutal and the ultimate cry is that of "grace and love".

Born in Cape Town, South Africa on February 9, 1940, Coetzee is the first author to win the prestigious 'Booker Award' twice. On 25 October 1999, this South African novelist was awarded the Booker Prize for the second time for his novel *Disgrace*. The other shortlisted novels over which *Disgrace* prevailed were *Fasting, Feasting* by Anita Desai, *Headlong* by Michael Frayn, *Our Fathers* by Andrew Hagan, *The Map of Love* by Ahdaf Sourif and *The Balck Water Lightship* by Colm Tobin.

Disgrace, a Booker Prize winning novel, is a heartbreaking one about grace and love shared individually and in its own recognisable individual ways by David Lurie and his daughter Lucy. Situating his character David Lurie in the fold of a crisis, Coetzee explores "What it means to be human". The lateral roots of his psychological abasement and physical torment lies in his insatiable desire to relate himself to Melaine (his student) after having failed in realising his being in his relation with Rosalind (his wife) and Soraya (a whore.) At the outset David comes out a full flesh human being, an English professor to whom the primary essence of love and sex defeats and the meaning is fathomed at the close of the novel when subjected to disgrace he rises to 'grace', which defines the art and dignity of living.

With David as a central character, Coetzee explores how a man of eminence may be a nonentity in a moral and philosophical way. Satirically he is depicted as an authority in 'Communication Skills' but ironically the basics of communication, which makes a fulsome living, is yet a remote territory in which fate would soon drive him in. He imagines himself with a disgraced face, a life no worth than an ugly reptile or a filthy animal. He imagines Melanie and his colleagues shuddering over him "as one shudders at a cockroach in the washbasin, in the middle of a night" and wonders how he can tame his sexual desires. The denouncement of David comes in the first early pages of the novel and much narration is devoted as to how David confesses his guilt but refuses to yield to pressure, to repent publicly, resigns and retreats to an isolated small holding of his daughter Lucy. 'Guilt' stares at Lurie's face that three rapists assault Lucy during passive helpless presence. Lucy "ashamed of herself" recedes into self-confinement. She refuses to go to the market and David for the sake of his daughter "endures the stares of the curious, responding politely to those friends of Lucy who choose to commiserate....:"[1]

This terrible sickness now confronts Lucy double-faced. The society declares him a moral and spiritual sinner and the "the sin and the crime" directed to his daughter staring with cruel eyes. The target of legislation now upsets his soul; he accuses his 'sexual self' as violent and unlicensed for the first time. This psychological and moral phenomenon gains visibility and meaning once the three rapists victimise Lurie's daughter. John Caroll in his book *Guilt* says:

> The existence of sensitivity in human relationship means that moral guilt is easy to provoke, and equally that remorse and desire to repair are even at hand.[2]

Lucy senses the intention of the rapists who poured hatred on her as a show of resentment for trespassing their boundaries of society, culture and 'living', she feels:

> They see themselves as debt collectors." Why should I be allowed to live here without paying?...When it comes to man and sex, you are a man; you ought to know... isn't it a bit like killing?[3]

As a matter of fact, guilt is the distiller, David is now ' a protective father' and not ' a body' enslaved to 'sex'. To channel his guilt in a viable way of life, he takes up a penance by sacrificing his career, his world of glamour, a quest for academic research and settles down in Grahams town to provide her companionship, parental love and humane refuge. The vital question now is, "Did guilt demand a righter answer?"

The archeology of David's trauma makes *Disgrace* a novel of intense feelings. David's experience, which schools him into a matured consciousness, constitutes its philosophical base. David's mutilated self (after Lucy's rape) initiates a soul-searching phase, yielding a better reasoning and a sensitive being who stands now fresh and eminently impressive. The traditional concept of romantic love is not communicated rather love and sexuality are clinically probed into through a microscope to seal the boundaries between the two. Lust is the modern version of love and the novelist lashes at it. He candidly admits:

> Repentance is neither here not there. Repentance belongs to another world, to another universe of discourse.[4]

This is how Coetzee records with fluidity the psychological metamorphosis that gradually glides through the fluidity of narration making a sensitive report of change at work within Lurie. Coetzee makes this change audible through his effective characterisation, with striking narration and neat and logical syntax, resounding with the "tick of a clock in a man's soul."

The novel is transparently plain. The setting with the use of local colour adds credibility to the surface and deep design of the novel. There is a noticeable "spiritual affinity" between the landscape and the changing climate of David and his daughter's lives. The meticulously detailed environment whether of Cape Town, George or Grahams town is not merely a background to the eventful happenings in the lives of the major characters but is a reflection of the "many vistas of a crowded larger world." Care is taken to avoid lavish strings of adjectives in the exposition of the physical background. Professor Lathrop suggests that the setting has become even more important in contemporary fiction because we increasingly recognise a man's background as one of the factors that shaped him. The active pressure of environment in forming personality is widely acknowledged now. The setting is seen as a force; the plot is often represented not as a thing in itself, but as something caused and conditional, possible and characteristic only in it's own milieu. Hence, the greater demand to have the setting authentic and realistic.

The book is in racy style, with intelligible details running one after the other in quick succession. Care is taken to avoid a heavy traffic of images, thoughts and details and Coetzee appears to be an ascetic who has subordinated the rules for writing properly. He seems to echo what Conrad had declared as his creed in the preface to *The Nigger of the Narcissus:*

> My purpose is by the power of the written word to make you hear, to make you feel-it is before all to make you see.

A scrutiny of Coetzeeian sentences bears this mark:

1. "Women can be surprisingly forgiving."[5]
2. "Eating is a ritual and rituals make things easier."[6]
3. Vengeance is like a fire, the more it devours the hungrier it grows."[7]
4. "Life from moment to moment is not as before."[8]

These sentences carry a sense of immortality transcending present, past and future with a heavy rhythm of knowledge and illumination.

To sum up, *Disgrace* is a representation of life as a victim of natural instincts, malignantly feeding upon the normalcy of those around and later upon consciousness within. It is a work of art in its own right for the universal validity confirms the expansive dynamism, the novel metaphorically ends in the triumph of both love and goodness; and the triumph of the integration of the 'man' and the "father figure". It tells us as to what is the strength of good novel promises to use T.S. Eliot's term 'superior amusement'. The fullness of his creative vision makes us feel what Srinivas Iyengar describes as:

> We must always come back to the soul quality in literature, for without it we have not literature but only bundle of dead words. This soul quality is the spark that gives life to literature and keeps it alive... great literature must, by the very intensity of its presentation of human characters and actions, transport the reader to the imaginative plain where soul communicates with soul, and rounded and serene apprehension of the true inwardness and rich manifoldness of life is possible.[9]

References

1. J.M. Coetzee, *Disgrace*, London, Secker and Warbug, 1999, p. 115.
2. John Caroll, *Guilt*, England, Routledge & Kegan Paul 1985, p. 17.
3. J M. Coetzee, *op.cit.*, p. 158.
4. Ibid., p. 58
5. Ibid., p. 69
6. Ibid., p. 111.
7. Ibid., p. 112
8. Ibid., p. 113.
9. Srinivas Iyengar, *The Adventures of Criticism*, New Delhi, Creative Book, 1995, p. 35.

27

Character Study Of Leela Benare in Vijay Tendulkar's *Silence! The Court Is In Session*

—S.K. Navin

Unlike an ordinary common human being, who may or may not react to things occurring in his surroundings, a sensitive writer is surely affected and moved by the ripples they form. The impressions create deep and often vibrant emotions in his mind which later find expression in several forms of artistic creation. The writer with a keen and genuine feel of social responsibility is usually fearless and intrepid and not ashamed of upbraiding the social follies and weaknesses. He reflects his society and its different moods and colours.

Vijay Tendulkar, a prolific writer for the last four decades, presents in his plays the middle class individual pitched against a hostile urban society of Bombay. Like the Urdu writer Saadat Hasan Manto and many realistic writers, Tendulkar portrays life as he finds it through his characters,their manners and behaviour. *Silence!The Court is in Session* is a satire on modern urban middle class society which is represented by the characters like Mr. Kashikar, the Chairman of The Sonar Moti Tenement (Bombay) Progressive Association, Mrs. Kashikar, house wife, Karnik, an actor in the experimental theatre, Ponkshe, Sukhatme, Rokde, Prof. Damle, Samant and Leela Benare—all belonging to a theatre group. The play exposes their sham orthodox nature and hypocritical behaviour. The theatre group in the play which comes to perform at a village is a miniscule cross-section of middle class society.

> Their characters, dialogues, gestures and even mannerisms reflect their petty, circumscribed existences fraught with frustrations and repressed desires that find expression in their malicious and spiteful attitudes towards their fellow beings.[1]

The play holds up a mirror in which we can surely see the weakest yarn of morality the society is composed of. Selfishness, seduction, character assassination is the goal of the world. The middle class people take immense delight in scandals and are not even ashamed of their coarse and mean behaviour.

Leela Benare, the central female figure and the protagonist of the play, is persecuted by the selfish and savage people of the society who plundered shamelessly the treasure of her body and made her pregnant. Her own maternal uncle seduced her when she was only fourteen and as Benare claims she didn't know what sin was. It appears that the playwright has cast her character to draw the readers' and viewers' sympathy. But to my mind Benare cannot be fully absolved of the sin of adultery that she committed. She cannot say she didn't understand the meaning behind the praise of her bloom everyday by her uncle. Her monologue at the end of the play throws some light on this aspect. She says:

> I was in love with my mother's brother. But in our strict house, in the prime of my unfolding youth, he was the one who came close to me. He praised my bloom everyday. He gave me love....How was I to know that if you felt like breaking yourself into bits and melting into one with someone—if you felt that just being with him gave a whole meaning to life—and if he was your uncle, it was a sin.[2]

It is true that she was drifted towards her uncle by adolescent love without giving much reason to the relation compelled by the sheer force of physical attraction. But that she was trespassing into a prohibited region she must be conscious of. A girl of fourteen cannot deny being ignorant of social and family relations.

Benare claims to be ignorant, whereas she herself says:

> I insisted on marriage. So I could live my beautiful dream openly. Like everyone else! But all of them—my mother too—were against it. And my brave man turned tail and ran. Such a rage—I felt such a rage against him then—I felt like smashing his face in public and spitting on it![3]

The passage glaringly underlines the fact that Benare understood well the meaning of marriage and sex.

Benare again falls in love as a grown woman with Prof. Damle and claims that her love was worship. It was love for an unusual intellect. So far it goes it is allright. But it doesn't go very far. Prof. Damle does sex with her and makes her pregnant. But he is not ready to give her the status of a wife for his reputation would be at stake. And moreover he has a family of his own. The question is why there was a need of offering her body on the altar of worship. Love could have flourished on the intellectual or spiritual plane. It could have prospered on a platonic or emotional plane. But, no. For Benare offering of the body was important. She seems eager to offer her body to please and appease her intellectual god. This is nothing but using a cunning known weapon against the man that Prof. Damle is. Towards the end of the play in her monologue while making a noble defence, she projects herself to be his adorer and makes him the person who sexually exploited her.

> It isn't love at all—it's worship! But it was the same mistake. I offered up my body on the altar of my worship. And my intellectual god took the offering—and went his way. He

> didn't want my mind, or my devotion—he didn't care about them! He wasn't a god. He was a man. For whom everything was of the body, for the body![4]

She cannot be so innocent as she projects herself in the play. Once she became aware of Prof. Damle's intention, she could have snapped her relations. She could have moved away from him. It is nothing less than a bold attempt to throw dust into the eyes of the reader-audience and win sympathy.

The playwright seems to have intended to win sympathy for Leela Benare. She has been portrayed as a teacher of outstanding calibre for whom public and private domains are two distinct areas. The one has nothing to do with the other. As an individual teacher she is sincere, honest and even meticulous. She is punctual, dutiful, gentle and generous. Above all she loves her profession. It is quite touching to hear her cry when she comes to know that her expulsion from her job is seriously considered. She says:

> Life is not worthy of life. Hold an enquiry against life. Sack it from its job! But why? Why? Was I slack in my work? I just put my whole life into working with the children.... I loved it!.[5]

However, it seems to be a justified step to expel her from the job of teaching in the school. She is morally a corrupt woman and should not be allowed to vitiate the school atmosphere creating unhealthy impressions on the young minds with her amorous episodes known everywhere.

It is true a person has an urge of the body and that needs to be fulfilled for very many healthy reasons. Who says no to this? Institution of marriage is there WITH social sanction. Lewdness has no end. If it is allowed unrestrained, it will create a social anarchy and disharmony and threaten the very foundations on which the society is based. A few Benares will spoil the social texture and the society will go to abysmal hell of immorality.

Prof. Damle, though he himself didn't come to Benare to quench his hunger for sex, is an unscrupulous man who used Benare's body to gratify his sexual desire and made her pregnant. The society expects from him to be a role model for his students. He is expected to be governed by his conscience and social ethics which he has thrown to the winds. He doesn't care. He couldn't keep a control on his nerves and accepted Benare's body as an offering to satisfy his lust. He, too, cannot be absolved of the sin of adultery.

Besides, characters like Mr. and Mrs. Kashikar, Sukhatme, Karnik, Ponkshe, Rokde and others join together and persecute Miss Benare in the mock trial laying first the charge of infanticide and later exposing personal and private affairs of her life.

Miss Benare who is to perform the role of a prisoner in the mock trial is held an accused with all seriousness as the play develops gradually. She reaches the point from where her escape is not possible and finally mutters in mortal pain a few punctuated sentences that the child in her womb will "need her...a father to call his name—a house—to be looked after—he must have a good name."

But Mr. Kashikar, the judge, pronounces the sentence that "no memento of her sin will remain in future and her child in her womb shall be destroyed." Benare, however, is not ready and she will not allow it to happen. Thus, she becomes a voice of the thousands of women in the world afflicted from the same cruel and unfortunate fate. The women around the world must be warned against making an offering of their body to Prof. Damle's kind, for they would never come to their help and the women would get their name tarnished.

References

1. Banerji Arundhati, *Introduction, Five Plays,* Oxford, Ninth Impression, 2007, viii.

2. Tendulkar Vijay, *Silence! The Court is in Session, Five Plays*, Oxford, p. 118.
3. Ibid., p. 117.
4. Ibid., p. 118.
5. Ibid., p. 116.

28

Post-Colonial Perspective in the Plays of Girish Karnad

—Priti D. Thakre

The term Indian Writing in English has recently attained respectable academic status. It is beyond doubt that the department of Indian Literature in English has now become a full fledged one, enriched with diverse writings. It is true that genuine Indian writer has to convey his own sensibility in a language which is not his own, if and when he chooses to write in English. Into the midst of this confusion came many grandmasters who witnessed the spectacular scenes of Indian Renaissance. These grandmasters have successfully made use of language capable of expressing the postcolonial predicament.

Postcolonial is the term that covers all the culture affected by the imperial process from the movement of colonisation to the present day. And postcolonial literature includes the cultural product as emerging out of the experiences of colonisation while in assuming, expressing or building a new identify as that of postcolonial, there is a conscious break away from the established system. Postcolonial criticism and theory interrogate the relations between culture and imperialism. It is concerned with creating consciousness for the marginalised and with recovering lost cultural awareness. In Indian context post-colonialism also describes a wide range of heterogeneous societies which themselves represent many different ethnic groups. In this paper

I have attempted to focus very briefly on the postcolonial perspective in the plays of Girish Karnad. How is the status of women in the institution of marriage and what is her predicament?

Modern women's predicament is focused on in Girish Karnad's *Hayavadana*. The predicament of Padmini, the female protagonist, can easily be compared with the predicament of a modern woman. Padmini marries Devadatta in order to find a complete man. But she gradually realises the weaknesses of him. The main line of argument seems to be revolving round the meaning and understanding of completeness and incompleteness. This leads us to a deeper structure which entails critical examination of social value and mass culture represented through human-nature struggling to rip it apart. Padmini, as a wife expresses her loyality to Devadata; as a woman reacts to physical charm of Kapila. She starts drifting towards Kapila hoping that she would find a perfect man in him. Kapila, an ironsmith, is the man of body.

The beauty of Padmini has succinctly been described as *Yakshini, Shakuntala,. Urvashi, Indumati*—all rolled into one. But after marriage she does not get what she deserves. Devadatta falls in love with her and marries not for her "intellect" but for her "appearance". Her intellect also does not find proper channel. This problem is generalised as the problem of a postcolonised woman. Padmini is asking for the right or freedom of woman to have ex-husband relationship. This is vey interesting as the drama depicts that Padmini is looking only for the best of the physique. That is, she is interested only in masculinity of a man. This is clearly from the dialogues between two Dolls.

> A head for each breast. A pupil for each eye. A side for each arm. I have neither regret nor shame.

It would of course be very dangerous to generalise this or that is what every woman wants. Then it would be a very superficial reading. Symbolically here the dramatist is attempting to put forward the change that is evident in the psyche of woman. It is their quest for individuality and right. It is their quest for their own status and self. And this is a modern postcolonial woman's problem which is very beautifully pictured by the dramatist.

The character role of Padmini can not merely be about her physical or sexual approach to Devadatta or Kapila. Her quest is not just for physical satisfaction or completeness. But it can also be considered as the right of a woman to express herself freely. To achieve what she really means. How far it is justifiable is another matter of debate. The death of Padmini reaffirms the authority of male. All the attempt made by woman may end this way only. Karnad has drawn out this very beautifully. Karnad's greatness as a dramatist lies in bringing forward the postcolonial frame of mind of Indian woman.

In this play, Karnad has described various problems faced by women and has questioned social conventions. Padmini wants to marry a perfect man and not finding all the qualities in one man she drifts towards another man. And the end of this quest is death. This can be led to multiple manipulations.

The Fire and the Rain can be considered as the best example of the situation of a woman in the postcolonial society. Both the female protagonists of the play, Vishakha and Nittilai seem as mere toys in the hands of males. Both of them are not allowed individuality. They act as if they were merely instruments. Yet both of them act independently and suffer. Vishakha loves Yavakri but is forced to marry another man that is Paravasu against her wish which she accepts unwillingly.

Paravasu, is in search of the universal knowledge, uses Vishakha as a device for his experimentation.

> He used my body, and his own body, like an experimenter, an explorer. As instruments in a search. Search for what ? I never knew.

And when he receives invitation from the king to be the Chief Priest of the seven year long Fire Sacrifice, he leaves Vishakha at the mercy of Raibhya and Arvasu. So when Yavakri comes to her, she suddenly feels hungry for words, of sympathy, and for human love. She says:

> The moment I heard you say you were hungry for words, I knew it was too late to go. I couldn't walk out on you after that I had lost the initiative missed the moment of decision. Because I knew that hunger well, Yavakri.

It indicates that she must have suffered psychologically. She must feel alienated. She is totally exploited at every stage and remains merely as a tool. First, she was deprived of her rights to choose her life-partner. Then she was forced to marry someone else. Thirdly, her husband too leaves her for a long time. Through the character of Vishakha Karnad wants to describe the predicament of the modern woman. She suffers at every stage but still she manages the situation. When Yavakri desires to enjoy her body, she submits her body to him consciously breaking all the norms and rules of the society:

> My husband and you ! He left no pore in my body alone. And you, you think a woman is only a pair of half-formed breasts.

This can be considered the predicament of woman in the post-colonial society. Though she is conscious about her individuality, she is deprived of all her rights and desires. Vishakha's gesture of submitting to Yavakri can be considered, symbolically, as a woman's answer to her suppressor. She, no more, is going to keep silent and suffer.

Nittilai, the only other female character, is treated in the same manner. She runs away from her husband on hearing the tragic plight of Arvasu, her lover. Her intention is pure, merely to help Arvasu get out of his hapless situation. At the end of the play, she has to die. For her society cannot permit ex-husband relations. She has an important solution to offer to her problem. She suggests to Arvasu to marry another girl whom he likes and she and Arvasu be together like brother and sister. She does not want anymore further disgrace for her husband.

Here Karnad is generalising the issue that if one goes for extramarital relations, then the end is death. Suppose one is attracted to the other sex, which is natural, but then there should be equal norms for man and woman. But all norms and rules are only for a woman and if she breaks the bondages, there is death. This is the plea of postcolonial woman. She wants the equality in norms of the society.

Naga-Mandala considers questions of marriage and the role of man and woman within this institution. Rani is married to Appanna. Appanna regularly goes to a concubine. Rani, feeling alone also falls in love with another man, first unknowingly and then consciously. A child is also born of this union. In the end Rani and Appanna realise the inevitability of the circumstances and decide to live together.

Here is the question on social attitude and norms of the society where a male is allowed to enjoy freedom enough to have extramarital relation. But the same thing when a female does, she is severely punished by the society. So the dramatist puts forward the problem of fidelity and morality within the institution of marriage. We are made to feel that this world is indifferent to both man and woman. And it is the woman who suffers more. Karnad's plays show this suffering of a modern woman. After all marriage does not mean mere living together. It is in fact a vow of fidelity. So any sort of extramarital relation means cheating eachother. But our society has rules only for women. But the modern woman wants social liberty and justice. Her quest is for her own status. She wants to express herself freely. The plays of Karnad show such female characters who suffer on account of this quest.

The female protagonists try to free themselves from the orthodox conventions of the society where the husband is the only man with whom she can keep touch. It is the society where husbands enjoy the status of demigod. The female in Karnad's plays seems to have started sensing that it is their right for freedom and individuality. There is an atmosphere of revolt. The male dominating society would definitely object to this. She does not want or mean a liaison or to justify extramarital affairs or relations. She just wants what she deserves.

Karnad's plays, while expressing the plight of his woman, have shown that the already oppressed woman has started reacting against the established notions of orthodox womanhood. The already suppressed and submissive woman has started realising her space, her individuality. This is, the effect of postcolonialism. In short, an attempt has been made to focus on a picture of woman in the postcolonial society in Girish Karnad's plays.

29

Anguish of Defenceless and voiceless Dalits in Praveen Gadhvi's *The Voice of the Last*

—Ram Sharma

The Dalit writers began their serious work in the 1950's. Although most of the writers have come out of the Buddhist movement, one of the earliest, Annabhau Sathe, who belonged to the Untouchable Mang caste, was deeply influenced by Communism. In the sixties, the flow of Dalit literary writings increased in the form of short stories, novels and drama. Conferences were held almost every year. In the 1970's, individual volumes of poetry began to be published by the Maharashtra Buddhist Literature Committee, Asmitadarsh Press, or the Marxist Magova Press. Dalit Sahitya has changed the face of Marathi literature and inspired similar literary creativity in Gujarat and Karnataka.

Praveen Gadhvi is a distinguished name in Dalit poetry. There are numerous anthologies to his credit, predominantly Dalit poetry and short stories. He is a prolific writer of Gujrati Dalit literature, whose works are replete with historical events and characters. These are included with a tinge of irony in his poetry. His collections of poetry are *Bayonet* (1985), *Padchhayo* (1996), and *Tunir* (2002). His short story collections are *Pratiksha* (1995), *Antarvyatha* (1995), and *Surajpankhi.*This volume comprises Gadhvi's translations of his own poems from the Gujarati original into English.

In the preface the eminent critic Dr. Rupalee Burke writes:

> It is an event that calls for celeberation and one heralds a new era not only in the history of Dalits in Gujrat. And the present writer feels extremely privileged to be a part of it. What more can one ask for his deeply committed bureaucrat –poet who provides his compassion for his deprived brothers over his own privileged social status [more so for exporting Dalit poetry from the regional Gujarati to the much wider realm of English]? (p.5)

The very first poem is a cry of a Dalit who wants that he should not be differentiated because he has been involved in history from Mohen-jo-daro. In every development he has been actively involved and he has made his history with his flesh and blood.

> There are prints of my steps on every stream of this nation
> There is fossil of mine under every rock of this nation
> The unreadable script of Mohen-jo-daro throbs in my blood,
> You cannot bury me as an untouchable
> (*I am the History of the Nation* p.13)

Taking the story of Shakuntala-Dushyanta the poet tries to divert our attention that Dalits have the same origin and they have the same contribution in the annals of the country. The poet is trying to remind everyone that blacks and whites are one but they have forgotten this. Or their ancestors have eradicated this.

> You see the origin of her race,
> Where is the origin of my race,
> It has been eradicated by your ancestors
> Though my black blood is rootless, it flows through all continents of the earth.
>
> (*Soliloquy of theUntouchable Shakuntala,* p.14)

The poet wants to eradicate the marginal mentality of the persons with waters of Ganges. There is no need of venomous *Manusmriti* which has divided the society between blacks and whites. He craves to brainwash all these things.

> There is no need of venomous curses of Manusmriti,
> This is centre of vision which gave me Black identity since centuries

Dear Bhudev,
See the blue sky of the winter, see the green woods.
Also see the seven colours of rainbow. (*Brainwash*, p.15)

The poet is doubtful whether persons will give equal rights to Dalits. He is ready to remove provisions for reservations in the constitution but will the society give the chance to the sons of Dalits. Will they be provided half the portion of harvest to them? Gadhvi also raises more serious questions like plundering of the virginity of Dalit daughters. He wants that they should remain untouchables and nobody should try to touch them. This is really an emotional cry of the poet because the situation is very dismal and they still have to suffer many hardships. The poet calls 'temples' 'slaughterhouses' because their ancestors sacrificed their lives for the service and safety of the temples but even then they were not allowed to enter the temples. Thus, their service and their sacrifices became useless.

They have covered the bloodstained walls with sheets of gold
They have made the golden peaks of the temple touch the sky,
The corpses of our ancestors are buried under the pillars of that temple, they groan,
Stop,
Don't step into that slaughterhouse.
(*Don't Enter the Temple*, p.19)

Gadhvi creates pitiful scenes to raise the sympathy of the readers. Dalits are everywhere amid the wolves and they have no protection. They have to work in the sun and bear all hardships that is the reason they became black, while others are white.

We suffered the pains of the earth
We were open to the sky,
You were in the graves
So that we are black and you are white.
(*We are Black You are White*, p.21)

The poet wants them to raise against the injustice done to dalits. They work hard and bear every hardship but in return what they get is only dark history and blank pages in the last five thousand years. He wishes them to stand up against their hardships, and disappear like Dinosaurs.

> No blank page of history to write
> Make yourself disappear like Dinasaurs from the face of
> the earth,
> Because might is right as Darwin said,
> Do you understand? (Question, p.23)

Dalits are legs of God Brahma and they have been walking throughout the ages but they have no dignity and respect. The poet desires that all blacks of the world should be united and they should have their own script and language. For Dalits it is very difficult to come out from their shadow of untouchability. They can change their appearance and language but still they remain *MARGINAL* and Dalits. The poet becomes the voice of the Dalits and he craves for his own village where they can walk with self respect. They want to have their own land and pucca house. In today's caste system, Dalits have no self respect.

> She had no village,
> She had no religion,
> She had no language,
> She had no dignity,
> She had no modesty,
> She was guilty
> Because she was untouchable by birth.
> (Barter System, p.33)

Changing of names and changing religion are not helping them. Even they are insulted more by these acts. Dalits can't draw water from the well, they have no lands of their own but in spite of that this country is theirs. They constructed the temple but they have no right to enter it. The poet salutes, Buddha, Gandhi, Shahuji Maharaj, Mahatma Phule and Ambedkar to raise the consciousness among the Dalits. Even in the whole history they weren't considered as human beings. They even couldn't get clothes and dignity. He doesn't want the division of human beings on the basis on caste and creed and they should remain only human beings.

He asked my caste
I was hurt
He asked my sub-caste,
I was offended
He asked my inner sub-caste,
I was disgusted. (Let me be a Human only, p.41)

Dalits were stopped from reading the religious scriptures and even their limbs were cut if they touched the scriptures. Even there is nothing for them in scriptures. Still today caste system is hovering there and there are titles to indicate the caste. Dalits are not even able to mingle in the society and their efforts have become futile. They are able to understand the efforts of Gandhiji and Ambedkar after their death. The brick-maker has no identity and everyone praises sky scrappers. This is quite humiliating for them. One can see the clear Dalit sensibility in this volume. The second part of this volume is dedicated to Mahatma Gandhi who has made efforts for the amelioration of Dalits.

Dr. Rupalee Burke writes in the preface of this volume:

> Mahatma Gandhi holds in the poems of the second section as is obvious from its title. No mincing of words for this poet and those expecting paeans in honour of the Father of the Nation are sure to be let down. Each poem in this section is laced heavily with anger, sarcasm, irony, violence and scorn [might we add hate?](p.9)

In this volume Mahatma Gandhi is dissected, examined from every possible skeptical angle and turned inside out, reducing him to the merest of mortals. In this country no one is following the teachings of Mahatma and he has not held in regard now. This nation has become a country of wolves now. He calls Gandhi as one without a crown and throne and we should respect him for his efforts to uplift the downtrodden. The poet also raises the questions why Gandhi or Ambedkar couldn't be successful in their efforts to abolish caste system. He has tried to scan Gandhiji in this volume. He gives a clarion call to all downtrodden—be united and make efforts to attain dignity and identity and he is quite hopeful of this.

The earth is mother of all,
There is no need of any walls,
The sun is father of all,
Nobody is untouchable to its shrine,
It is better to die by their sticks-spears than to face insults,
Rise, awake (Invocation, p.22)

In conclusion I can say that Praveen Gadhvi is the voice of the voiceless and comes in defence of the undefended in this volume of poetry.

WORKS CITED

Gadhvi, Praveen, *The Voice of the Last,* New Delhi, Yash Publications, 2008. (All poetry lines have been taken from this volume).

Lal, Sheo Kumar and Nahar, Ummed Raj, *Extent of Untouchability and Patterns of Discrimation,* New Delhi, Mittal Publication, 1990.

Pilla, Sivashankar, *Scavenger's Sons,* A Seminar on Dalit Literature in Marathi and Gujrati was held on February 18-20, 1988 in Surat.

30

Kshemendra: Our Own Horace

—Rajiv K. Mallik

I

G.N. Devy in *After Amnesia: Tradition and Change in Indian Literary Criticism* observes that Indian literary criticism is in such an utter state of bankruptcy that when it comes down to it, most Indian critics gravitate towards imported Western aesthetic concepts. He further comments that our present critical debility is due to the fact that we have forgotten all about the traditions and the literary riches of Sanskrit and Tamil and Kannada and Persian and so on.[1] It is a sad commentary that even after sixty-two years of independence, quite a few critics have been employing only Western theoretical tools to analyse texts written in English in India. The influence of Western criticism was quite noticeable right from the very beginning. Even today, only the fads and fashions and credos have changed with the changes in Western theoretical canons. These new 'labels' or critical 'tools' are perhaps potently inadequate to analyse and thus understand the English writing in India.

In the background of Marx's dictum that no one can transcend his/her culture, we have to de-Anglicise and decolonise our critical discourse because of the fact that our own categories have potent concepts which are natural components of our own social and literary psyche. The history of postcolonial Indian criticism in English since early 1980's has seen varied responses to arrive at some critical canon that might help in understanding the utility of our own 'labels/categories'.

The present paper attempts to extend, develop and reinterpret Auchitya in order to apply its concept to texts and genres *vis-a-vis* Horace's Decorum/Propriety.

II

In Indian poetics the concept of *Auchitya* has not been taken seriously. Though Bharata, Anandvardhan, Kuntaka, Vamaha, Dandin and others had spoken of *Auchitya* in oblique references, it was Kshemendra, the court poet of King Ananta of Kashmir in the eleventh century AD, who propounded and established the theory of *Auchitya* in poetics on a firm basis. It is equally true that when we ponder over the elements of *Auchitya* in correspondence to *Rasa, Alankara, Dhvani, Riti* and *Vakrokti*, we do not have the same intensity in literary appreciation. Nonetheless the literary appropriateness of *Auchitya* in itself has its own importance. The reasons are not too far to seek.

By the end of the ancient period, historically speaking ninth and tenth century AD Rasa Kavya was in much vogue and this genre, at that point of time, did not attach much importance to the use of appropriate words at the appropriate place. Its sole purpose was to please the peanut gallery in general and gentry in particular; it was panegyric in nature and, therefore appealed to courtiers, who, after the fashion of the day, employed and patronised pseudo men-of-letters.

Historically speaking, northern India, i.e., Kashmir at the time, was an area of peace where and when distinction could no longer be achieved through war. So, men turned to literature to gain such attention and distinction. The consequence was that poetasters were churning inferior poetry of no literary merit at all, and were therefore, corrupting and degrading public taste. The outpouring of such scribblers required constant critical attention and hence the concept of *Auchitya* by Kshemendra became all the more important.

Similar is the case with Horace (65 BC-8 AD), Roman critic and poet, and the author of *Ars Poetica*. The criticism of Horace was part of an Augustan classical movement back toward the high seriousness of Greek classical art. The main thing assumed in the criticism of Horace is the normative value of the literary 'species', the genre, kind, or type, and the companion principle designated by the term 'propriety' to Prepon in Aristotelian criticism, Decorum in Latin.[2] In *Poetics*, Aristotle had observed that tragedy, having passed through many stages of growth, had reached its final and perfect stage, and where characters should be true to life and internally consistent. In *Rhetoric* also he insisted that style should be appropriate to theme. He also wrote of the differences between poetic and prose styles and the three main oratorical styles, matching the three main types of oratorical purposes, forensic, deliberative, epideictic. But by the time of Horace, such notions had undergone a marked development in the subdivision and multiplication of fixed literary types and had acquired a new legislative prestige. The aim of criticism was to expound for each of these types an *operis lex* and its corollaries.[3]

Both Kshemendra and Horace made constant efforts to perfect their own art. From the very beginning, both seem to have been markedly conscious artists, with a definite theory of their own. Both were keenly alive to the immediate literary problems of their time. Throughout their literary output runs a critical strain, a criticism of contemporary manners, morals, thoughts and serious literature.

It is to be noted that Kshemendra's *Auchitya Vichar Charcha* and Horace's *Ars Poetica* have similar purposes, i.e. both are, in a sense, practical guides, rules and precepts for the guidance of the would-be poets. There is, however, one fundamental difference to bear in mind at the outset while comparing oriental and occidental purposes of literature. Oriental poetics is more concerned with beauty—the ultimate realisation or elaboration of *Rasa* (aesthetic experience) whereas occidental poetics is concerned with practical utility of formal beauty. (Practical utility, in my opinion, is absent in Indian poetics). Another difference is that Horace aims, it seems, to guide literature along the lines laid down by Hellenic poets and critics. He accepts the basic theories of the Greeks but circumscribes and narrows them down: "Be Homer's works your study and delight. Read them by day, and meditate by night".[4] Kshemendra, on the other hand, as a critic, no doubt, also appeals for some kind of order (propriety) in writing, and never alludes to the poets of yore.

III

Kuntaka had termed Vakrokti the life-breath of poetry (*Vakroktikavyajivitam*), Kshemendra believes *Auchitya* to be the life-blood of poetry (*Authityam rasashidyas sthiram kavyashya-jivitam*). In his opinion, it is not only the Shiva-energy and dignity of a creation, it is at the same time adbhuta (unique) i.e., a magical wonder, a miracle which intensifies the elaboration of *Rasa*. For him, in the absence of *Auchitya*, the grandeur and stateliness of Alankara and the gravity of poetry itself has no meaning. He considers *Auchitya* indelible, indestructible and intransient attribute of poetics, and hence poetry.

Alankara or *Vakrokti* used in proper context is grandiose, but if separated from its function and virtue, the very nature of *Alankara* or *Vakrokti* transforms/descends into imperfection and becomes calumny. Defining *Auchitya*, Kshemendra says that the very *Bhāva* (idea/meaning/feeling/design) of *Auchitya* (proper) is i.e., everything has to have its appropriate measure. The aim of each type of fine art is to give the pleasure proper to it.

Uchitam prahuracharyah sadrisham kil yashya yata,
Uchitashya ch yo bhavastdauchityam prakchate.[5]

This *Auchitya* is the soul of Rasa and it is marvelously unique.

Auchityashya chamatkar karinascharu charvane,
Rasa jivit bhutashya vicharah kriyatedhuna.[6]

Yashovarman, the king of Kanauj, mentions the term *Auchitya* for the first time in his drama *Ramavadhya*. The text is traceless. But

Bhoja, the king of Dhara from AD 1018 to 1063, in his, mentions one of its shlokas. In this particular shloka/couplet we recognise the *Shringar Prakash* satisfaction of *Rasa* in relation to *vachan* speech/utterance and *patra*-character. In Bharata's *Natyashastra* we get the seeds of *Auchitya*. For the proper realisation and satisfaction of *Rasa* appropriate character, dress, code, proper action, etc., are ultimate prerequisites. In other words, the whole structure of a poetic creation would be travestied if the rules of prosody are not adhered to. Kshemendra almost echoes the same sentiment when he says, "A girdle in the neck, a necklace of bright/shining gems round the waist, an anklet circling the wrist, an armlet on the ankles, terrorising a refugee and pitying an enemy would invariably evoke sardonic derision. An *Alankara* or a *Vakrokti* has neither merit nor grace if not used properly." The above translation, it seems, is an extension of Bharata, but Kshemendra prefers *Auchitya* to *Alankara* and *Vakrokti* not only for the genre of poetry, but also in life and behaviour.

Ars Poetica opens with stress upon the need of observing organic unity and propriety. He says, "If a painter should try to unite a horse's neck to a human head, and to add various features of limb collected from every kind of animal, so that a woman's fair form above should end in a foul and ugly fish beneath, tell me, my friend, could you control your laughter, if admitted to a private view?"[7] In other words, both Horace and Kshemendra believed that poetry is not mere imitation. It is creative. Poets are free to indulge in fancy, to use their imagination, but they must remain true to life. Imagination must not be overdone, freedom must not degenerate into licence, otherwise the result would be sheer absurdity. Poets must seek their models in nature, life and manners, and must remain true to nature even when they indulge their fancy in writing stories and fiction. *Ars Poetica* declares, "a place for everything and everything in its place."

Kshemendra has discussed *Auchitya* at length in relation to all the manifestations and dimensions of poetics. Nowhere in *Auchitya Vichar Charcha* he considers *Rasa* the corporal characteristic of poesy. For him, *Rasa* is produced only when pleasure and elegance combine together. When we review his theory in totality we note that he lays stress equally on the various elements of poetry and not on any one principal element, viz., *Rasa* or *Alankar* or *Vakrokti*. He elaborates his concept by citing the metaphor of a wheel: a wheel is in action only when all the spokes in it are at their proper places and in proper positions, even one crooked spoke renders the wheel immobile. Similarly when a poem offers a complete meaning and satisfies the wits, the poem becomes immortal. All the elements ought to have their appropriateness so as to convey a pattern to make a poem different from ordinary speech, and only then it provides *Vibodh* (knowledge) to the *Abodh* (ignorant).

Dhvanists like Rudrata, Anandvardhan and Abhinavgupta, firmly believed *Rasa* to be the essential element of poetry. The appropriateness and propriety of the different attributes of poesy is to complement and aid in the realisation of *Rasa, Bhava*, etc. and as such *Auchitya* is the ultimate revelator of *Rasa*. They unanimously accept the *Acuhitya* of *Alankara* only in relation to Rasa. Regarding the *Auchitya* of *Alankara* Kshemendra attests that only when it assists in producing a *Rasa*, it is indispensable otherwise it loses its meaning. If an *alankar/a vakrokti* is inserted intentionally without being fully aware of its meaning, the very purpose of the use and effect is lost in the haze and maze of erudition. It is like rowing the boat against the current. Kshemendra cites the beautiful example of a woman who turns her face away the very moment one looks at her. Without proper context *alankar/vakrokti* can never become an essential component of the whole structure of the poem.

Every work of art has a special language, i.e., "a language within a language' (Paul Valery, 1958).[8] This language is, to quote Matthew Arnold, "the most perfect speech of man'; it is "the language at full stretch" (Nowottry, 1962).[9] The poet makes words and their combination serves more than their ordinary function. It exploits more consistently the full potential of that language. In other words, both Kshemendra and Horace believe that the poet is the one who 'sees' and is able to express in appropriate and revealing words what he has 'seen'. Both of them tried to universalise the theory of Auchitya/Decorum from minimum to maximum. A sentence structure always follows a definite pattern which is the function of *Auchitya*/Decorum which provides uchit (proper) words to the structure. Horace says, "Let the author of the poem show taste and care in linking up his words; let him embrace one word and reject another...."

Kshemendra says that if 'Jivit Shabda', i.e., living speech is not used, the poetry is not poetry for, there is no distinction between a current word and its usage. The 'jivit' and the 'usage' are one. Horace also stresses the use of 'living speech'. Both with regard to obsolescence, the passing away of fine old words, and with regard to revivals, the norm is usage; usage is the final count of appeal: "Many words that have perished will be reborn, and many will perish that now live respected if usage says so. Usage is judge and law and rule of speech."[10]

Both Kshemendra and Horace nowhere discuss the subject-matter of poetry. Both of them, however, advise the poet to choose his subject wisely for, the source and fountain head of a good writing is right thinking and "only right thinking will get you 'Shahridaya Pathak' (the empathic/competent reader).

Thus, we need to develop a distinct theory of our own free from western influence. In the above discussion we have noticed the similarity of the categories. But Kshemendra's *Auchitya* as compared to Horace's Decorum has the wholeness of a tradition—a tradition where different categories (*Rasa, Alankar, Riti, Dhvani, Vakrokti* and *Auchitya)* combine to produce *Saundarya Darshan.*

References

1. Devy, G.N., *After Amnesia: Tradition and change in Indian literary criticism.* Bombay: Orient Longman, 1992.
2. Wimsatt, J.R., W.K. and Cleanth Brooks, *Literary Criticism : A Short History,* Calcutta: Oxford Book Company, 1964, p. 80.
3. Ibid., p.81.
4. Prasad, A. (ed.)., *Ars Poetica,* New Delhi: Orient Longman, 1992, p. 68.
5. Mishra, Dr. S.K., *Bhartiya Kavya Chintana,* Patna: Anupam Prakashan, 2001, p. 66.

6. Ibid., p. 67.
7. Prasad, A., op.cit. p. 74.
8. Valery, Paul, The Art of Poetry, London: OUP, 1958, p. 64.
9. Nowottry, W., The Language Poets Use, London: CUP, 1962, p. 123.
10. Wimsatt, J.R., op.cit., p. 88.

31

Negotiating Postcoloniality: An Interview with Jaydeep Sarangi

—Sudhir K. Arora

Jaydeep Sarangi, Head of the Department of English, Seva Bharati Mahavidyalaya (Vidyasagar University), Kapgari, Paschim Medinipur, W. B. (India) is a critic, bilingual Indian English poet and the author of a number of significant publications on postcolonial issues, Indian Writing in English, Australian Literature and Linguistics and ELT in reputed journals/magazines in India and abroad.

His doctoral thesis *Indian Novels in English: A Sociolingustic Study* (pub.2005) has been reviewed as a welcome contribution to post-colonial studies in different journals including, "Revista de Lenguas para Fines Especificos" (Spain). His articles have appeared in journals like *Across Cover, DOST,* The Dept. of Oriental Studies, University of Turin (Italy), *Percorsi di Flesssibilita Dell' Indian English, Hindusthani Innovator, Indian Literature, Atlantic Literary Review, The Visvabharati Quarterly, Glimpses* (Ontario, Canada), *Litcritt, The Commonwealth Review* and *Summer Hill.*

Dr Sarangi, at present, lives with his family in the small, forest-enclosed town of Jhargram in West Bengal. He edits two research journals including the *Seva Bharati Journal of English*

Studies (a refereed journal) and has been taken on the editorial board of *Pegasus* (Agra), *The Okigbo Review* (Nigeria), *Unheared Melody* (Chapra), *Pernasus* (RaeBarelly) *Prosopisia* (Ajmer), *Mascarapoetry* (Australia), *Indian Journal of World Literature and Culture* (Bhubaneswar), *IJPCL* (Kerala) and *Reflections* (Tezu). He has been serving as one of the executive (regional) members of the *Indian Associations for Commonwealth Literature and Language Studies.*

Awarded with Associateship (UGC) at IIAS, Shimla (H.P., India), 2006, he is a dedicated teacher who loves teaching in different universities as a resource person or guest faculty, known for his passion for helping smaller children and young adolescents, especially coming from less privileged backgrounds.

Sudhir Arora: Being a critic you have the credit of covering the interviews of the popular literary personalities. Now how do you feel being interviewed?

J.S.: (smiles....) I feel honoured.

My hands speed the clock towards the rotting of living flesh. I am curious to sit with you. It was great feeling when I interviewed popular literary personalities like Jayanta Mahapatra, Bibhu Padhi, Tabish Khair, Sunny Singh, Shanta Acarya, Basavaraj Naikar, Meena Kandasami and Niranjan Mohanty. Great personalities have influenced me a lot They taught me the lesson to work hard; "Always set a goal and go for it."

S.A.: Your interest is in postcolonialism. Don't you think that this postcolonialism still reminds us of the colonial period? Don't you think that it is a negative term? Don't you feel that it must be replaced by the term post-independence literature or any other?

J.S.: Postcolonialism is a top-heavy theoretical toolbox that involves the shifting of understanding the world with available empirical experiences. It is the re-location of the cultural space in the post-colonial (hyphaneted) time. Interdisciplinary and transcultural studies are undertaken so that people understand one another better. Everything is perpetually in process of cohesion and dissolution. Postcolonialism is a pluralistic and all-inclusive outlook to value, judge the effects and after effects of colonialism. It is defined as a set of theoretical approaches, which focus on the direct effects of the Emipre, and aftermath of colonisation. I fully agree with your claim that postcolonialism is a negative term, a crude reminder of the colonial practices. 'Open Period' may be an alternative we can think of. Now things are open; anything can go to any direction; all are equally conscious of their rights; no one is beyond the codes of conduct; geographical space is not closed and the notion of the global village is in the air. Awareness of *being* is the hallmark of people living in a free state. But, the proposal for 'post-independence literature' as an alternative term for postcolonialism needs to be used with caution. Do we need to refer back to the days of pre-independence? If 'pre' is a harsh prefix why do we need to use 'post' as prefix to Independence? We can continue the debate in seminars and conferences until we arrive at a consensus. Let me quote a poem from Marshal Hembram where the Santhali poet expresses the sense of postcoloniality as the rhetoric of resistance.

We Shall Take the Bow and Arrow

Marshal Hembram

(Original text is in Santhali: translated from Bengali by Jaydeep Sarangi)

All by a thunder
they say,
this land
this pond
this farm house
are not mine.

Red eyes pierce us
to leave
all these
and to be without address.

But, with these
there are stories numberless.

We fought to make
this untrodden territory of forest
for a land
to live in;
with happy family.

If you ask all these
from me
my land
my pond
my farm house.
What else can I do
but to take the bow and arrow.

S.A.: Postcoloniality is nothing; it is simply globalisation, a well-planned conspiracy of the west meant for destroying the native culture. Do you feel that decolonisation of the mind is equally a necessity to retrieve our identity?

J.S.: Why not? We are indirectly under the hang over of colonialism. Our orientation still loves for colonial buildings and architecture. The mind set is NOT open to access new changes. I have reasons to differ with your observation, "Postcoloniality is nothing; it is simply globalisation." Postcoliniality is the subjective orientation of mind based on new experiences. It is more than a political or literary term. It is a new set of cognition in man.

Decolonisation doesn't mean getting freed from colonial obligation. It is a continuous process to accept changes around man. It can only happen when there is awareness. It is a code of resistance to injustice as well as a denotative term which has metonymic significance.

S.A.: How far do you feel that your suggestion for 'glocal language' and 'linguistic hybridity' are going to help in maintaining the sociolinguistic identity?

J.S.: I think whatever language one uses is his or her 'concrete' expression of self. It is as real as roaring of the lion and the babbling of the infants. I am reminded of Niranjan Mohanty's lines from *Prayers to Lord Jagannatha*:

> It's half Orissan, half-Indian
> It gives me the flavour of watered rice.

Linguistic code-mixing and code switching result in linguistic hybrididty which is the reality these days. Post-colonial Society is melting pot—monoculturalism is a myth; different languages contribute to each other and remain alive. Otherwise, linguistic death is on the card. It happened to some of the old/classical languages. Only the fittest (flexible) can survive.

S.A.: Nativisation of English language is one of the tools of postcolonial theory. You always trace out Indianness (applying available critical parameters) in Indian Writings in English. How far do you get success in assessing the literary work with this critical parameter?

J.S.: Nativism is the socio-cultural reality these days. It is the age of representation of the total culture. It includes the regional subjectivity too. *The God of Small Things* by Arundhati Roy is a glaring example of this regionalism as the textual matrix. Truth is all. If one needs to be true he must present the truth. My articles on Indiannisation of English in Indian context reflect Nativism as a positive assertion of the cultural experiences in India. Vernacularisation as a sociological as well as sociolinguistic reality has been faithfully portrayed in Indian literary writings in English. I must accept the fact that the Queen's tongue has been widened enough to represent Indian experiences. It replaces the traditional role of language with language as the most powerful and controlling agency in society.

I don't know whether I have succeeded propagating my voice around the world or not. At times, I receive constructive observations by e-mails, letters, reviews of my books, etc. I am not unaware of the possibility of heated debate on the subject and presume that one may end up by breaking a pot of husk under the sweltering heat. Let me refer to a Bengali Dalit poet, Manohar Mouli Biswas' poem 'Phulondevi':

PHULON DEVI

(Translated by Dr Jaydeep Sarangi from Bengali poem of Manohar Mouli Biswas)

Manohar Mouli Biswas is the current Secretary, Bengali Dalit Sahitya Sanstha.

Who gave you the strength
to challenge,
to take revenge against twenty four strikes?
Your pride hurt or promises to safeguard shame?
You were a Sudra.
In the far off village who raped your
innocent womanhood
must know
Phulan is every woman.

S.A.: While assessing a literary work, you have the sociolinguistic point of view. Do you not feel the need of pluralistic approach to have a true estimate?

J.S.: If the society is plural the pluralistic approach is only way through which one needs to assess the texts that represent a plural consciousness. No conscious critic can deny the role of sociolinguistic approach to interpret role-relationships in society which have been consciously represented by writers in India. At times, critics are more carried away with the wind of literary flavour, top-heavy theoretical tools and literary intertextuality that they unknowingly ignore the sociolinguistic approach for literary analysis. No truth can be a burden. I've been working on it to make a point that working knowledge of Sociolinguistics is a must for honest appreciation of literature.

S.A.: What is Indian English? Your seminal work, *Indian Novels in English: A Sociolinguistic Study (2005)* has been reviewed as a pioneering contribution in Postcolonial Studies, your articles on sociolinguistic approach to Indian English Novels have appeared in prestigious journals like, *Across/Over,* The Department of Oriental Studies, University of Turin, *Percosi di Flessibilita Dell'indian English.* What's your opinion regarding the future of this approach of study?

J.S.: Indian English is the sociolinguistic reality in India. It is the vortex of truth—India is a multi-cultural, multilingual country where regional languages are powerful, is a land of diversity; an ethnological mosaic. English in Kerala can never be the same as English in Gujarat or West Bengal. Indian English, therefore, is more of an abstract concept than its concrete implications. I'm aware of researches going on to arrive at a comprehensive model on this. Professor B.K. Kachru, Priya Hosali and Professor S.V. Parashar have enriched the parameters and prospect with their pioneering contribution through books and articles. I must mention the name of Prof. Alessandro Monti of the University of Turin for his continuous research on Indian English. Some of his PhD and MPhil scholars have worked on Indian English. I am glad that I was able to help them during their research. Broad-based field study is on the card for a generic description of the model of Indian English.

S.A.: Do you believe that cultural criticism is a tool for proper understanding of postcolonialism?

J.S.: Yes. It is a must; cultural criticism should be applied for a proper understanding of postcolonialism. The cultural heritage, disfigured by the colonialist is the challenge before the Orient. In the present scenario, it is being re-constructed, re-shaped and re-discovered without loosing its base. Postcolonial writers engage themselves with "race retrieval" (Wole Soyinka).

For example, to study the dominant trend in Nigerian poetry today one needs to appreciate aesthetics of resistance the poet evolves for himself in order to be relevant to his society. The relevance is manifested in the confrontational attitude he developes towards the authorities in his society, whom he accuses of leading the society astray politically and economically. At times, a postcolonial text becomes the socio-cultural dialogue between the author and his art in order to contribute to the solutions of the postcolonial crises of his nation.

S.A.: Your book on postcolonialism has come out recently. How far is it going to enrich the Indian English Literature?

J.S.: Indian English Literature is a powerful literary discourse. My book sets out to explore the limits of postcolonialism as a literary discourse. Postcolonialism, moving beyond plot of the so-called critical practice has come to represent a complex web of meaning produced through multiple strategies of reading and interpreting it. The book opens the possibilities that indicate the gap between the experience of sociological place and the language available to experience/describe it forms the matrix of postcolonial texts.

S.A.: What is your opinion about the 'discourse study of a text'?

J.S.: Modern developments in 'discourse study of a text' have added a new avenue to look into a text. It is an approach that demands sincere and honest professionalism. Language is an artifact of society. Knowledge of linguistics is a must to go into a literary text. Discourse study is an analysis of connected speech or written speech. It assumes that a text is an organised speech process. Addresser, addressee, topic, code, channel and context determine a discourse process. The Conceptual Dependency Representation (CDR) is one of the key models to analyse discourse.

S.A.: Prof. C.D. Narsimhaiah, who left an indelible impact as a literary critic, always preferred to assess literature in English employing Indian critical cannons. Would you like to name some of the critics who are following the same trend?

J.S.: I read the works of Professor Meenakshi Mukherjee, Prof. G.S. Balarama Gupta, Prof. Makarand Paranjape, Prof. Jasbir

Jain, Prof. John Oliver Perry, Prof. M.K.Naik, Prof. Christopher Rollason, Prof. Basavaraj Naikar, Dr G.J.V. Prasad, Dr Subhendu Mund and Prof. Alessendro Monti with interest. They have preferred to assess literature in English with Indian critical cannons.

S.A.: In the critical space, you have established yourself through your original critical knack. What are your future critical explorations? Are you satisfied with your work as a critic?

J.S.: I think I need to improve a lot more; a solid base to launch sincere and honest criticism. I'm not at all satisfied with the job I have done so far. I look forward to contributing even more substantially. Imagination is the resource by which I must regulate my comprehension of reality, and literary consciousness connects my imagination and reality. As a literary critic, I want to evolve constructively.

S.A.: Are you satisfied with the kind of criticism that is being churned out? What suggestions would you like to give for its improvement?

J.S.: I admire some critical works but not all. Scholars may not be all alike. They differ in their orientations. I would like to see more sincere and honest criticism emerging as regards literary studies. Intensity in logical formulation of an analysis should be the bedrock for assessment of a literary corpus. A text is formless and undefined space, unless it is properly tuned in. Serious scholars have room to expand their tools to investigate the problems honestly.

S.A.: What is your message to the scholars, critics and the lovers of literature?

J.S.: Be honest and sincere to the profession. One needs to be sincere and honest when any job is assigned to him or her. Light minded critics cannot make any substantial appeal to anyone. Intensity is the hallmark of scholars, critics and the lovers of literature. True scholars are intense scholars.

S.A.: Thank you for enriching (almost pioneering) the field of criticism with your sociolinguistic approach, application of discourse study and favouring Indianness in Indian Writing in English. Thanks for sparing your time and sharing your views.

J.S.: Thank you, Dr Arora. The feeling is mutual.

32

Pioneer of Post Colonial Literary Criticism: C.D.Narasimhaiah

—T.S. Chandra Mouli

Ananda Coomaraswamy asks, "What has India contributed to human welfare?" He himself answers "Indianness." C.D. Narasimhaiah successfully blends the best of East-West poetics. Born to a semi-literate shopkeeper, he grew up listening to the folk tales and songs from his mother and folk version of Ramayana sung sonorously by his father. W.G. Eagleton, his teacher at Maharaja's College, Mysore, arranged scholarship for his study at Cambridge University and young Narasimhaiah was assigned to F.R. Leavis as supervisor of his studies. He visited America on Rockefeller scholarship. At Princeton he used to meet Einstein, the scientist who inspired him to recover wisdom of ancients. He also perceived the spiritual streak in American Literature, though the nation is known to be interested in materialistic pursuits.

C.D. Narasimhaiah's visits to Australia were illuminating, kindling interest in commonwealth literature. He was able to comprehend the common features of aborigine philosophical ponderings and Indian perspective. As he himself states in his address on being conferred D.Litt by Bangalore University in 2005, "Aurobindo in my own country taught me to reject Aristotle's kindergarten theory of Catharsis and look for the *rasa, dhvani, auchitya vichara* to realise through them the *purusharthas* of *dharma, artha, kama, moksha...*"

Global exposure, keenness to focus on the best in east and west theories enabled C.D. Narasimhaiah carve a niche for himself and emerge as a pioneer holding the torch of literary appreciation aloft, shaping a new class of literary critics.

While K.R. Srinivasa Iyengar wrote to justify the existing order to substantiate his own stand, Narasimhaiah dismantled that order to offer strength to his way of criticism. The former was sincere and transparent, while the latter was a passionate critic, maintaining remarkable consistency. Narasimhaiah had functioned with a purpose, of acquiring respectability and reputation due to Indian writing in English.

He understood the significance of humanism and adopts scientific humanism of Nehru in his works. "The function of criticism for Narasimhaiah is elucidation and evolution" (Narasimhaiah, *The Function*, 87). His humanism turns him anti-colonial. His opposition to imperialists is on account of his being a humanist and a great patriot. His passionate plea for according due regard to Indian aesthetics is purely due to a conviction that culture and criticism go together. Culture for him incorporates one's spiritual experience.

"It is almost axiomatic that literature is primarily a cultural pursuit...Literature and cultures have been interchangeable terms..." (Narasimhaiah, *Indian Critical Scene*, 201). Hence, his regard for Shakespeare, T.S.Eliot and Raja Rao. His approach encourages comparative study of writers, texts and literatures. He details the manner in which a British writer's text may be viewed and appreciated in the light of *rasa* and *purusharthas*. He goes on to elaborate how *rasa, dhvani* theory can be extended to include salient features of Western aesthetic theories.

He analyses Blake's famous poem *The Tiger*. It is of interest to note that Blake was an engraver, like our own goldsmiths who give a shape and life to ornaments. The Tiger has been created in the foundry where the anvil and the hammer have been effectively employed to give it a shape infusing life. C.D. Narasimhaiah convincingly asserts that 'The Tiger' is an *udbhavamurthi* and not a mere artifact *utsavamurthi*. The *chinmaya ananda* of the creator of such a wonder is presented in the line:

> Did He smile his work to see?

The critic declares that wonder *vismaya* deepens fusion of emotions *rasaikya,* culminating in *adbhuta* (explicit wonder) intensifying the insightful mystery:

> Did He who made the lamb make thee?

Narasimhaiah delineates how Wordsworth fails to create *ahlaaada* (pleasantness) in *Daffodils*. Unlike Blake who is totally involved in depiction of the process and impact of creation of Tiger, Wordsworth drifts away in gay abandon like the dancing daffodils and pretends to present a pleasant poem. T.S.Eliot and Coleridge were justified in their criticism of the poem. *Karunarasa* marks Lucy poems and the lines haunt a reader endlessly.

> The song in my heart I bore
> Until it was heard no more.

Narasimhaiah's emphasis on native critic is not based on narrow parochial view or misplaced regard for the nation. For him culture is a source of identity, personal and natural, which are inalienable. He rightly observes, "What one has in mind is a shared tradition, a community of interest, a set of values people live by, all of which gives a sense of identity to individuals and nations."

Narasimhaiah's love for Indian philosophy stems from his idea of a literature that would be purely Indian in sensibility. "A zest that springs from a sense of purpose and strength of conviction, vibrates through Narasimhaiah's criticism. One may disagree with him, but his ideas are infectious because they are sincere." (Bandana Sharma & L.R. Sharma, 1998, 86)

A discerning reader will find that C.D. Narasimhaiah is at his best as a critic of Indian English fiction. His autobiography *'N' for 'Nobody'* reflects his abiding love for English studies in this country. It is not a book of confessions. He pulls a joke at himself at times.

His lecture delivered as a part of Sahitya Akademi's Samvatsara lecture series brings out his innermost thoughts about Indianness of Indian English literature. He gives an exquisite account of Nehru's contribution to this country in this regard. "To a bare intellectual understanding of India, he added an emotional appreciation". (Narasimhaiah, 2003, 19)

He showers encomiums on the first prime minister of India. As the lecture progresses he himself says, "From the lofty heights of Vivekananda, Tagore and Nehru let me come down to the plains, to see how our novelists function." (Narasimhaiah, 2003, 25). He wonders what makes a writer choose a language to exhibit his creativity. It should come naturally. A writer should endeavour to enrich his grasp of the idiom.

Narsimhaiah's assessment of Mulk Raj Anand, R.K. Narayan and Raja Rao is apt and unbiased. He sums up admirably Anand's art, "Mulk Raj Anand is a novelist who is not interested in portraying the beauty or ugliness of life and poverty and suffering, but the heartlessness of the few which thwarts the promising life of the helpless young" (Narasimhaiah, 2003, 29).

About R.K. Narayan he states, "His world was South Indian middle class which he knew how to handle in fiction, not for an audience 6,000 miles away as his jealous detractors accused him but for his own English knowing countrymen....Himself a product of the Hindu middle class, sharing their beliefs and superstitions in a small town, he had qualified himself to be a writer of that class and the provincial town" (Narasimhaiah, 2003, 29).

We admire Narasimhaiah's astuteness when he declares, "Narayan's sense of the comic is sustained, not by the Dickensonian kind of exaggeration, but rather some thing home-spun and close to what one may find in the Tenali stories in Telugu" (Narasimhaiah, 2003, 31).

As he says, Raja Rao's three well known novels sum up his main contribution to Indian English novel. The language in *Kanthapura* makes one feel quite at home, because most of us speak that way in our own mother tongues. People in the West and India come to know what India is really through *The Serpent and The Rope*. "Raja Rao has demonstrated in convincing terms, in terms of fiction that is, that human relationships, no less than man's union with the Absolute; are not the result of bridges on rivers or bridge parties but temporary suspension over gurgling space" and, alone with silence. The enactment of this truth is the lasting contribution of Raja Rao" (Narasimhaiah, 2003, 35-36).

Narasimhaiah dismisses the works of all prize-winning writers for their artificiality, lack of Indian sensibility and unabashed liberties taken with English language. He praises the creative imagination of Toru Dutt. *The Lotus* is a simple poem with abundance of feminine charm and delicate idiom. Aurobindo's overhead poetry witnessed in *Savitri* is explained with illuminating examples from the epic.

Narasimhaiah advises an Indian critic to go back to his own tradition and make literature yield benefits like *kamadhenu* or *kalpavriksha* — the more one knows how to seek, the more one gets. He goes on to apply the rich concept of *rasa, dhvani,* and *purushartha,* the Indian value system and evaluate Shakespeare's *Tempest* and Blake's *The Tiger*. Thus, he has initiated a new mode of literary criticism as regards Indianness in Indian English literature.

Any attempt to understand the contribution of C.D.N., as he is affectionately and reverentially called, as a literary critic will be incomplete without a reference to *Dhwanyaloka,* a Saraswati Kshetra, conceived and nurtured by him painstakingly, with loving care for the benefit of visitors, scholars in search of material and guidance, and well-wishers who felt sanctified in the balmy presence of the Acharya. Located in midst of pristine beauty of nature, this hallowed place is an ashram where learning and dissemination of knowledge goes on eternally, silently, soothingly. Sharing food and information collectively under the cool shades of pleasant trees is an unforgettable experience. *Dhwanyaloka* is spiritual fountain slaking the thirst of the seeker and student alike. The Acharya's blessings radiate from a leaf on a tree, fragrance of flowers and lyrical ripples in the pond there.

C.D. Narasimhaiah has given a shape and conferred recognition and reputation on Indian English literature, which was earlier known as Anglo-Indian Literature, through decades of selfless service rendered with peerless patriotic fervour. He inculcated a sense of adventure to explore, examine and evaluate Indian English Literature by blending the best of east- and west theories. His modesty, novel approach and work heralded a new era in post-colonial literary criticism. May he continue to inspire the new generation of literary critics.

Works Cited

Narasimhaiah, C.D. (ed.), Shakespeare's Last Plays, in *Shakespeare Came To India,* Bombay, 1954.

Jawaharlal Nehru, Mysore, Rao & Raghavan, 1960.

______________, *Fiction and the Reading Public in India,* Mysore, University of Mysore, 1967.

______________, *The Human Idiom: Three Lectures on Jawaharlal Nehru,* Bombay, Blackie & Sons, 1967.

______________, *The Writer's Gandhi,* Patiala, Punjabi University, 1967.

______________, (ed) *Indian Literature of the Past Fifty Years* Mysore, University of Mysore, 1970.

______________, *Raja Rao,* New Delhi, Arnold-Heinnemann, 1973.

______________, *The Swan and the Eagle.* Shimla, 1977.

______________, *Moving Frontiers of English Studies In India,* New Delhi, 1977. *The Function of Crticism in India,* 1986.

______________, *Indian Critical Scene,* 1990.

______________, *'N' for Nobody: Autobiography of an English Teacher,* Delhi, 1991.

Index